UNDERSTANDING
GRAHAM SWIFT

Understanding Contemporary British Literature
Matthew J. Bruccoli, Series Editor

Volumes on

UNDERSTANDING
GRAHAM
SWIFT

David Malcolm

University of South Carolina Press

© 2003 University of South Carolina

Published in Columbia, South Carolina, by the

University of South Carolina Press

Manufactured in the United States of America

07 06 05 04 03   5 4 3 2 1

Library of Congress Cataloging-in-Publication Data

Malcolm, David, 1952–
    Understanding Graham Swift / David Malcolm.
       p. cm. — (Understanding contemporary British literature)
    Includes bibliographical references and index.
    ISBN 1-57003-515-6 (cloth : alk. paper)
    1. Swift, Graham, 1949– —Criticism and interpretation.
    I. Title. II. Series.
PR6069.W47 Z75 2003
823'.914—dc22   2003016361

for Cheryl Alexander Malcolm

Contents

Editor's Preface

The volumes of *Understanding Contemporary British Literature* have been planned as guides or companions for students as well as good nonacademic readers. The editor and publisher perceive a need for these volumes because much of the influential contemporary literature makes special demands. Uninitiated readers encounter difficulty in approaching works that depart from the traditional forms and techniques of prose and poetry. Literature relies on conventions, but the conventions keep evolving; new writers form their own conventions—which in time may become familiar. Put simply, *UCBL* provides instruction in how to read certain contemporary writers—identifying and explicating their material, themes, use of language, point of view, structures, symbolism, and responses to experience.

The word *understanding* in the titles was deliberately chosen. Many willing readers lack an adequate understanding of how contemporary literature works; that is, what the author is attempting to express and the means by which it is conveyed. Although the criticism and analysis in the series have been aimed at a level of general accessibility, these introductory volumes are meant to be applied in conjunction with the works they cover. They do not provide a substitute for the works and authors they introduce, but rather prepare the reader for more profitable literary experiences.

M. J. B.

Acknowledgments

I thank Zina Rohan, without whose kindness and help much of the research for this book could not have been done. I am also grateful to the University of Gdansk, which provided funds for me to make visits to the British Library in London. I thank Dr. Philip Brindle, who gave me a copy of *Waterland* in 1985. I also thank Craig Brandhorst for his expert job of copy editing.

I thank William and James Malcolm for their toleration of their father's work. My main thanks, always, go to Cheryl Alexander Malcolm for her help, support, advice, and much else besides.

UNDERSTANDING
GRAHAM SWIFT

CHAPTER 1

Understanding
Graham Swift

Graham Swift is one of the most successful and highly regarded novelists writing in contemporary Britain. The basic facts of his life are well known, but beyond those, little is a matter of public knowledge. He was born on May 4, 1949, in Catford in South London, the son of a civil servant. He has described his childhood as "a very ordinary suburban existence" and as "really quite happy." He was educated at prestigious institutions. He attended Dulwich College (an English public school) and went on to Queen's College, Cambridge, from which he graduated in English in 1970; and York University, where in 1973 he completed an M.A. thesis on the city in nineteenth-century English literature. After his studies Swift worked as a teacher in Greece and in London, but with the success of his first three novels he decided to become a full-time writer. His home is in London, where he has lived "with the same lady friend for about twenty years." They have no children. In *Who's Who 2000,* he gives fishing as his sole recreation and his agent's address as his own. He is clearly a writer who values privacy in his personal life.[1]

Despite the lack of detail in Swift's biography, certain elements in it are of interest to the readers of his fiction. It should be noted that although he frequently turns to a South London setting for his novels, many aspects of those novels are not directly drawn from his personal experience. His immediate family background is not that of the shopkeeper, William Chapman,

in *The Sweet-Shop Owner,* nor that of the wealthy arms manu-
facturing family, the Beeches, in *Out of This World.* It is not that
of the working-class and lower-middle-class characters of *Last
Orders* (people from that background do not attend Dulwich
College). Nor—most surprisingly of all—is he from the East
Anglian Fen country described so closely in *Waterland.* The dis-
crepancies between depicted worlds and authorial background
are striking. Swift is an author whose biography does not particularly illuminate his work, nor does it seem to give rise to it
in any straightforward way.[2]

Swift's career has been a very successful one. He now produces novels at relatively long intervals—usually, since 1983,
every four to five years—but these novels are respectfully, and
sometimes even rapturously, received by professional critics,
scholars, and other writers in major journals and periodicals.
His novels are published by major British and U.S. publishers,
and they win prizes in the United Kingdom and abroad. They
have been translated into many languages. His first novel, *The
Sweet-Shop Owner,* was first published in 1980. *Shuttlecock* followed in 1981, and a volume of mostly previously published
short stories, *Learning to Swim and Other Stories,* appeared in
1982. His most celebrated novel, *Waterland,* was brought out to
great acclaim in 1983. Since then he has published only four
novels—*Out of This World* (1988), *Ever After* (1992), *Last Orders* (1996), and *The Light of Day* (2003). His œuvre is quite
slim, but it has won widespread recognition. *Shuttlecock* took
the Geoffrey Faber Memorial Prize in 1983. Although *Waterland* was shortlisted for the 1983 Booker Prize (Britain's most
prestigious award for fiction), it did not win the prize. *Waterland* was, however, awarded the Winifred Holtby Award of the
Royal Society of Literature and the *Guardian* Fiction Prize in

1983. Swift has also won highly regarded foreign prizes for his fiction, receiving the Italian Premio Grinzane Cavour for *Waterland* in 1987 and the French Prix du Meilleur Livre Etranger for *Ever After* in 1994. In 1996 *Last Orders* took the important and remunerative Booker Prize, as well as the James Tait Black Memorial Prize. In 1984 Swift was elected a fellow of the Royal Society of Literature, and he has received honorary degrees from the University of East Anglia and the University of York. Films have been made of *Shuttlecock* (in 1991), *Waterland* (in 1992), and *Last Orders* (in 2002). Although these films have had mixed receptions, they have attracted highly distinguished actors. Alan Bates takes a leading role in the film of *Shuttlecock,* Jeremy Irons and Sinead Cusak in that of *Waterland,* and the film version of *Last Orders* contains performances by some of the best postwar British film actors: Helen Mirren, Tom Courtney, Michael Caine, Bob Hoskins, and David Hemmings. Apart from his novels, Swift has published only an anthology of literary writing on fishing entitled *The Magic Wheel,* which he edited with David Profumo in 1985. He has not allowed himself to be diverted from his fiction, and he has not produced the essays, screenplays, and reviews that many of his contemporary fellow novelists have. His is a career of almost singleminded dedication to the novel.

The reception of Swift's work by scholars and critics has always been respectful, and often more than that, but it has on occasion been somewhat negative. Hostile commentary focuses on four (at times related, at others contradictory) qualities of his novels: a deployment of what are seen as one-dimensional, ultimately uninteresting, and unconvincing characters; an overshematic, insistently intellectual organization of his texts; excessive ambition; and the use of melodramatic story material that makes too great demands on the reader's emotions. Such criticisms emerge very strongly after 1983. For example, with regard to Swift's skills in character construction, Michael Gorra insists that "*Waterland* lacks passion, or rather its passion is all for history itself and not for the people who are affected by it." Also in a review of *Waterland,* Derwent May complains that characters are only presented "in two or three arresting postures" and that the reader is not provided with enough detail about central figures. In an intemperate review J. L. Carr accuses the characters of *Out of This World* of being limited, coarse, and boring, while Lynne Truss sees them as simply the author's mouthpieces. Hilary Mantel describes *Ever After* as fatally flawed by the choice of a tedious, overreflective narrator, too persistently the porte-parole of Swift's thematic concerns. The same problem applies to the other characters: they are "afloat, barely, in a pale sea of abstraction." Oliver Reynolds's praise for *Last Orders* is set against the critic's uneasiness about Swift's characters in earlier novels. "Occasionally . . . in Swift's previous books, one is aware of the novelist attending to the nuts and bolts of the plot or buffing up his themes to the detriment of the independent life of his characters."[3]

A corollary to this sense of Swift's inadequate technique in characterization is the critics' concern that his novels are over-schematic and overburdened with ideas. For example, Harriet Gilbert, in a review of *Out of This World,* welcomes its status as "a novel of contemporary *ideas,*" but describes it as "overschematic, more like a game-plan than a game played out, with symbols sticking up like marker flags and a structure of crossword puzzle symmetry." Hermione Lee joins in such criticism of *Out of This World:* "It is a book to respect, but not to fall in love with." Its "ideas" are too abstracted, not adequately embodied in the text, a view shared by Truss, and by Lorna Sage, who describes *Out of This World* as a "'dry' book—abstracted, diagrammatic." This is the burden of Hilary Mantel's strictures against *Ever After:* this novel "may have deeply advanced Swift as a thinker, but sadly it has not advanced him as a novelist."[4]

One might see Anne Duchêne's suggestion that *Out of This World* is too ambitious in the range of historical events it attempts to cover, or Stephen Wall's and Kirsty Milne's insistence that *Ever After* tries to deal with so many concerns that it fails to cohere, as consistent with the above strictures. A set of hostile comments on Swift's novels, however, seems to point to a radically different feature of his fiction, and one which sits uneasily with accusations of an overshematic intellectualism. Many reviewers attack *Waterland* for being melodramatic and emotionally overheated. In fairness one must note that Sage argues that *Out of This World* is dry and diagrammatic, while *Waterland* and *Ever After* are overly sentimental, and that different critics stress the melodrama of *Waterland* from those who argue that Swift's fiction is overschematic. But several critics do handle *Waterland* very roughly in this matter. The anonymous reviewer in *Kirkus Reviews* suggests that *Waterland* "doesn't quite manage to hide the melodramatic, even gothic, nature of the central story," a view which underlies Marion Glastonbury's witty, and very hostile, review of Swift's most celebrated novel. In his *Listener* review of *Waterland,* May endorses this criticism when he argues that "all the accomplished story telling leaves us in the end with a rather weightless melodramatic or Gothick tale."[5]

Positive comments on Swift's work are, however, much more common than the above. Indeed, several of the critics cited in the previous three paragraphs combine censure with approval when they write of Swift's novels. This is true, for example, of Gorra's review of *Waterland,* Lee's of *Out of This World,* and Mantel's of *Ever After.* Swift's fiction has always elicited applause from a wide range of critics and scholars. Gorra writes that *The Sweet-Shop Owner* is "on the whole a remarkable novel," and compares Swift with Joyce, concluding his review by insisting that this novel "joins with *Waterland* in establishing him as one of the brightest promises the English novel has now to offer." Reviewers such as Hermione Lee and Michael Wood take *Waterland* very seriously indeed, placing Swift in the company of major world writers. Academic scholarship quickly focused on Swift's fiction and praised it highly. In an important essay on Swift published in 1989, Del Ivan Janik declares that Swift has "already established himself as a major novelist and may prove to be the most outstanding English novelist of the final quarter of the twentieth century." In a similarly insightful piece published in 1991, David Leon Higdon sees Swift, along with Julian Barnes, as one of the "most promising authors" of the 1980s, who has "consistently broadened [his] appeal with each new work, demonstrating astonishing mastery of fictional structures and burking little in [his] pursuit of complex ideas."[6]

The role of *Waterland* in the reception of Swift's fiction is very important, and not always positive. "Graham Swift may sometimes have wished he had never written the damned thing," the eminent Irish novelist John Banville speculates in the *New York Review of Books.* Since 1983 Swift's work has been constantly compared to *Waterland,* usually unfavorably. The praise *Waterland* has garnered is, indeed, very high. In the early 1990s Higdon writes that it "remains truly extraordinary. It is Swift's most powerful, most ambitious, most technically accomplished novel." The success of *Waterland* has, however, meant that his three later novels have sometimes not been given their due. "It seems to be a convention," notes Hilary Mantel in a review of *Ever After,* "that when you are writing about Graham Swift, somewhere in the first paragraph or two you refer to '*Waterland,* his best book.'" She proceeds to make adverse comparisons between *Ever After* and the earlier novel. In another fundamentally sympathetic review of *Ever After,* which appeared in the *New York Times Book Review,* MacDonald Harris still insists that "It remains clear that *Waterland* is the brightest ornament" of Swift's fiction. "It must long have vexed Graham Swift that everything he writes is measured against *Waterland,*" writes the anonymous reviewer in the *Economist,* who then, unusually, goes on to declare that *Ever After* is "something just about as good." It is clear that Swift himself has reservations about the effect that such an early success may have had on his subsequent career.[7]

There is no doubt the success of *Waterland* has meant that the achievements and complexities of Swift's later novels have not been fully appreciated. But these other novels have also won very high regard from readers. "Not a book the reader is likely to forget, *Out of This World* deserves to be ranked at the forefront of contemporary literature," writes Linda Gray Sexton in the *New York Times Book Review.* In addition, not all reviewers see *Waterland* as the pinnacle of Swift's career. In the *Times Literary Supplement,* Oliver Reynolds declares unambiguously that "*Last Orders* is his finest book to date." Summing up Swift's work to *Ever After,* Michael Levenson strikes a note of peculiarly grudging admiration. "[Swift] is a figure to learn from," he writes, "the hard-working novelist with one significant success (which may never be repeated, and so what?), the professional in the imagination business who delivers his goods every few years, who raises no boasty thumbs in praise of his own talents, but who doggedly composes two hundred pages of serious story, without pandering to those who write the reviews or to those who write the checks." This seems too-faint praise for a novelist who has written some of the most serious, provocative, and technically ambitious fiction of the late twentieth century in Britain. John Banville's summation in a review of *Last Orders* expresses a more just (and more widespread) opinion: "Book for book, Swift is surely one of England's finest living novelists."[8]

In his rather hostile study of postwar British fiction, entitled *A Vain Conceit,* D. J. Taylor notes that in the early 1980s new writers and new concerns emerge in British novels. Although he damns these with faint praise, he insists that "to dwell on the deficiencies of the literary scene is to ignore the existence of a new strain in English writing whose effects have been profoundly felt, and resented, over the last ten years. The names are familiar: Martin Amis, Graham Swift, Timothy Mo, Peter Ackroyd, James Kelman" (114). Positive assessments of the changes wrought in early 1980s British fiction can be found in more balanced essays by Valentine Cunningham and Peter Kemp, while Malcolm Bradbury unambiguously celebrates the emergence of something new in British novels after 1980. The decade, he argues, was "not a period of traditionalism but of considerable exploration and much new and original talent."[9]

Although the radical nature of any shift in British fiction in the late 1970s and early 1980s can be exaggerated, one can identify four main aspects of this decade's novels that stand out in sharp relief against those of an earlier period and that, it must be noted, endure on into the 1990s and the early twenty-first century: a fascination with historical events and processes of the distant and more recent past; a cosmopolitan opening out to settings and characters from beyond the geographical limits of the British Isles; a very substantial amount of mixing of genres within individual texts; and metafictional concerns (that is, the writing of fiction that constantly advertises, in a variety of ways, its own textuality and fictionality—in short, its "madeness"—and of fiction that prominently takes as its theme the difficulties and sometimes the necessity of giving an account, telling a story, or producing a reliable narrative of any kind).[10]

Swift's place within these new concerns will be discussed fully below. However, it is worth noting here that his work very clearly represents three of these general aspects of post-1980 British fiction. His novels are very mixed in terms of genre; he is a writer obsessively fascinated with the role of historical events in his characters' lives; and much of his writing is deeply metafictional. The one aspect of 1980s and 1990s fiction that Swift shows little interest in is the cosmopolitan opening out to African, Asian, Latin American, U.S., and Continental European settings and experience one finds, for example, in the novels of Ben Okri, Salman Rushdie, Timothy Mo, Louis de Bernières, Martin Amis, Ian McEwan, Jeanette Winterson, or Tibor Fischer. Swift favors English settings, and although parts of *Shuttlecock, Out of This World,* and *Last Orders* are set in Continental Europe, these settings (except in *Out of This World*) are few in number and are outweighed by English—and often provincial or suburban English—settings.

There are five general issues that need to be discussed with regard to Swift's novels: the high degree of intertextuality and genre mixture in his fiction; narration and narrative (the voice of the story teller and his/her organization of the story material); issues related to characters (the family, insanity, entrapment, the commonplace, and the presentation of women characters); motifs of history and nation; and metaliterary concerns, specifically Swift's relationship with the traditional British novel.

One can certainly discuss Swift's novels to date as forming a unified body of work. In his review of *Ever After,* MacDonald Harris remarks that this novel "takes its place in what is now a familiar family of novels that resemble one another like siblings who have, perhaps, an odd marital infidelity or two in their heritage. The plots change, the characters are different, but the same patterns recur." Although John Banville thinks differently— "His novels differ greatly from one another; indeed, were it not for the evidence of his name on the title page, one might think that all six of them had been written by different hands"—one is rather struck by the sameness, within considerable differences, that mark Swift's novels (and even his short stories).[11]

Swift's fiction is always full of intertextual echoes of other major texts.[12] As William H. Pritchard notes regarding *Waterland,* "Mr. Swift has some strong writers behind him as precursors." Commentators point to similarities between his work and that of various major British and world writers, such as Henry Green, Virginia Woolf, Ford Madox Ford, Gabriel Garcia Márquez, and Günter Grass.[13] The experienced reader can see a wide range of local echoes of other writers (and not only novelists) in Swift's fiction: poets like Thomas Gray and Philip Larkin in *The Sweet-Shop Owner,* Wordsworth in the epiphany that concludes *Shuttlecock,* John Fowles's *The French Lieutenant's Woman* in *Ever After,* Chaucer's *The Canterbury Tales* in *Last Orders. Ever After* is the Swift novel that is most full of references to other texts, particularly to Shakespeare's *Hamlet.* The substantial and general use of references to other literary works, however, mainly involves two kinds of text and one particular author—classical literature, Victorian fiction, and the novels of William Faulkner. References to classical literature run through much of Swift's fiction. "I've always had a fondness for the classics," he says in the *Salon* interview, and critics have remarked on the Heraclitean ideas (concerning flux and change) that underlie *Waterland,* and the classical, Trojan War models that the characters and action of *Out of This World* reflect.[14] The chapter on *The Sweet-Shop Owner* in this study will also point out the occurrence of classical motifs in that novel. In addition, the Oedipal echoes in Prentis's pursuit of his father's past, and his own elder son's hostility toward him, are very clear in *Shuttlecock*.

Swift's scholarship has frequently shown that his novels constantly refer to the tradition of the canonical British nineteenth-century novel. His novels, it is argued, echo and engage with those of Dickens, Trollope, George Eliot, and Hardy.[15] There are good reasons for this perception. Swift can be seen to celebrate a modest lower-middle-class and, in *Last Orders,* working-class milieu that is the stuff of Dickens's and Hardy's fiction. It is also part of George Eliot's subject matter in *Adam Bede* and *The Mill on the Floss.* Both Hardy and Eliot are precursors of the detailed evocation of rural and small town settings in *Waterland,* while the characters in *Last Orders* travel through a world replete with Dickensian associations. Swift's fascination with the family, and the disrupted family in particular, has its antecedents in Dickens's *Bleak House* and Eliot's *The Mill on the Floss.* The dark secrets hidden within these families (insanity, illegitimacy, misplaced parents) echo Dickens and Wilkie Collins.

It is, however, to the novels of William Faulkner that Swift's texts most consistently refer. Swift has acknowledged his admiration for the work of Faulkner, and critics have always stressed how much Swift draws from the great novelist of the southern United States. Landow, for example, relates *Waterland* closely to *Absalom, Absalom!* (1936).[16] One can readily see why. Both novels present their story material in an extremely complex way; both are deeply concerned with history and its shaping of individual lives; both are regional, yet also national, in their focus; both engage with dark secrets and extreme psychological states. One can go even further in this matter. The mentally retarded Benjy in Faulkner's *The Sound and the Fury* (1929) is a prototype for Dick Crick in *Waterland,* although Dick is never allowed his own monologue as Benjy is. Jason Compson's demotic monologue, however, is surely echoed in the narrations of *Last Orders.* This novel also clearly refers—in story material, social origin of characters, and narrational strategy—to Faulkner's *As I Lay Dying* (1930), to the extent that some readers have suggested (quite unjustifiably) that it plagiarizes the earlier text.[17]

Thus, one can see that Swift's novels are deeply and consistently intertextual, both on a local and a more general level. The functions of such intertextuality are multiple, and they are discussed in chapters on individual novels in this study. However, in overall terms, intertextuality serves to universalize and to dignify particular characters and their fates. What happens in *The Sweet-Shop Owner* or *Last Orders* may be limited to unglamorous parts of South London, but the lives of those within those "narrow bounds" can be seen to echo the grand experiences of classical heroes and heroines, and the subjects of both British and U.S. canonical literature. Although one must allow for differences, the same is true of Swift's other novels.

Genre mixture is also a prominent feature of all Swift's novels, and this is something he shares with many of his contemporary authors in the 1980s and 1990s. Few novels by any author are generically pure, but Swift's fiction is particularly variegated in the range of genres that individual texts include. *Waterland* is most striking in this respect, juxtaposing folktale and legend with history textbook and encyclopedia entry, and the novel of psychological development with a nonfiction essay on the breeding cycle of the eel. However, other novels are no less varied in terms of genre. *Shuttlecock* is a psychological social novel with strong elements of war fiction and the espionage novel. *Out of This World* is part family saga, part psychological study, and part essay on British history, photography, and the possibilities of knowledge. *Ever After* is a campus novel, psychological study, and historical novel rolled into one. *Last Orders* is perhaps the least mixed of Swift's novels in terms of genre, but even it combines passages of metaphysical speculation with the novel of working-class life (a subset of the social psychological novel) and contemporary television soap opera. As with intertextual references, genre mixture has several functions in individual texts. But certainly the genre kaleidoscope of *Waterland* serves to draw the reader's attention to the text's own narrative procedures, reminding him/her that what one encounters in any text is an account of a particular kind (folktale or historical narrative in this case), and that reality and truth can be captured only through a variety of different genres, and often only provisionally. A similar function underlies the genre mixture in *Shuttlecock, Out of This World,* and *Ever After.*

The second topic to be considered with regard to Swift's fiction as a whole is that of narrational and narrative technique. These are remarkably consistent throughout his novels. All of them, except for parts of *The Sweet-Shop Owner,* are first-person narrations (almost all the short stories are as well); many of his novels also have more than one narrator. There are elements of multiple narration in *Shuttlecock, Out of This World, Ever After,* and (very strikingly) in *Last Orders.* Even *The Sweet-Shop Owner* has a brief passage in which the speaker/narrator is surely Irene. The major narrators usually deliver their monologues to no one in particular. *Waterland* is in some measure the exception here, as several of Crick's monologues are given to his class (whether they are listening is another matter). In *Out of This World,* too, Sophie is addressing her psychiatrist (although perhaps she would prefer to be speaking to her father). But William in *The Sweet-Shop Owner,* Prentis in *Shuttlecock,* Harry in *Out of This World,* Unwin in *Ever After,* and all the speakers in *Last Orders* ultimately speak to no one, apart from themselves. No one hears them; their monologues pass each other. In addition, the narrator in a Swift text is almost always a sad, self-scrutinizing man, middle-aged or older, delving into his unhappy past in order to try to work out how he got to the rather dispiriting situation in which he finds himself.[18] Swift very rarely chooses female narrators, although he does so in *Out of This World* and in *Last Orders.* It is also a striking feature of his choice of narrators that at some points in certain novels the dead speak. Matthew Pearce does so through his journal in *Ever After,* but Anna speaks directly to the reader after her death in *Out of This World,* as does Jack in *Last Orders.* Even William Chapman is dead by the time he completes his narration in *The Sweet-Shop Owner.*

There is a certain degree of uniformity in the language used by Swift's narrators. Although they employ a spectrum of stylistic levels, they are all relatively articulate and sophisticated in their vocabulary and syntax. Prentis in *Shuttlecock,* Tom Crick in *Waterland,* Harry Beech in *Out of This World,* and Bill Unwin in *Ever After* stand out as users of an often highly formal, educated discourse, often playing with language and drawing the reader's attention to their linguistic fireworks. Even characters of much less formal education, such as William Chapman in *The Sweet-Shop Owner,* and Ray and Vic in *Last Orders,* achieve a rather formal style on occasion, perhaps at time stretching the reader's sense of probability. Most of Swift's major narrators use language very skillfully (and often in a self-advertising fashion); however, their speech is also marked by severe breakdowns of language. The Swiftian narrators' speech is distinguished by incomplete utterances (frequently as aposiopesis—the intentional failure to complete a sentence). Many narrators allow their utterances to trail off into dashes and ellipsis points. Usually the reader is well able to complete the unfinished sentences, while still getting a strong sense that some characters are unwilling to say certain words, or to look at certain issues directly. This is coupled with one's sense that there are deep silences in some narrators' lives, areas of their experience that they will avoid at all costs. This is true of Tom Crick in *Waterland,* who seems reluctant to speak in detail of his mother or his wife. It is also the case with Harry Beech and Sophie in *Out of This World,* who delay in revealing what it is that Harry did when his father was blown up by the Irish Republican Army (IRA). *Ever After,* it can be argued, circles round Bill Unwin's avoidance of his wife's possible adultery. In *Last Orders,* Ray constantly postpones certain revelations about what he has done for Vince and for Jack in both the recent and the distant past, and why he did those things. Swift's narrators talk constantly, but they do not always reveal everything.

Narrative, that is the organization of the novels' story materials, also takes a particular and homogeneous configuration in Swift's fiction. Although there is an overall linear progression to all his texts, none of his narrators tells his/her story chronologically.

This is as true of *The Sweet-Shop Owner* as it is of *Last Orders.* There is always a movement backward and forward between the narrator's present and the past events recounted. In addition, the events recounted are frequently not given in their chronological sequence. Thus, in *The Sweet-Shop Owner,* Willy's crucial race as a schoolboy is not related until chapter 34. The interweaving of past and present scarcely follows a more chronological order in *Shuttlecock,* and in *Waterland* the dislocations of linear narrative are quite radical. The narrator moves freely among the various time levels, and the last four chapters reverse chronology, moving back from the late 1970s through 1947 to 1943, where the novel stops. The same is true of *Out of This World,* which like *Waterland* ends at an earlier point than it began, having crisscrossed large parts of the twentieth century in a seemingly arbitrary and digressive fashion. Like *Out of This World, Ever After* follows its own associative chronology, starting in the 1980s and ending in 1957. The four travelers in *Last Orders* make their way from Bermondsey, in South London, to Margate in the course of a few hours, but during their journey they recount events from the 1930s to 1990 in a succession that bears little relation to the traditional sequence of years.

Such narration and narrative organization are very important features of Swift's fiction. They embody a particular vision of the world, in which the past weighs heavily on the present. His narrators are all badly wounded by history (even, or especially, the dead), compelled by their own desire to understand, to retrace the past, to seek out some patterns in its destructive flux, to work out why and how they got where they are. But the associative chronologies of his novels, and his use of multiple narration in some texts, emphasize the particularity of the narrative accounts that are given. Breaches in linear narrative and multiple points of view emphasize the textual nature of the account, and the partiality of the narrator's version of things. These are individual, shaped versions of events, not objective, generally valid reports.

The battlefields from which these narrators bring back their accounts are, above all, those of family life. This is third major aspect of Swift's fiction that requires general discussion. Critics point quite rightly to the centrality of the family in Swift's novels.[19] From *The Sweet-Shop Owner* to *Last Orders,* fathers, mothers, daughters, and sons are embroiled in conflict and hostility. Willy Chapman waits in vain for his estranged daughter Dorry to come to him; Prentis pursues his father's heroism or lies through the years, while his own son struggles against his authority; in *Waterland,* Tom and Dick Crick compete for Mary Metcalf; Bill Unwin's relationship to his mother and stepfather is fraught and hostile; daughters and sons (Vince, Mandy, Sue, Sally) usually turn against their fathers in *Last Orders,* and relationships between mothers and daughters (for example, Amy and June, Carol and Sue) are scarcely better. Adultery runs like a scarlet thread through Swift's story materials: Prentis's father is probably an adulterer, as is Anna in *Out of This World,* and her daughter Sophie has casual sex with workmen; Sylvia Unwin and Sam Ellison are adulterers in *Ever After* (and Bill Unwin nearly is one), as are Ray and Amy in *Last Orders;* in *The Light of Day* Kristina's and Dr. Nash's affair is central to the novel's action. Indeed, sexual irregularity bedevils the families in Swift's novels. Prentis has turned his wife into a quasi prostitute; Tom Crick's mother has an incestuous relationship with her father; wives betray their husbands throughout *Ever After;* Vince pimps his own daughter in *Last Orders.* The only traditionally stable family in Swift's fiction is Vic's in *Last Orders,* although the Prentises do seem to have come to some kind of accommodation at the end of *Shuttlecock.*

Insanity, too, runs through Swift's families. Irene is pathologically afraid of life in *The Sweet-Shop Owner;* her illnesses are a kind of self-destruction. Similarly, Prentis's father has withdrawn into silence and is confined to a mental institution. Sarah Atkinson and Ernest Atkinson become deranged in *Waterland,* and Mary Crick is in a psychiatric hospital at the novel's end. Sophie delivers her monologues to her analyst in *Out of This World.* The institution for the insane or for the mentally handicapped looms large in Swift's novels—in *Waterland* and in *Last Orders,* for example—and mental handicap affects two major characters: Dick Crick in *Waterland* and June Dodds in *Last Orders,* the latter of whom spends almost fifty years in an asylum.

Over his whole output, Swift's characters are drawn from a wide social range, from working-class figures like Lenny in *Last Orders* or Mr. Crick in *Waterland,* to the lower-middle-class shopkeepers and businessmen like Willy Chapman in *The Sweet-Shop Owner,* Jack Dodds, Vic Tucker, and Vince Dodds in *Last Orders,* or Frank Webb in *The Light of Day.* Swift's social range also includes professional middle-class figures like Tom Crick in *Waterland* or Prentis in *Shuttlecock,* the glamorous actress Ruth Unwin in *Ever After,* and the very wealthy Beeches in *Out of This World.* At both the beginning and the most recent points in his career as a novelist, Swift has focused on an unglamorous, drab South London world of small businesses, while in between the social scope of his work has been quite broad.

Swift's choice of characters, however, has been criticized on two accounts. It is clear that female characters play lesser and often quite specific roles in his texts. Very few of Swift's narrators are female. The principal exceptions are Sophie and Anna in *Out of This World,* and Amy and Mandy in *Last Orders.* They are given extremely strong voices and very important roles in their respective novels. Those roles are very traditional female ones, however, and very negative. They are all, in Amy's words, "hardnosed little tricksies," sexually unreliable and sometimes quite calculating women who cause (usually for very good reasons) their husbands and fathers a great deal of grief.[20] Indeed, this is the role that many female characters play in Swift's novels —Mary Metcalf, Helen Atkinson, Sylvia Unwin, Ruth Unwin, Sally Tate, and Carol Johnson. Another similar criticism that has been leveled against Swift's choice of characters in *Last Orders* is that it is not ethnically inclusive enough. Kate Flint notes that in this novel "Swift's South London, or at least the South London of his characters, seems self-protectingly free of all possible multiculturalism."[21] The only nonwhite character in the London parts of *Last Orders* is a rich Arab client of Vince's, whom he heartily dislikes. The gender and ethnic selectivity of Swift's range of characters is striking. Individual readers must decide whether this severely undermines the status of his fiction. Like any serious author, Swift does have a particular vision of the world, and women play specific roles within that vision. It should be noted, however, that men are scarcely viewed more positively in it. Nor is it clear that a certain version of gender should always determine an author's status. It is worth remarking that women reviewers have given very positive accounts of Swift's novels. As regards the lack of black and Asian characters in *Last Orders,* it might be suggested that that is how the narrators would see the world, given their age and ethnic and social background.

The fourth central issue with reference to Swift's fiction is its concern with history. This is a commonplace of Swift criticism, and even a cursory glance at the novels will show to what degree they are fascinated with historical events and processes.[22] For example, dates are extremely prominent in all of Swift's novels; the reader's attention is constantly drawn to the particular year or month of events, as in a historical account. In addition, these dates and characters' experiences are constantly related to grand, national occurrences and developments: wars especially, but also technological, social, and cultural change. William Chapman viewing the altered face of his high street and the new demands and behavior of his customers, or Vince Dodds reflecting on the motor car and social attitudes in the 1960s, are representative of the way in which historical processes impinge on characters' lives. The rise of the Atkinson family in *Waterland*—based on the technological, social, and economic changes of the Agricultural and Industrial Revolutions in Britain, and Britain's subsequent imperial expansion—is also a clear example.

Grand events impinge, too, above all in the shape of war. Almost no major character in Swift's novels is not affected in some way by twentieth-century warfare, especially by the Second World War. Willy Chapman is unusual in his detachment from armed conflict, but even he thinks a lot about the war during its course, although it scarcely touches him directly. The heroic fathers of *Shuttlecock* and *Ever After* are men whose lives (and therefore their sons' lives) have been shaped by the Second World War. Jack Dodds meets Ray Johnson while serving with the British Army in Egypt in the 1940s; Lenny Tate's career as a boxer is destroyed by his six years in the Army; Vic Tucker's view of the world is partially shaped by his experiences in the Royal Navy. In *Waterland,* many of the events in the Fens are set against a backdrop of the war in Europe: flights of U.S. bombers take off from the Fenland to bomb Hamburg. Tom gains a sense of the importance and fragility of civilization in bombed-out German cities. Other twentieth-century conflicts alter characters' lives too. Robert Beech is badly wounded during the First World War and is killed by an IRA bomb, while his son Harry makes his career out of photographing the wars of the later twentieth century. Vince Dodds learns his trade and some of his attitudes in the British Army as it fights to hold on to and then withdraws from Aden in the 1960s. In *The Light of Day* Kristina is a Croatian refugee from the Balkan wars of the 1990s. Swift constantly interweaves the personal and the historical. Characters' lives are deformed and formed by their involvement in the events and processes of their particular time and place. Swift's emphasis on war is because wars—with their enormous upheavals and savage destruction—show the brute force of history in clear terms. Robert Beech and Henry Crick are literally the walking wounded of history.

In a review of *Out of This World,* Hermione Lee notes that in *Waterland* and the earlier novels the reader encounters "secret family pasts that come to stand for a national history."[23] Indeed, throughout Swift's fiction, one has a sense that he is describing and discussing aspects of the nation. He appears to be celebrating and scrutinizing a particular lower-middle-class England in *The Sweet-Shop Owner* and *Last Orders.*[24] The generational conflicts of *Shuttlecock, Out of This World,* and *Ever After*— heroically flawed fathers being rejected by their sons—also have a specifically English dimension. Prentis Sr., Robert Beech and Philip Unwin are not just universalized heroes, but specifically English ones. *Waterland* is concerned to examine and question a particular English (or, in this case, unusually for Swift, British) narrative of historical progress.

This last element in *Waterland* points clearly to the metafictional concerns that underlie much of Swift's writing. In this novel, both the narrator and the author scrutinize the validity, power, and usefulness of a variety of narrative texts. This is, in fact, closely related to a concern with history. The word "history" denoted not only a set of events, but also the narrative account that tells of those events. Indeed, the *New Shorter Oxford Dictionary* (1993 edn.) indicates that this second meaning is older than the former. The entire genre kaleidoscope of *Waterland* involves a consideration of how best to give an account of events, if indeed good accounts are possible at all. This metafictional element in *Waterland*—and in Swift's fiction in general—has generated a large quantity of essays and articles.[25] Individual novels' metafictional concerns and strategies will be discussed in chapters on those novels. Only his first novel, *The Sweet-Shop Owner,* and his short stories are without strong metafictional focus. Suffice to say that Swift is manifestly a writer who, in almost all his fiction, is deeply interested in the procedures, claims, and difficulties of giving both fictional and nonfictional accounts of the world. Different aspects of his art—intertextuality, intermittently baroque vocabulary and syntax, nonchronological narratives, explicit discussion of the problems of telling events and of knowing the truth—all show this clearly. In this, Swift participates in a general worldwide tendency of late-twentieth-century fiction.

He also engages in a critical scrutiny of the achievements and problems of traditional British fiction. As has been suggested above, Swift's novels position themselves in relation to a Victorian tradition of novel writing. Swift clearly sees Dickens, George Eliot, and Hardy (among others) as his predecessors. His metafictional concerns, however, are in part a questioning of the generally much less problematized approach to the literary presentation of reality in the earlier authors' works. Yet, in his novels' rich story materials, in their interest in the details and complexities of their characters' lives, and in their fascination with the world as well as with the problems of talking about the world, Swifts also identifies himself closely with a Victorian (and nonexperimental twentieth-century) tradition of storytelling.

Like his contemporary fellow authors—Ian McEwan, Martin Amis, Rose Tremain, Kazuo Ishiguro, Pat Barker, and others—Swift's career is far from over and may develop in at present unexpected ways. The pattern that is observable in his fiction to date is, however, clear. He writes deeply intertextual and metafictional novels, with self-questioning narrators who tell their stories in far from linear fashion. These stories involve disrupted families whose experiences are embedded in the destructive flux of history. But such a summation does not do justice to the richness and variety of the individual novels. Although the short stories may be, to some extent, apprentice work, Swift has not written a single novel that is less than fascinating and complex, and, for many readers, profoundly moving. *Waterland* will perhaps always be valued above his other novels, but the outstanding quality of all his fiction should be emphasized and celebrated.

CHAPTER 2

A Narrow World? (I)
The Sweet-Shop Owner (1980)

The Sweet-Shop Owner establishes many of the features of the representative Swift text: the monologue of an isolated speaker; a fascination with time, memory, and history on the part of narrator and author; an examination of the limits of knowledge; classical allusion; the motif of the seaside; the focus of the text on three generations of a family. The only unusual feature of *The Sweet-Shop Owner* is its lack of any metafictional concerns. But like the rest of Swift's novels, this one maintains its uniqueness. *The Sweet-Shop Owner* takes as its frame the last day of William Chapman, the sweet-shop owner of the title. In the course of this single day the protagonist recalls and reflects on his life and that of his wife, his daughter, and his wider family from the 1930s to the mid 1970s. As he moves toward his death, his day is interwoven with memories of his marriage, the Second World War, his wife's illness, and his estrangement from his daughter. He dies on the final page, still waiting for his daughter to return to him. Like all Swift's novels, it is remarkably ambitious in its attempt to span decades of social and personal history. It is one of the most crushingly sad novels of the postwar period, its bleak despair recalling the desperate emotional landscape of Graham Greene.[1]

Narration is both more and less sophisticated than in Swift's other novels, with a complex manipulation of point of view and shift in narrators. The principal point of view in the text is that of William Chapman himself, although he does not speak in his own voice until almost halfway through the novel. The largest part of the first half of the text is narrated by a third-person omniscient narrator, but usually through free indirect speech or thought. For example, the novel opens with William lying in bed in the early morning.[2] Here, and again in chapter 3 (22–23), when he recalls his wedding, the point of view is predominantly William's. But it is worth noting, too, that the point of view can shift, at times within one paragraph, toward that of other characters (for example, to that of William's parents on page 23) so that it is finally rather elusive.

Just after the account of William's daughter's birth in chapter 15, the narration changes, and William starts to narrate events in his own voice, usually addressing his (absent) daughter Dorry as he does so (103). For the rest of the text, the narration slides from William's narration to a more neutral, omniscient narrator, and from that to further representation of William's point of view through free indirect speech. Chapter 36 is a good example of the text's movement among these possibilities. Throughout the novel, however, the reader encounters other points of view and even one other speaker. Both of William Chapman's assistants in his sweet shop—the long-suffering, thwarted Mrs. Cooper (chap. 14), and the youthful Sandra (chap. 16)— are allowed substantial portions of the text in the form of free indirect speech. Also, in a remarkable passage (reminiscent of the way Anna, the dead wife and mother in *Out of This World, speaks*) Irene, William's enigmatic and beautiful wife, narrates (or at least speaks) *in propria persona*. The opening sentences of chapter 7 illustrate the shifting, elusive quality of the novel's narration: "Sit back Willy; drink your tea, rest your head, if you like on my lap . . ." (49). Does the narrator change again in the parenthesis in the first sentence of this passage ("he did not hear, there in the autumn evening . . .")? It is very hard to say, and the complexity of the narration here is increased by the fact that Irene's account of her past is followed by William's waking up from sleep. How much has he dreamed of what has gone before? The narrational jigsaw puzzle is completed by correspondence—for example, the brief letter that William writes to Dorry (186), Dorry's letter to her father (which stands at the beginning of the novel [9]), and the extracts from William's and Irene's wartime letters to one another (chap. 8).

In terms of language, the third-person narrator and William do not differ substantially. Both use a relatively neutral English without formality or informality. This may be considered a defect in the novel. William, after all, informs the reader that he does not understand Shakespeare (145). But William does not come from a poorly educated working-class background. He attends a grammar school in the 1930s and is apprenticed to a printer (24). His language, when he speaks for himself, is far from improbable.

The functions of Swift's narrational technique are clear. William is highlighted by being a narrator for part of the novel, and by the way in which his point of view is so central to other sections of the text. An objectivity is maintained, however, by giving other characters' perspectives their due weight through the semi-immediacy of free indirect speech. The fact that William only starts to tell his own story after the birth of his daughter is surely also very important. Is she his only chance to escape from the traps of his strange bargain with his wife, his allotted role, or the silence of death? If this is so, it is a chance he loses. Part of the wrenching sadness of the text lies in the fact that Dorry will never hear her father's long monologue and will come too late and perhaps just for the sake of the property. The monologue, like those of so many of Swift's characters, is delivered into an unlistening void. (Hermione Lee gives another verdict on this aspect of the text when she criticizes the novel's "wistful narrative methods which have the characters silently addressing each other.")[3]

The novel's narrational strategy allows the humdrum central figure, William, the sweet-shop owner himself, to speak directly or indirectly to the reader. It puts the dull, the prosaic, the unadventurous at the center of the text, with echoes of those masters of the drab quotidian—Thomas Gray, George Eliot, and Philip Larkin. But like these earlier writers, Swift aims to give his humble milieu the dignity and weight of classical tragedy. The narrational frame of William's last day observes the classical unity of time, while throughout the text the principal characters seem bound to one limited milieu. For large parts of her life Irene is virtually confined to her home. As William remarks toward the end of the novel: "We never moved out of these narrow bounds. Born here, schooled here, worked here. And even when I met her I stood here on the common and thought: enough, now everything is in its place, and I in mine" (184). There is an echo of Gray's "Elegy Written in a Country Churchyard" here (except that William speaks for himself), and of the unity of place common to classical tragedy. Elsewhere in the novel there is an echo, too, of Shakespearean drama. In a school production of *The Merchant of Venice,* Dorry declines to play Portia and chooses instead to play Jessica, Shylock's daughter, thus anticipating her own estrangement from her bookkeeping, seemingly miserly father (144–45).

Names, too, carry classical allusions. Irene paradoxically suggests peace (ειρηνη [eirini] means peace in Ancient Greek), while

Dorry is short for Dorothy, which means, as William learns, "God's gift" (112). William recalls Dorry's bedroom and the books on her desk, "faded ink-splotched school copies of Latin texts, Virgil and the *Metamorphoses,* whose contents I puzzled from the English heading before each extract: 'Narcissus and Echo,' 'Diana and Actaeon'" (147). As a schoolgirl and a student, Dorry studies Keats. Her university dissertation is titled "Romantic Poetry and the Sense of History" (216), and it is particularly the "Ode on a Grecian Urn," with its classical subject matter, that William reads as he looks over his daughter's shoulder. "You were doing your project on Keats and over your shoulder I read lines of verse (did you know, Dorry, how I peeped into those books when you weren't there?) which I didn't understand: 'Bold lover, never, never canst thou kiss . . .'" (147). The reference to Keats is echoed later when William is looking over old letters from Irene. The third-person narrator notes that a "china shepherd and shepherdess on the dressing-table still anticipated their embrace" (219–20). The pastoral couple does not kiss. Like the references to Keats, this motif is very appropriate to William and Irene's life together. They surely are the lovers who can never finally embrace; he is the "bold lover" always pursuing the elusive Irene, who is always "slipping away" from him (45, 99, 116).

All these references serve both to dignify the humble, the everyday, the life that has "never moved out of these narrow bounds," and also to generalize it, to make the "action" of William and Irene's life archetypal. Through the classical and literary references of the text, their experience, humdrum and limited though it be, becomes both tragic and typical. William reflects on the injury (he has prosaically fallen off a ladder) that will keep him out of the war: "He wouldn't have the opportunity, as they put it, 'to see action.' Such a strange phrase and such an odd notion—as if there were no action besides wars" (56). The novel emphasizes that there is "action" elsewhere, and that it is of consequence. As Gorra puts it, "There is a touch of Joyce in Graham Swift's revelation of the hidden poetry of small men's lives."[4] The references to Keats and especially to the "Ode on a Grecian Urn" also form part of the opposition between the human and the material—between people and things—which runs throughout the text. Just as the urn and its figures will outlast the lovers and singers of the human world, so objects and money survive after Irene's death and Dorry's separation from her father. In the last hours of his life William looks around his and Irene's living room at all the things she has bought as investments. He hears her voice saying, "See, things remain" (218).

Just as Irene slips away from her lover/husband, so she remains elusive for the reader too. William's and Irene's relationship is highly complex, especially in terms of the motives which are suggested (or better, hinted at) for Irene's behavior. Individual psychological and social elements interweave in their marriage and its development, but at the end there remains a mystery, an elusiveness about the whole affair. One should note that Dorry never seems to understand her mother. After one of the last attacks of Irene's illness, Dorry asks her father numerous questions about him and her mother. "So many questions, Dorry, about the past—when you had stepped so boldly into the present," William muses (168–69). Her questions reveal an attempt to understand her mother and father, and also a lack of knowledge about them. For her, too, the relationship is mysterious, opaque. And William's answers are scarcely revealing (169–70).

Motifs of obscurity and mystery abound in the text. Gorra suggests this is a defect in the novel ("its defective analysis of the emotional web within Willy's family, which leaves Irene's and Dorry's motives obscure"); this, however, seems rather a deliberate element.[5] For example, when William reflects on Dorry's knowledge of the relationship between Hancock, the estate agent, and his wife, and between her and Dorry's Uncle Paul, all he can do is pose unanswered questions (151). The reader never knows who won the race at the school sporting event between William and Irene's brother Jack (chap. 34). The account of the race simply ends with William deciding to accelerate toward the boy in front of him (198). Irene and William employ codes that are not always understood by those to whom they are addressed. For example, in the early days of their marriage Irene and William have a ritual exchange when he returns from the sweet shop in the evening. "'Good day?' It was a sort of code. 'Four pounds. And I sold out of lemonade'" (46). When Irene tries to tell her mother that Hancock has had intercourse with her she employs coded "coy evasions she [her mother] would have used" and is not understood (52). During the war, Irene and William conclude their letters in code. "He [William] wrote, '5520 helmets,' meaning, 'I love you'" (65). This continues throughout the war, and in her own way Irene joins in. But William is nagged by one question: "12,840 helmets, 25,700 packs. When she wrote now from London she added at the foot of her letters numbers of her own. 4,000, 5,000 ration books. Was it the same code?" (79). William sees the money Irene leaves him when she dies, and which he will not give to Dorry, as some kind of "token," though of what he does not clearly reveal (188). At the very opening of the novel, we find him musing over a letter from Dorry. "He sat up, in the double bed, holding the letter before him, looking at it fixedly as if it were really a code in need of breaking" (9).

A further motif of mystery is a stylistic device of which Swift is very fond, although it is not nearly as prominent in *The Sweet-Shop Owner* as it is in his later novels. This is the uncompleted utterance, the statement or question syntactically incomplete, tailing off into ellipsis points, not wholly clear or often unanswered. For example, William recalls what seems to him a perfect evening in the early days of his marriage to Irene.

> We walked back over the grass of the common, under the trees. How green this part of London always was. And up in the bedroom, behind the green curtains, the scent of Pimms and lemon on her lips. . . . I let you touch me but I'm not touched, I let you take me but I'm not possessed, I let you . . . (175)

After a disastrous encounter between Dorry and her young man and Irene, William overhears the fragments of the young people's conversation.

> Later, as you washed up the things together, dutifully in the kitchen, I overheard snatches of your talk: "That was fun, wasn't it? . . . I told you, didn't I? . . . *He* doesn't say much, does he? . . . Oh you were lucky he took time off from his precious shop to see us—he'll be straight off again after this . . . this bloody china . . . so we know what to do now, don't we Mike? Don't we? . . ." (180)

Questions and mystery recur throughout the text. For example, Dr. Cunningham tries to probe into the possible causes of Irene's illness by asking William questions. He gets no satisfactory answers. William reflects at the end of the interview:

"The smooth face eyed him as if it might be withholding some vital piece of information—or as if he were" (127).

The reader, too, is compelled to ask questions about Irene, questions that receive at best partial answers only. One is finally left with a mystery. Why does Irene choose William? Why does she move inexorably toward death, in effect welcoming it? The text suggests hostility toward her family as one motive for her marrying William. They have not believed her, they have ostracized her, sent her to a "home" after Hancock has had intercourse with her, and she has complained (chap. 7). Is there an implication that they would have liked to marry her off to the acceptable Hancock, and that her refusal to do so—to play her prescribed role—leads them to punish and confine her, and then guiltily to dispose of her to the first best suitor like soiled goods (55)? Certainly she continually expresses a hostility toward her family, and her choice of William and much of her subsequent behavior become one long act of vengeance (rather like a piece of modern Jacobean tragedy or Gothic fiction). In chapter 3, the narrator, who is here half William, half a third-person narrator, suggests this when he tries to guess what is in Irene's mind on her wedding night (28).

When she buys the shop for William, her father and brothers presume that it will remain in her name. She makes sure that it is William's. She says: "No, you must sign. The solicitors know, Jones knows. Only Paul and Jack don't know. The shop will be yours." William notices that "over her lips had passed—was it? you couldn't tell in the firelight—for the first time without its seeming like an act of charity, a smile" (41). In chapter 9, Irene's refusal to have her photograph taken with her family, and then her subsequent acquiescence, embodies her hostility, her distaste for them. As her father's business and health crumble at the end of the war, she remarks caustically: "He talks of 'saving the business.' Then again, he says it isn't the money—'Money won't bring Jack back.' It's a matter of principle. I don't know what he means by principle. I've never known him distinguish principle from money before" (81). When her only surviving brother, Paul, falls on hard times, she refuses to give him any financial help and never replies to his letters (chap. 23). It is the lumpish, lowly William—unambitious, malleable, controllable—who becomes her agent of revenge, her "solution" (55). The irony is that it is she who prospers financially, and it is William who becomes the well-off shop owner, while her brother is reduced to being Hancock's dependent.

Irene, the text suggests, also feels her beauty as a burden, as something from which she must escape (50). In this respect, the heavy, dull, ordinary William becomes her perfect partner, her way of escaping from the burden of her good looks. But William is finally only an agent, an instrument for her—respected, liked, but never loved. He is always held at a distance, always made to feel that in everything in their marriage she is only fulfilling a duty, her part of a bargain. "I let you touch me but I'm not touched, I let you take me but I'm not possessed, I let you . . ." (175). "And didn't you see," William asks the unlistening Dorry, "how when I lifted you up in my arms and kissed you, she wouldn't kiss *me*?" (116).

Irene seems in continual flight from life itself—from joy, from spontaneity, from sex. As the crowds celebrate V-E (Victory in Europe) Night, William notes to himself: "Victory, victory. But not for her. Along the path by the privet hedges and blossoming trees her face had tensed, as if to a vigil still to be maintained" (88). Her subsequent sexual intercourse with her husband is a matter of joyless acquiescence. "Later, up in the bedroom, she said suddenly, spreading her legs: 'All right'" (88). Sex—the unexpected, new life—seem to terrify her (99).

"You know," the young doctor remarks to William in chapter 18, "there are times when your wife almost seems not to want to get better. We can't have that" (126–27). But Irene, willfully it seems, pursues death throughout most of the novel. After withdrawing from life, she seems to embrace her illness as her desired fate, her desired role. "What does she want?" Dorry asks her father after one of Irene's serious attacks. "I think what she wants is peace," William replies (142). Dorry makes an enemy of her mother, not by discovering that her uncle Paul has had an affair with Hancock's wife, but by the "note of adventure" in her voice when she tells her parents of it (152). Only sterile withdrawal, hiding, or standing joylessly apart from life are acceptable to her mother. Her illness is a clear metaphor for this antipathy to life. She suffers from asthma; breathing is difficult, the air itself hostile, dangerous. "She could never get enough air," William reflects at the end of the novel, only to ask immediately, "Or was it that air assailed her?" (218). The reader is left once more with an unanswered question.

The questions concerning William and Irene's marriage are never satisfactorily answered, but what the novel does present through that relationship is an understated, though utterly devastating, critique of a way of life: a life based on money, things, and bargains; a life based on playing a part; a life based on standing back from the processes of life; and one based on a fear of "events," and "action," and "adventure." Criticism does underlie the depiction of their relationship despite the fact that both William and Irene are narrators, that William's narration forms the central consciousness of the text, and that both figures are in real ways victims of the social and personal circumstances in which they live. The novel is ultimately a tragedy—a tale of loss and failure—and these stem from Irene's and William's choices, from the lives and the roles to which they commit themselves. They are both victims and agents of their own fate.[6]

Theirs is a life of money, of things, and of bargains. The novel is packed with references to material transactions, to money and material bargains that take the place of love, of emotional commitment, of gifts of self. The question of Dorry's 15,000 pounds, which Irene has left to William instead of to her, is symptomatic of this aspect of the novel. It opens the text and is on William's mind at its conclusion, as he waits, dying, for the daughter who will arrive too late. Throughout, we see William paying off those who have worked for him—the newspaper boys first, then Mrs. Cooper, Sandra, and finally the employees at his second shop. These are all undeniably acts of generosity, but they are symptomatic of William's approach to the world. Payment must be made, but the only kind of payment possible is a material one. Janik suggests that at the close of the novel William "ends a life in which all attempts at the expression of love had been thwarted."[7] Swift's attitude is, however, finely balanced between a recognition of William's kindliness and generosity, and a recognition of the limits of his view of human relationships. It is a remarkably unsentimental balance. The issue is especially acute with regard to his treatment of Mrs. Cooper, his employee for sixteen years. Mrs. Cooper is predatory; she wants to take over Irene's place, to possess her employer. But it is also suggested that there is a cruel, unyielding limitation to William's treatment of her. She, too, will be "paid off" with a monetary gift, not with any kind of human warmth (38).

These limits, this insistence on striking material bargains with the world, are qualities William draws from Irene. Their marriage is one in which Irene grants William her wealth and her body, but insists that in return there be no question of love, of passion, of strong emotion. The text's presentation of William's and Irene's honeymoon is complex, subtly sympathetic and damning simultaneously. Irene "did the right things," lets William make love to her, plays the young bride, but will never say she loves him, nor let him say he loves her. That is not part of the bargain. "Wasn't the rest enough?" is William's paraphrase of her thoughts (30–31).

The rest is certainly a great deal. Irene is, in her strange way, fiercely committed to William. They form a unit defying the world about them. She is the making of the easygoing young man, at least socially and materially. But the reader must sense some kind of impoverishment in their relationship, in which the birth of a child is part of an unstated bargain (103), in which something as simple as Irene's wading in the sea with her husband and daughter becomes a "concession"—to life, to happiness, to them (118). The perverse bargain between William and Irene must be one whereby Irene gives her body, her wealth, and a child to William, who in return must make no emotional demands on her and, above all, not try to hold back her slow progress toward death, toward "peace." In its way it is as horrifying as a Faustian pact; only, of course, it is inverted—Faust (William) must let Mephistopheles (Irene) be damned.

The text continually emphasizes how Irene is concerned with money or things rather than love or other less material values. She buys things as investments, and when William comments on their beauty, she replies, "her tired eyes somehow disinterested: 'They will keep their value'" (148). All she says on learning that her daughter is going to Greece with her boyfriend is: "He'll pay for her I suppose" (181). William notes that she says this "as if she were washing her hands of something." After her death, William is left with a house full of objects. They surround him as he sits near death at the end of the novel (chap. 39). But the reader's response to William and Irene's marriage cannot be simple. As was noted earlier, there is a kind of fierce, if limited, commitment on Irene's part to William. There is also at least a double irony in the end of Irene and William's life together. First, the Keatsian echoes of the last chapter do point to a real truth within the text: things survive, people do not. Second, William has loved Irene devotedly for many years, and the novel takes the form of a long, sad love story. But despite this, the sense of impoverishment remains.

Irene is far from alone in her approach to life. Elsewhere the novel points to a similar materialism, a similar transactional attitude. Irene's family, after all, has treated her as property and disposed of her as such (chap. 8). Sandra, too, deals in sexual favors (105). Hancock seeks to possess Irene's body and beauty (and perhaps her family's wealth) (chap. 7); he certainly wants his wife as "a prize on display" (149). In return, his wife Helen demands things—not love—in their marriage (149). Even the predatory and devoted Mrs. Cooper belongs among the materialists and bargainers. In return for her years of devotion to William, she demands the money, the security, the ownership of Mr. Chapman and his property (chap. 4).

The effect on William of Irene's cold transactional approach to life is marked. It is as if the family begins to separate into discrete units as Irene withdraws more and more into the limits of her bargain (120). William slips more and more into the role of the miserly shopkeeper, always working, with no time (only occasional checks) for his daughter. At the end of the novel, he dies surrounded by cold "unmoving objects" (220), his wife and daughter distant, lost. He reflects on "memorials," on things left behind instead of people, substituted for people, for love, for emotional closeness, for what he describes as "the real thing." In a quite complex passage, the text reveals its ambitious scope as it talks about the impoverishment of a marriage, of a whole way of life, and of a country and a century. Irene's money and her property have come from her uncles, killed in the First World War. Instead of them—their living bodies, their lives—there is only money, and, of course, the "bronze memorial outside the town hall" (221–22).

Money, things, bargains. A life based on these seems to lead to impoverishment, sorrow, loss, and loneliness. But these are not the only aspects of Irene's and William's life which the text presents as leading to disaster, and which it subjects to the same devastating but complex critique. Irene and William lead a life based on the playing of a part, on standing back from events, and on a consuming fear of events and action. These also entail severe impoverishment—not of a material, but of an emotional kind.

Direct or indirect references to playing a role or part abound in the text. Janik comments extensively on this aspect of the novel.[8] From the very beginning of the novel, one is aware that William sees himself as an actor inhabiting a role, even as a puppet which needs to be jerked into life to play its part (11). When he first acquires the shop, William reflects that he will, with time, assume the part of a shopkeeper (42). This motif is repeated throughout the text with regard to William. He is a performer, an actor; most of his life is one long role, that of the shopkeeper. At the end of the last day of his life, he sits in his shop alone, the doors locked. "He felt like a conjurer, amidst his tricks, for whom, alone, there is no illusion" (213). His departure from the shop is described thus: "Then he turned his back on the shop and passed through the plastic strips. Best to go by the back. Actors slip out by back-exits, leaving their roles on the stage" (215). As he drives away for the last time, he thinks: "No, there was no longer a sweet-shop owner" (215).[9]

Irene, too, is a role-player. From the early part of her life, she has the role of the beauty thrust upon her, just as later her family will decide she is mentally unstable (chaps. 3, 7, 18). When Hancock rapes her, the incident is described as "like a performance," but one "in which people were really stabbed and wounded" (52). On her honeymoon she plays the role expected of her—to a certain point—just as she will be a mother only to a certain point (chap. 3). Indeed, her whole life with William seems like a conscious assumption of a role—half wife of a shopkeeper, half puppet-mistress. Her feelings as she recovers from the "insanity" for which she has been put in a nursing home are somewhat opaque, but they echo her future with William—in which she takes responsibility for her own and another's life, avenges herself on her family, and is also trapped in the role she creates for herself (54).

From another perspective, her decline into ill health and death is seen as an attempt to escape life, as if living itself were an unwelcome role thrust upon her. William reflects that peace can mean different things to different people—beating the Germans, for example, or death. "But he didn't know what it meant to him or her. Save perhaps a kind of not acting" (77). When Dr. Cunningham tries to persuade William to have Irene allow her doctors to help her, the sweet-shop owner clearly sees Irene as someone trying to renounce an unwelcome role, to give up life for death and peace (127–28).

A related motif is that of patterns. As Irene and William play their roles—or try to abandon them—so the novel sees those lives and those of others, and also historical events, in terms of pattern. "The world's events were gathered into those patterns," the narrator remarks of the newspapers William sells but never reads (17). The soldiers marching outside William's army stores at Carbury Camp form "patterns for the sergeant" (56, 78). William sees Dorry's life, as well as Irene's, as a "pattern" (114, 125). When Dorry comes to his shop, he feels that she "disturb[s] those patterns" of his life which he has established (138). Mrs. Cooper's distress at being asked to go to lunch first comically echoes the word "pattern." "Change? She always went to lunch second; the pattern had never changed" (156).

The words "role" and "pattern" are allowed to develop complex, perhaps not wholly resolved or integrated connotations within Swift's text. William's role is something he falls into, that he finds to be easy, that gives his life order and discipline, but which eventually leaves him lonely and ghostlike when, after Irene's death, he sheds his shopkeeper persona. Irene's role, as a beauty or a madwoman, is thrust upon her, and she seems to spend most of her life dismantling the mask of beauty, trying to escape the role of being alive itself. She allows herself to play roles—as a newly wed wife, as a mother—but with a certain reservation, a holding back, an ironic distance. Perhaps William only achieves this distance at the end of the text, and at the end of his life. Surely this is, in fact, the shopkeeper's tragedy. All through his life he has insisted that he is not his role, that it does not touch the truth of his identity. This is something he shares with his wife. Irene feels as a young woman that her "looks didn't belong" to her (50), and William thinks of her as she becomes more and more ill that if she could, "she would have torn off that thin mask of loveliness at the very beginning. For that was never the real thing" (128). Such a sense of the separation of role and person is very marked in William (132). But the sadness of all this lies in the fact that there is so little apart from his role—his consciousness, certainly, his love of Irene and Dorothy. But what does William have at the end of his life? A "monument" of things only. He dies alone.

"Pattern" points to the roles characters play, the rituals, the repeated behavior by which they define themselves. It seems to be either something at least partly adopted (as in Irene's case, she, to some degree, determines the pattern of her decline), or as a metaphor for the powerlessness of individuals in the grip of history, of the patterns of life itself (aging, death, birth).

This sense of powerlessness is very marked in William's view of himself. "He had planned nothing," he muses. "Not for himself. And yet he knew: plans emerged. You stepped into them" (24). "History came to meet you," he reflects on his honeymoon (32). Before the school race, he has a sense of individual powerlessness. "He stood on the grass at the track-side, bending and stretching his legs mechanically, as if he, the favorite, were not really a participant, as if the race about to be run were already decided. For wasn't it?" (192). Of Henry VIII and his wives he reflects, "They weren't real, but they didn't know it. History fitted them into patterns" (44). As he dies, he feels as if he "was a powerless skittle towards which was hurtling an invisible ball" (222).

Although the connotations of these two key terms in the novel ("role" and "pattern") are complex and perhaps contradictory, they do nevertheless fuse, at a certain level, to suggest that the principal characters see themselves as finally trapped and powerless within roles that are thrust on them or which they partly assume, and from which the only escape is the peace of death. As with basing a life on money, things, and bargains, the consequences of a life of role and pattern seem ultimately wasting and destructive.

Both Irene and William also continually withdraw from life, from events. Just as Irene is often described as "slipping away," elusive as Keats's nightingale, so William, too, stands back. Both seem to wish to be spectators at a remove, watching the world's events from a safe distance. The motif of the detached observer is established early in the text. William recalls Irene's reading of newspapers, not because she likes news, but rather, partly, to hide behind the pages of the newspaper (17). William takes this a stage further. He does not even read the papers, but only sees them as "columns, captions and neat gradations of print." "The world's events," he thinks, "were gathered into those patterns" (16–17). Later in the novel, he describes the passersby in the street as bobbing "like figures carried in water past the cluttered port-hole of the shop-window" (142), while he observes, detached, seemingly untouched. The moment in the day he and Irene appear to like best is in the very early morning as they sit together, silently (it seems) before he goes to work (137). This is valued as a moment of peace, separation, and superiority vis-à-vis the rest of the world.

Such a sense of superiority has been an important aspect of Irene's character from the start of their relationship. William slides down the children's slide on her suggestion while she stands back and watches him. William knows then that it will always be this way: "She wouldn't join in. She would watch; he would do" (27). On another occasion, Irene stubbornly refuses for some time to come out and join the rest of the family for a photograph (165). Mrs. Cooper again comically echoes this aspect of the Chapmans' characters when, vexed by William's friendliness toward Sandra, she sits in the stock room "like a hidden observer, spying on the others through the veil of the plastic strips" (158).

On Irene's part, the standing back—which she largely imposes on William; it becomes part of his shopkeeper's role—is motivated by a horror of "events," of risk, change, occurrence, process (these are surely part of the Keatsian echoes throughout the novel). When William falls from a ladder in 1938 (sustaining the injury that will keep him out of "action" in the Second World War), he feels Irene has a "knowing look" as she helps him. "That is what you get for adventuring," she seems to be saying, "that is what you get for wanting things to happen" (44). William himself looks at the recruits marching outside his army stores (an observer observing patterns), and he too adopts a knowing attitude. The recruits are prisoners of events, while William is the detached observer (59). When, after the war, he returns to his shop, he considers that "you seemed to walk (but perhaps you always had) through a world in which holes might open, surfaces prove unsolid" (96). In such a world, it is the very irrelevance of the sweet-shop that appeals. "Sweets, cigarettes. Useless things" (chap. 15). Dorry's boldness in walking along the breakwater is horrifying to her mother. The risk, the adventure, and the excitement in it are all anathema to her (119). Limit, caution, a horror of event—these are all things that Irene imposes on William and tries to impose on Dorry; on the husband who was once the fine runner, the man who would slide down a children's slide for her; and on the daughter who once "stood up, unafraid, high over the swimming pool, over the blue tiles wobbling beneath—that was no adventure, you knew how to keep your balance" and who then "plunged, with a perfect arch, and bobbed up again, to take second prize, with a laugh" (146–47).

At times William pushes against the limits of the detached, withdrawn position Irene forces on their lives. As Irene holds his head on her lap, she notes that William, too, wants things to happen, and this scares her (49). At least the sexual demands that William might make—and also, perhaps, the demands of love—clearly terrify Irene. Sex brings the change of childbirth, the involvement in life that that entails. For Irene, this must be controlled, avoided even though William occasionally frets under her power (76). William might also rebel against his shopkeeper's role, against the routine, the constant playing of a part (136). Toward the end of the novel, William reflects on the limits ("these narrow bounds") of his life (184). This complex passage is part of the author's insistence throughout the novel that the humdrum, limited lives of the Chapmans are worthy of literary treatment, that their unglamorous existence can also be a focus for intensely felt love, loss, and tragedy. But the passage also notes an impoverishment. William's and Irene's are lives lived within emotional limits, marked off by fear of events and change, by a fear of adventure which leaves William (if not Irene) isolated, hesitant, and unfulfilled at the end of the text. The very vagueness of what "the real thing" that he talks of (184) might be for him is very important and very telling. It might be anything, but it is certainly not what he has gotten from Irene.

The scrutiny which Irene and William's lives are held up to is, like the "narrow bounds" passage itself, very complex. It is, on the one hand, sympathetic. The reader understands, at least in part, why Irene behaves as she does; one knows William in detail; theirs is a love affair; and Irene has, in her way, a fierce commitment and dignity. But, on the other hand, the scrutiny is utterly devastating. Irene's is a life given over to emotional coldness, to things, and ultimately to death. She is William's puppeteer, and she both molds and destroys a likable, if weak, young man. He becomes what she makes him, and in the end he dies alone in a house empty of people, full only of objects. So complex is the balance of the text that no description of it quite does it justice. In this respect, the novel seems a very subtle and balanced piece of writing.

Can the way of life depicted in *The Sweet-Shop Owner* be given a social classification? The answer is probably yes. Here one can note echoes of George Eliot's fiction. The Chapmans and the Harrisons are clearly descendants of the Dodsons in *The Mill on the Floss*. Indeed, the parallels between the two novels, and the broader echoes of Eliot's fiction in Swift's (in, for example, *Waterland*) are complex and unavoidable. The Chapmans belong to the English trading middle class, the small shopkeepers of London and provincial towns. No British reader, certainly, could miss the social connotations, the class identification of William and Irene's life. It is the life of the English commercial petty bourgeoisie that Swift is subjecting to such close scrutiny. The Chapmans embody many of the qualities associated in literary and nonliterary texts with the shopkeeping class—materialism, hard work, and emotional restraint. One might argue, therefore, that there is an element of sociopolitical engagement in the text, inasmuch as it is the representatives of a specific social class that the text is examining. In this context, it is also perhaps worth noting that throughout the 1980s, the British Prime Minister was herself the daughter of a provincial shopkeeper.

If the text ultimately condemns Irene and William for how they conduct their lives, it also points to aspects of its world that make their behavior at least comprehensible and perhaps partly defensible. "What randomness," William muses as he observes the ebb and flow of people in the high street and the blooming prosperity of Britain in the 1960s (132). "See, things remain," he thinks, recalling Irene's words as he sits alone in his empty house (218). In a world of constant flux and change, perhaps it is defensible to hold on to objects which remain, which retain some value, just as the desire is understandable to stand back, to build up a pattern of behavior, a role against the randomness of history.

"History. Now I've always been fascinated by history," William says lamely to Dorry's history-graduate boyfriend (179). History is clearly brought to the foreground in a variety of ways in *The Sweet-Shop Owner*. The word itself is repeated constantly. The whole novel—as is the case with all Swift's novels—is an act of memory, a recollection and a reliving by a dying man of the steps that have brought him to this end. "And what do you first remember, Dorry?" William asks his silent and distant daughter (114). As he gets up in the first chapter he almost immediately plunges into a memory of the day Dorry was born (10). The novel has William explore his own personal history, that of his wife and his marriage, of his part of London and of his nation from the 1930s through the 1970s. Soon he "would be history," he reflects in chapter 1 (10). Passing time, the exploration of the past, and the interweaving of past and present are integral to the organization of the text. There is a continual movement between levels of time, and even past events are not given chronologically. For example, William's race as a schoolboy is not recounted until chapter 34. *The Sweet-Shop Owner* is pervaded by a sense of history in a number of its forms.

History in terms of chronology is marked very clearly, even as the novel deviates from linear chronology so completely. Dating is quite insistent. The reader knows the years, at times even the months, of all the major occurrences and episodes in the novel. History in another sense is present throughout the text. Personal history, national history, and world historical events are continually counterpointed. William stands in his shop before the customers enter, the day's newspapers (of which he reads only the headlines) piled in front of him. One headline ironically mocks his own failure to repair his relationship with Dorry. It reads: "Peace Bid Fails" (17). This moment is echoed later in the novel (although not later chronologically) when William is shown standing in the same place and position, and the headline from September 1938 reads: "Will Germany March?" (47). (For a similar use of newspaper headlines see chapter 21.) William and Irene's correspondence, and their humdrum store-keeping activities, contrast throughout the war with the terrible events going on around them, elsewhere in the world (chap. 8). Once again, Mrs. Cooper's experiences echo those of the Chapmans. As German bombs fall outside, she is seduced in the darkness of the air-raid shelter. "That was action, that was excitement; something was happening in her life" (81).

History is associated with danger and death. The earliest historical reference point in the novel is to Irene's uncles, killed in the First World War (49–50). Ironically, it is the uncles' money that allows Irene and William to set up the sweet-shop. William recalls their memorial, and that to the millions like them, as he dies at the novel's close (221–22). The recruits parading outside William's army stores are given over to history; this is the "action," "the real thing" they have desired since schooldays. The implication is that this history is deadly and menacing (59). It kills Irene's brother after all. Where it is not associated with death, history seems a matter of random, hectic flux, as in the high street outside the Chapmans' shop (113, 132). William and his shop seem symptomatic of this constant change. For all that he stands to one side of it, he is a purveyor of the transitory and the useless. William delights in the very triviality of what he sells: "Sweets, cigarettes. Useless things" (98).

Throughout the text emphasis is placed on personal, individual experience, but this is often bound up with (not just juxtaposed to), and at times influenced by, national and global events. One of William's fellow shopkeepers is said to carry the physical scars of war on his body (98), and this figure, typical of Swift's fiction, is representative of the power of historical occurrences over the inhabitants of the novel's world. As was noted above, Irene's money comes in the first instance from her uncles, killed in the First World War. Her father dies on V-E Night, an embittered man, his business ruined by bombing, one of his sons lost at sea. William's shop prospers as it offers relief from postwar austerity, and as it participates in the prosperity of the 1950s and the 1960s. Irene's and William's fear of events, and the emotional and existential limits they impose on themselves, may well be understood against a background of global death (1914–18, 1939–45) and random social flux. They try to escape history by putting their faith in things ("See, things remain"), in money, in the "pattern" of a repeatedly played humdrum role, in their avoidance of the new, the adventurous, the event. Hence Irene's fear of her daughter. Dorry represents change and risk. She dares to jump from upright to upright on the breakwater (119). There is "that note of adventure" in her voice when she speaks of her uncle Paul's affair (152). She goes beyond the narrow bounds that confine her parents—to university, to Greece, into an affair. And in her final encounter with her father, she carries off some of the signs of her parents' attempted escape from history—the property, the things which Irene has accumulated (chap. 35). Her university dissertation is titled "Romantic Poetry and the Sense of History" (216); her lover is a history graduate. As he is dying, William asks the absent Dorry: "And what will you buy with it [her mother's money], Dorry? History?" (222).

Irene and William manage successfully to evade great historical events, to profit from the socioeconomic changes of the 1950s and 1960s ("that mad boom," [187]), although they lose a daughter to those changes. But, of course, they cannot avoid another kind of history, that represented by time and change—the history that is embodied in death and transience. In fact, one way in which Irene's character can be interpreted is to see her as someone who—like a baroque poet—realizes this, who realizes the hollowness and the vanity of all roles, and who embraces death, gradually shedding beauty and health, as an escape from existence. Her life seems one long process of self-mortification. There is a kind of grim satisfaction in her response to her doctors' failure to cure her, in her acceptance of her disease. Indeed, there are a number of motifs of transience in the text. Some are established by contrast. For example, the things that do not perish are contrasted with human lives that end. Irene's beauty and William's strength as an athlete (surely these are strong echoes of classical and neoclassical *topoi*) are juxtaposed with their inevitable fading.

Other motifs of transience are brought to the foreground as well. At important moments the clock that stands in the Chapmans' hall is mentioned. And, on two occasions, William notes the flower-seller preparing her flowers outside the hospital. The echoes of the flower as a symbol of transience (especially in conjunction with the hospital—here a place of death, not of life) are unavoidable (128, 166). The echoes of classical and neoclassical motifs (and of Ecclesiastes in the Bible) are an indication of the ambition of this bleak novel. It is a complex picture of complex personal relations and psychological development; it is an attempt to chart the movement and the cost of a long period of British (or specifically English) history; it is an uncompromising and subtle analysis of a way of life; and it aims, too, at a kind of generalized perspective, the universality of the classical, even the high tragic. In all these, it is typical of Swift's output throughout the 1980s.

CHAPTER 3

Secrets
Shuttlecock (1981)

The mystery that lies at the heart of *The Sweet-Shop Owner* becomes the very substance of Swift's second novel, *Shuttlecock*. Like the earlier text, it too circles round historical events (in this case, the Second World War), interweaving individual lives with those great occurrences; like *The Sweet-Shop Owner,* it is concerned with the recovery and scrutiny of the past, of an individual's past and perhaps (by extension) a nation's.

Shuttlecock is narrated by Prentis, a senior clerk, an archivist in a British civil service department which stores the records of crimes which the police have not been able to solve or which they have ceased to investigate. "In the official phrase," as Prentis notes, these are "dead crimes."[1] The son of a war hero who has recently lapsed into some kind of mental alienation, Prentis begins to reexamine his father's behavior in the war. Along with his superior, Quinn, he comes eventually to suspect that his father, far from being a hero, became at a moment of ultimate testing, a traitor, a collaborator with the Germans. This suspicion, which is never confirmed, seems to act as a kind of liberation on the narrator-protagonist, and allows him to restore his crumbling relationship with his wife and sons. At the end of the novel, he is also promoted to be head of his department and to preside over the files of secrets of men and women like his father.[2]

Shuttlecock has none of the subtle shifting of point of view found in *The Sweet-Shop Owner*. It is narrated, predominantly in a straightforward autobiographical manner, by Prentis himself. However, narration is not without its complexities in this novel. Prentis, at times, adopts certain significant stylistic traits as he writes his account (and one should note he is writing, not speaking, throughout) of his investigation of his father's past. For most of the text the narrator uses a standard educated English, relatively neutral, casual in its syntax certainly, but marked really only as a contemporary middle-class dialect. A passage from the end of chapter 11—three paragraphs beginning, "All right, so you've gathered it by now"(75–76)—is representative of the narrator-protagonist's style. This style is sophisticated and eloquent ("a preposterous, an obsessive, a pathetic affair"; "Systematically and cold-bloodedly, like a torturer bent on breaking his victim, I am turning my wife into a whore"), is flexible enough to deal in sentence fragments where necessary ("This same woman . . ."), and is marked by an unmistakable contemporary simplicity in terms of lexis and syntax. (The sentence beginning "And are there really crimes . . ." is complex, but the pattern of subordination is a relatively unsophisticated one.) The parenthesis—"(All right, *bits* of other women)"—in its syntax, its lexis, its marked intonation, and its ironic self-deflation and self-questioning, also seems contemporary. But note the shift in the lexis at the end of the second paragraph ("shamefulness of my proclivities," "healthy and normal") to that in the next paragraph ("shilly-shally"). It must be stressed that these items are not used ironically—and that this is important—for they seem quite inconsistent with the predominant contemporary register of the previous sentences. In fact, they seem rather dated and old-fashioned, not quite the style one would expect from someone like Prentis. In a manner that is unmistakable, Prentis's narration frequently exhibits such stylistic shifts. A selection of decontextualized examples must suffice, but this is a widespread occurrence in the text. For example: "information sometimes of a nefarious and inflammatory nature, the subjects of which would, to say the least, feel uneasy if they knew such information were stored" (15); "extremely thrusting breasts" (22); "Real enquiries don't come our way thick and fast" (23); "I am particularly grateful that she hasn't slumped as some women do after they have had their children. You could say that my wife has her share of beauty" (27); "From what I gather from Martin and Peter, Nature Study is not a subject they teach any more in primary schools—and that, I can't help thinking, is a bad thing" (33); "Needless to say, I punished it severely" (36); "You will have gathered that my relations with Martin and Peter aren't exactly harmonious" (53); "So Quinn was a lover of plants, too, a devotee of the flower-pot; like Marian" (173).

George Steiner has noted that it is remarkably difficult to pin down the stylistic coloration of texts and utterances that are close to the reader in time, but somehow alien and distant too.[3] This is true of this aspect of Prentis's style. He speaks, at times, like someone a generation older than he—like, in fact, his father. Prentis himself is aware of his father's—and his father's generation's—distinctive style. After a conversation with Quinn, his boss as well as an acquaintance and contemporary of his father, Prentis reflects on the "old-fashioned" exchanges, on "the suave chummy talk" of his father and his companions (67–68).

When Prentis thinks of *Shuttlecock,* the war memoirs of his father from which the novel's title derives, he notes that his father discusses his feelings in them "in a bluff, almost light-hearted way" (52). It is that slightly dated bluff pomposity, the use of cliché without irony, and the slight heightening of lexis and syntax that mark his father's memoirs and aspects of Prentis's own use of language. The passage in chapter 18 ("For with the German retreat . . ." [106]), in which Prentis quotes from his father's memoir, is representative. The frequent modifying adverb phrases, along the slightly heightened lexis and syntax ("often savage it is true, but localized and in the majority of cases directly influenced by ourselves," "carnage," "This was a period"), create the dated impression here. In his echoes of his father's style, Prentis reveals both his own imprisonment in his father's shadow and his need to break out. It is noteworthy that the stylistic shifts from contemporary to rather dated seem less numerous after the first third of the novel. This stylistic aspect of the novel must be partly responsible for Patrick Parrinder's judgement about *Shuttlecock* and *Out of This World* that "both novels rather blatantly set out to debunk a *Boy's Own Paper* ethos."[4]

Unusually for a Swift narrator, Prentis almost always completes his sentences. He is a bureaucrat and his father's son, after all. But one other aspect of narration in *Shuttlecock* suggests mystery, uncertainty, and an inability to tell or understand all. This is genre mixture, in places marked by the presence of text within the main text of the novel. Prentis's account of his investigation into his father's past quotes extensively from his father's war memoirs, *Shuttlecock,* in which his father tells of his experiences as a British agent in occupied France during the Second World War. This immediately produces one aspect of genre mixture within the text. It contains not just Prentis's narrative of his own actions and experiences in contemporary Britain, but also a war story—an autobiographical account of wartime experiences—although one should note that the father's text is contained in, and controlled by, Prentis's own.

In addition, Prentis's narrative itself contains disparate generic elements. On one hand, it possesses genre markers of the detective story (the "dead crimes" department, an investigation, quotations from police files); on the other hand, its focus is quite clearly that of a piece of psychological fiction (Prentis's relationship with his wife and sons, his relationship with his father, his father's retreat into insanity). Few novels are pure in terms of genre. In *Shuttlecock,* however, the psychological, personal material is very foregrounded for a piece of detective fiction, and the aspects of the detective story are unusually prominent for a psychological novel. Once again (as will be noted with regard to *Waterland*) genre mixture functions as an indication of the difficulty of understanding the world. The text tries to capture the truth through two narratives and three discrete genres (the detective story, psychological fiction, and the war memoir), and in the end Prentis still is not sure whether his father was a traitor or not. *Shuttlecock* anticipates the genre kaleidoscope of *Waterland* and its function.[5]

Prentis is continually concerned with the pursuit of knowledge and the acquisition of information—knowledge about secrets, mysteries which, he suggests, lie at the heart of human life and action; knowledge of the past, covered over by layers of time and fiction. The very words "knowledge," "information," and "know" are repeated insistently throughout the novel. Prentis wants Quinn's job, not merely because it means promotion, but because he would "be in a position where I would *know;* where I would no longer be the victim, the dupe, no longer be in the dark" (71). Making love, for Prentis, is a pursuit of "enlightenment," a search for "the very secret of nature itself," for "nature's purpose" (73). Prentis sees himself like one of his father's interrogators, probing his father's secrets (106), and before he visits Quinn for the final revelation of the truth of his father's actions in the war, he declares: "On Wednesday I will see Quinn; on Wednesday I will know" (155). As Quinn remarks during his discussion of truth and knowledge with Prentis, "You see, it's the knowledge that matters, it's the knowledge that makes the difference. Only that" (197).

The knowledge that Prentis and Quinn possess and seek is a knowledge of secrets and hidden mysteries. On the tube (the British term for the subway), Prentis suspects that all those around him are doing what he himself does, pursuing each other's humiliating secrets (25). He feels his wife "doesn't know who I am," while he senses that he could mold and shape his wife in a variety of ways without touching her inner being (27). Prentis's father's wartime activities as a spy are particularly appropriate here. It is the spy's job to discover the secret piece of information that the possessor wishes to conceal. It is the enigma of his father's past—the hint of shameful secrets concealed in an exemplary life, in an admired biography, and finally in the silence of the insane—that Prentis himself chases throughout the novel. His own profession, archivist in a "dead crimes" department, seems most appropriate too, surrounded as he is by the records of unsolved, dark mysteries.

The repeated motif of nakedness is relevant to this concern. Prentis's father "escapes" from the Gestapo without his clothes on; Prentis reflects that he and Marian used to make love naked by the sea, but now no longer do so (he now even fears the intrusion of their sons into their bedroom) (75–76); while Prentis is visiting his father in his "institution," one of the patients strips naked and runs through the grounds (46). Nakedness is associated in each case with shameful exposure. Similarly, Prentis begins to question whether the revelation of knowledge, the laying bare of what is secret, is necessarily good. Quinn asks these questions directly (118).

For some time, Quinn has been using (or abusing) his position as director of the department to destroy records of people's misdeeds, follies, and shameful secrets. "You've been withholding—or destroying—information so as to spare people—needless painful knowledge," says Prentis in amazement (176). As Quinn questions the absolute value of knowledge, Prentis modifies his purpose. Finally, he decides he does not want to know the truth about his father's actions. "And then suddenly I knew I wanted to be uncertain, I wanted to be in the dark" (199). "'I don't know,' I said resolutely. It seemed to me this was an answer I would give, boldly, over and over again for the rest of my life" (200).

Prentis seeks knowledge of the past above all—of his father's past, of the secrets of his past actions. His department, similarly, is concerned with storing information about past events and actions. Like William in *The Sweet-Shop Owner,* Prentis probes and scrutinizes the past—of his father and of himself, and also (by implication) of his nation. The process is, for him, one of self-discovery and self-placing (as it is for William too, although Prentis seems much more perceptive about his own situation and actions than the shopkeeper).

> Before I went to sleep I thought: I was born in August 1945. I must have been conceived when dad came home, after his escape, from France. Mum and Dad together in the autumn of '44. A honeymoon hotel amidst tangy, woody air. I am a product of those times and of all that happened in the Chateau Martine. (151)

All Swift's novels involve historical inquiry, a probing of personal history and of those grand, public events usually identified as "history"; they also stress, as in the above quotation, the interweaving of the personal and the public, the domestic and the grand event. Public and private intersect, too, when Prentis learns that his father's treachery may be paralleled by adultery after his wife's death. Memory, a faculty and an activity obviously intimately connected with either form of history, is constantly referred to in *Shuttlecock*. It is central to the action of the text, the means whereby Prentis uncovers (and his father conceals) the truth of those events in France forty years previously. The novel begins by recording an act of memory: "Today I remembered my hamster" (5), and immediately the fallible, selective, distorting nature of memory is stressed.

This kind of comment on memory recurs throughout the novel: from both Prentis *père* and *fils* (138–39), and from Quinn (191–92). Prentis's department itself is like a huge institutionalized memory. His very impulse to write down his thoughts and feelings is prompted by the memory of torturing his pet hamster when he was a child (39–40). By chapter 7, it begins to become apparent that Prentis's focus is on his father—on his mysterious "language-coma," and, crucially, his wartime past. The father himself has given an account of this past in his war memoir, *Shuttlecock: The Story of a Secret Agent*. Prompted by Quinn, perhaps by his own obsessive desire to talk to his now silent father, Prentis slowly uncovers the possible evasions, the possible lies that comprise part of his father's memoir, of this written memory. Significantly, Prentis's own memories play a role in uncovering his father's past—his memory of discovering his father writing late at night and seeing him start, as if guilty (104, 188); and his memories of the golf-club companions of his father (146). Quinn delivers the final blow to Prentis's doubts by recounting his memory of his own failure of courage in the war (191–92).

Motifs of memory and genre mixture combine in *Shuttlecock* with repeated motifs of storytelling to problematize, in very typical 1980s fashion, the possibility of a true account, the notion of the truth itself. Prentis's father is a storyteller; he can only speak now through his book. "The book *is* Dad," Prentis asserts (52); "I stare at the page. I read the words as though, if I read hard enough, other words will appear: Dad will begin to speak" (60). At times Prentis fears—as Quinn leads him by the nose—that he is the victim of his boss's "imagination," as if the latter were some sadistic, manipulative author, bent on playing with him (chap. 13). Z's wife's evidence is seen by Quinn as "the wife's story" (87), as "fabrications" (89). For much of the novel, Prentis probes his father's book (his story), obsessively scrutinizes and analyzes it, and tries to square its account with his suspicions, his memories, and other documents. Finally, he refuses to find out the truth. Would the document which Quinn has stolen, and which he and Prentis destroy together, be conclusive? Prentis prefers not to know the truth for certain, but he is adamant at the end about the untrustworthiness of any account and any text (213–14). The "knowledge" of which Prentis speaks so often is finally a very elusive thing and something that he ultimately turns away from—even if it were really attainable.

The primary focus of Prentis's investigation and his father's memoir is the Second World War and one individual's conduct in it. It is worth noting here the prominence of the war motif in Swift's fiction and the recurrence of children whose lives are profoundly shaped by their parents' or forebears' experiences of either of the two world wars of the twentieth century. In *The Sweet-Shop Owner,* Irene's sense of the chaos—of the brutal destructiveness of time and history—is connected with her uncles' deaths in the First World War. She also loses a brother in the Second World War. Prentis, in *Shuttlecock,* lives in the shadow of a heroic father and what may or may not have occurred in the Chateau Martine. In *Waterland,* Tom's parents meet in a home for soldiers seemingly incurably disturbed by their experiences in the First World War. (His half-brother Dick might be seen as a product of his grandfather's despair at this war and the Boer War.) In *Out of This World,* Harry, himself scarred by his albeit secondhand experiences in the Second World War, is the son of a man physically and emotionally maimed by the First World War. The Cricks' father limps because of his war wound. Prentis's father presumably carries the psychological wounds of his torture and possible treachery, wounds that he attempts to conceal in his memoirs and that eventually drive him into his silent withdrawal from the world. Swift's picture of twentieth-century Britain is of a world littered with physical and mental cripples, a world savagely scarred by the twentieth century's brutality, especially in the shape of its two world wars.

But in *his* war, Prentis's father seems to have behaved with outstanding heroism, seems to have emerged from it unscathed, to have had, in a phrase current after 1918 and 1945, "a good war." But just like Harry in *Out of This World,* Prentis feels compelled to reassess this heroic past, to probe at it, and to uncover a partial hollowness, a partial lie within it. His father emerges as a hero, certainly, but also a traitor—one who collapsed under unbearable pressure. His heroism is still there, but balanced by a flawed, ordinary humanity. This reassessment of a father's past emerges in the course of *Shuttlecock* (as it clearly does in *Out of This World*) as part of a conflict of generations, of a power struggle between them. One should note that Swift's novels often possess elements of the popular "family-saga" subgenre. Once he discovers his father's likely failure, Prentis is a free man, freed from his father's shadow, able to reestablish his relationship with his wife and his own elder son, able to assume the position of director of his archive, and to hold his own, at least, in the struggle that is now beginning with his elder son.

Motifs of father/son conflict are frequent in the novel. Indeed, only Z's son seems to have had no conflict with his father, and ironically his mother's story presents them as enemies (89). Even before he starts to write of his own father (and surely this is an indication of the driving force behind his investigations and writing), Prentis recounts a "routine" case from his department's files. The oppressive weight of a father's past and a son's guilty response (he "systematically disfigured and mutilated his father's body" [23–24]) in part anticipates Prentis's own situation and what he will do in the course of the novel (although to his father's past, not to his body). Although loyal to his father, considerate to him in his illness, Prentis has always concealed his "admiration" for him (41). He confesses he wants "to step into Dad's shoes" (71). "Now his mind was gone," he continues, "now Dad was no more: I wanted what he had had. To be even with him" (71). His complicated sexual activities with Marian become a pursuit of the "adventure" that his father knew as a spy and that he, as a modern petty bureaucrat during peacetime, is denied (51, 74). He feels the discovery of his father's failure as a liberation. "Something had collapsed around me; so I couldn't help, in the middle of the ruins, this strange feeling of release. *I* had escaped; I was free" (183).

Prentis's relationship with Quinn partakes of his relationship with his father. He wants to replace Quinn, just as he wants to step into his father's shoes (71). Quinn, the male authority figure inspecting him from above as he works, is associated with Prentis's father, whom he knows, in fact, and even speaks like (67). Prentis fears Quinn's crumbling—his loss of authority before him—just as he does concerning his father (115, 128–29). For there is nothing gleeful in Prentis's pursuit of his father's failure, but rather a hesitation, a fascinated compulsion to know the worst (which he turns from finally and never knows for certain). The conflict of fathers and sons will be repeated down the generations. To his own sons, Prentis is no hero. They prefer robots on TV and even dent their grandfather's heroic glamour (to them he is "Grandpa Looney" only). Prentis is in constant conflict with his older son Martin whose qualities impress him and remind him of his own father's (84).

Only once he finds out almost everything about his own father (but refrains from gaining final certain knowledge in what is perhaps also a gesture of power), and once he replaces the fatherlike Quinn, can Prentis's relationship with his son improve. He recognizes, however, that his older son will develop into a bold, resolute figure, much more like his grandfather than his father, while his second son is doomed to have his own weak, hesitant qualities (218). Prentis has gained a certain stability and authority, but Martin has gone his own way already, and Prentis seems pleased enough. Martin no longer spies on his father (as Prentis spied and spies on his?) but pursues his own ends, almost indifferent to his parent (212).

As with the lives of the protagonists in *The Sweet-Shop Owner,* one senses a depth to the characters, a resonance beyond their own particular fates. There is a metaphorical pressure in Prentis's reassessment of his father's heroic past, of his role in that at once very real and also highly mythologized event that is central to the British twentieth century. Prentis's father's matter-of-fact derring-do seems so clearly, to a British reader at least, representative of a certain type of Second World War heroism, depicted, for example, in many British wartime and postwar films.[6] In the culture of postwar Britain, the Second World War assumes a very great importance. Prentis's scrutiny and questioning of his father's past surely echoes beyond the individuals involved, and becomes suggestive of a postwar generation's reassessment of its country's glorious past—a discovery that it was still heroic, but flawed and more human than it had presented itself. This is a process to which Prentis acknowledges, with considerable wisdom, his own account of his actions, the novel *Shuttlecock*, will be subjected by later generations (214).

But Swift is concerned to move the novel onto an even more general plane of significance. The text aims to depict not only individual and national destinies, but also tries to show how these may be bound up with very general, natural processes. The word "nature" and ideas associated with it are clearly foregrounded in *Shuttlecock*. Prentis writes of his fondness for "Nature Study," of his desire to have a hamster, "a part of nature" (34). He and his wife used to make love outdoors, in nature, "quite spontaneously, in the open air—in fields, amid ferns, in secluded parts of beaches" (76). Despite his guilt about their present erotic experiments, he feels he should try to justify his and his wife's contortions as normal (75–76). Under terrible pressure, Quinn suggests, Prentis's father followed his own nature in betraying his comrades (190).

The father's memoir is highly suggestive at this point. Although the word "nature" is not used here, it underlies his account of the escape from the Chateau Martine. He does so naked—a bare, unaccommodated, natural man. When he appears before the French woman who helps him, "Some trace of civilized delicacy still clung to me in my primitive state and I tore a leafy branch from a bush for purposes of decency. I stood like Adam after the Fall" (166). Pursued by the Germans, he abandons shoes and clothes—"it seemed that quite deliberately and actually—not as some metaphorical gesture—I was trying to turn myself into an anonymous creature of the woods" (169). Finally, he does indeed become like an animal, burrowing into the undergrowth, covering himself with leaves (170).

He, too, seems to become a "piece of nature" at this point (220). (His betrayal diminishes him as a hero, but makes him more natural.) This is the phrase—"a piece of nature"—with which Prentis Jr. closes his account, as he thinks of how his wife and he have once more made love in the open air, in a landscape that resembles naked "human flesh," and after he has described his sons ("naked, fleeing creatures") running towards the sea. Perhaps it is possible to see Prentis's confession as an examination of nature, a piece of "Nature Study," a discussion of the possibilities and drives of human nature under specific circumstances.

In *Shuttlecock,* human nature (what is normal, natural) and the circumstances in which it operates are marked by cruelty and brutality. The whole novel starts with Prentis's memory of his hamster and his tormenting of it—a comic, if not so humorous, anticipation of things to come (chaps. 1, 5). The savageries of the Second World War are clearly set out in his father's memoir, savageries that he perpetrates, observes and experiences directly. On a different level, Prentis's relationship with his family, especially with his older son Martin, is one of brutal struggle for power. When the boy steals and hides a copy of *Shuttlecock,* Prentis has a vision of his own possibilities for violent action (79–80).

As a subtext to the novel, one can perceive that Prentis, too, fights his father and, in the end, hunts down his father's guilt until he has power over him. Prentis still visits his father twice a week. He could, he reflects, ask the questions about betrayal, adultery, and failure that "might restore and destroy my father" (212). But Prentis does not ask the questions. He refuses to be one of his father's Gestapo interrogators, and in their mutual agreement not to speak and not to ask, he feels he has found "the perfect balance" between himself and his father (212–13).

Like Prentis and his father, the novel itself tries to achieve a "balance." Prentis does not ask the questions; he does not strike his son. The "nature" of the torturers and the traitor of the Chateau Martine, and of Prentis's and his family's ugly clashes, are matched by the forgiving landscape of Camber Sands and of the woods, by the shelter of the institution where his father lives, by the son's holding back from destroying his father. The novel is full of incongruous juxtapositions of this sort. As he reads of war's brutality, Prentis thinks of his wife and children by the river at Richmond (60, 62–64). He moves from a "chink of bare flesh" above his wife's jeans to the Gestapo torture chamber of the chateau (131). In the chateau itself, his father is struck by the harmony and beauty of the gardens and the house as opposed to the vicious brutality of their present uses (136). Prisoners are executed in the rose garden. The novel strikes an ambiguous balance among these motifs. As he remembers torturing his hamster, Prentis asks: "What became of my love? For what else is love—don't tell me it is anything less simple, less obvious— than being close to nature?" (35). Nature seems to comprise both the cruelty of the torturer and the love and forbearance of the son. It ends on a note of joy, of at least temporary balance— Prentis reconciled with his family in the open spaces of Camber Sands. But even here there is ambiguity. Rusty Second World War defenses dot the landscape. Martin's character (his nature?) contains the seeds of future conflict; his younger brother is a future replica of his father; and Prentis has already anticipated their scrutiny of their father (chap. 33). But for the moment there is reconciliation and balance, even perhaps a momentary escape from the brutal exigencies of history and human nature.

CHAPTER 4

The Novelist's Workshop
Learning to Swim and
Other Stories (1982)

Swift has published only one collection of short fiction, containing eleven stories; short stories form a small part of his output. The reasons for this are likely to be personal to the author. He is clearly a writer who works most happily in the greater space that the novel offers. It is also, however, worth noting that since the Second World War the short story has not enjoyed the same interest of publishers and writers in the United Kingdom as it has in the United States or the Irish Republic.[1] Swift's short stories themselves have usually met with a lukewarm reception from critics. For example, Jonathan Penner remarks in the *Washington Post* that they are "of thoroughly mixed merit" and that some "fall into contrivance and melodrama." Michael Gorra criticizes Swift's inability to render distinctive voices for his narrators. He sums the stories up as mostly "minor—pleasant reading but no more." If Hilary Mantel, writing in the *New York Review of Books,* does not share these negative views, she clearly understands that the primary value of the short stories lies in what they tell the reader about Swift's development as a novelist. European commentators have been much kinder to these short texts. The eminent Polish critic Jerzy Jarniewicz describes the collection as integrated, poetic, and substantial, while the French scholars Liliane Louvel and Richard Pedot have written extremely complex (and, in Louvel's case, convincing) analyses of individual stories from *Learning to Swim*.[2] Although these stories are, indeed, of interest above all because of their relationship to the rest of Swift's oeuvre, they are by no means negligible individually, nor is the collection unintegrated.

All but one of the stories in *Learning to Swim* is told by a first-person narrator. The only exception is the title story, "Learning to Swim," which has a third-person omniscient narrator. In this, they reflect Swift's practice in his novels (only *The Sweet-Shop Owner* employs a third-person narrator, and that only for part of the novel). There is a wide range of narrators in the ten, first-person stories. Two of the stories ("Gabor" and "Chemistry") are told from the point of view of children, by adult narrators looking back on crucial episodes in their lives. The narrator of "The Tunnel" is an adult recounting the experiences of one summer when he and his girlfriend were in their late teens. The narrators of "Hoffmeier's Antelope" and "Cliffedge" tell of events that occurred to them at a somewhat later age, while those of "The Hypochondriac," "Hotel," "Seraglio," and "The Son" are clearly much older characters, and "The Watch" is narrated by a very old character indeed. The majority of narrators relate events at a certain temporal distance, but in "Cliffedge," "The Hypochondriac," "Seraglio," "The Son," and "The Watch," the time of the story and the time of the narration overlap at the end of the texts.

The narrators also vary in terms of social class and ethnic background. Wealthy middle-class narrators (in "The Hypochondriac" and "Seraglio," for instance) interweave with a modest hotel proprietor (in "Hotel") and a relatively unsuccessful Greek immigrant restaurant owner (in "The Son"). But they do have a great deal in common. All the first-person narrators are male.

They also use remarkably similar language, to the objection of some critics. Most of the narrators (including the third-person omniscient one in "Learning to Swim") speak a neutral to slightly formal discourse. This is largely a matter of vocabulary, although Swift's narrators can, on occasion, produce sentences of considerable length and complexity. One can observe this in the case of the educated narrator of "Hoffmeier's Antelope" (see, for example, his description of his uncle on pages 29 and 30) and of the elderly narrator of "The Watch" (see his discussion of his wife on pages 172 and 173).[3] But it is also striking that the same is intermittently the case with the omniscient narrator of "Learning to Swim," and the narrators of "Gabor" and "Seraglio," but also with the far from well-educated central figure in "Hotel" (see page 105, for example: "the ambition was sown in me," "My efforts matured slowly"). The narrators' language usually shows a slight formal tendency, with the exception of the Greek narrator of "The Son," although even with regard to this story, one critic feels that Swift has not captured what he feels would be the character's distinctive demotic voice.[4]

In her admirable essay on "Cliffedge," Louvel points out the deep unreliability of the story's narrator.[5] This is a component of the narrators of several of Swift's novels—Prentis, Tom Crick, Harry Beech, and Bill Unwin—but it is the exception in *Learning to Swim*. Even the emotionally damaged narrator of "Seraglio" is frank about the silences and evasions at the heart of his account, while the other narrators do their best to set out the full complexities of the experiences they relate. If these experiences are obscure and ambiguous, that lies in the nature of things, not in the narrators' evasiveness. "Gabor" and "Hotel" are good examples of this. In addition, the very complex, highly unchronological ordering of events that is so much a part of

Tom Crick's, Harry Beech's, and Bill Unwin's narrations is absent in the stories in *Learning to Swim*. Events are recounted in chronological fashion, and when there are retrospects (as in "The Hypochondriac," "Seraglio," or "Chemistry"), these are clearly marked.

Despite this clear organization of events, the narrators' stories are far from simple. They are usually open-ended. What is going to happen when the young son swims away from both mother and father in "Learning to Swim"? Where has Uncle Walter gone at the conclusion of "Hoffmeier's Antelope"? What is going to happen to Gabor and the narrator after their trip to London in "Gabor"? What does the future hold for Clancy and her lover at the end of "The Tunnel"? Only "The Watch" has a clear conclusion. Further, what actually has happened in several stories remains obscure. Did Hoffmeier sleep with Aunt Mary (39)? Has Uncle Walter eaten the antelope (note the "smell of frying onions" (42))? What did the narrator see in the face of the young girl in "Hotel"? What happened in the Turkish hotel in "Seraglio"? Did Grandfather kill himself in "Chemistry"? Was Neil murdered by his brother in "Cliffedge"? It is in these unresolved questions that Swift's short stories most clearly echo his novels. (Compare, for example, the mysteries at the heart of the Chapmans' marriage in *The Sweet-Shop Owner*).

Narration, narrators' language, the ordering of accounts, and the nature of events unify the collection of short stories. They are also integrated in terms of genre. All are psychological studies of characters in complex personal situations. Almost all lack any substantial political or social resonance. "The Tunnel," recounting as it does an act of teenage rebellion against well-off parents, is an exception. Penner notes this lack of social reference; "Swift's forte is psychological dissection," he writes.[6] "The

Watch," however, stands out from the rest of the collection in terms of genre. The magical watch that bestows longevity on its owner is a motif that belongs to folktale, legend, or the supernatural story. But even in this story, the primary focus is on the narrator's wrestling with his peculiar existential situation, rather than on the watch's magical properties. Two other stories contain hints of supernatural motifs. M., in "The Hypochondriac," has some of the sinister, disturbing features of a Gothic doppelgänger ("His features had this flat quality, as if there was nothing behind them," reflects the doctor [61]). In "Chemistry" the young boy is visited by his drowned father in a dream (145–46). In both these cases, however, the supernatural is simply hinted at and is subsumed in psychological portraiture. The boy's dead father in "Chemistry" is a figment of his dreaming and his hostility toward his mother.

The stories are also unified through recurrent motifs, figures, and concerns. It will be readily seen that these are the same as those found in Swift's longer fiction. Many of the stories in *Learning to Swim* focus on family conflicts of different kinds. Seven concern disturbed relationships between parents and children—"Learning to Swim," "Hoffmeier's Antelope" (Uncle Walter is *in loco parentis*), "Gabor," "The Tunnel," "The Son," "Chemistry," and "The Watch." In all of these, except "Hoffmeier's Antelope," a child disappoints his or her parent. Similar disappointment and failure bedevil stories that present the conflict between husband and wife—"Learning to Swim," "Hoffmeier's Antelope," "The Hypochondriac," "Seraglio," and "The Watch." "Learning to Swim" sets the tone for this subject with its first sentence: "Mrs. Singleton had three times thought of leaving her husband" (9). This story and the bleak and suggestive "Seraglio" paint a complex picture of marital relationships, with subtle intricacies of blame and self-condemnation (18–19, 118–19). Given the fraught atmosphere in the marriages in *Learning to Swim,* it is not surprising that the motif of adultery recurs—in "The Hypochondriac," "Seraglio," and "Chemistry." It may even be hinted at in "Hoffmeier's Antelope" when Uncle Walter fails to complete a sentence and tell his nephew where, or with whom, Hoffmeier slept when he visited (39). In "Hotel" the guests and the narrator assume that a couple is actually a father and daughter in an incestuous relationship, while Mrs. Singleton in "Learning to Swim" relishes the "admiring glances" of men on the beach, and makes love, in her imagination, to "the moody, pubescent boys" she sees around her (25). The panorama of family conflict is filled out with antagonism between brothers in "Cliffedge," and the ebb and flow of tensions and boredom between young lovers in "The Tunnel."

Critics have long observed the centrality of the disrupted family in Swift's fiction.[7] Another central motif from the novels echoed in these stories is that of uncertain knowledge. Like Tom Crick or Bill Unwin, the narrators of several stories worry about what they know and what basis they have (if any) for their knowledge. The desire for knowledge drives Adoni to try to establish his parentage in "The Son." Here knowledge is unproblematic (although its consequences are not), but this is not the case in "The Hypochondriac." How can the doctor-narrator be sure he is right about his patient? How can the patient insist that he knows he is unwell? In "Hotel" the narrator takes a long time to see what the other guests see very quickly. How can he (or they) be sure? Knowledge—of adultery, of what happens in the hotel, of who is responsible for the death of the couple's child—and uncertainty are central motifs in "Seraglio." They are also raised, in a humorous way, in "Hoffmeier's Antelope" when the narrator teases his uncle about the existence of species that are unknown to science. As indicated above, mysteries and silences run throughout the collection of stories—concerning Uncle Walter and the antelope, Gabor's response to the sight of the naked girl, and Neil's death (in "Cliffedge"). Silence is the essence of the relationship between husband and wife in "Seraglio," and here it is seen as not entirely negative (as it is not seen negatively at the end of *Shuttlecock*). In "Seraglio" the couple lies side by side, not exploring guilt, not reproaching each other, but not harming each other either (119).

The vision of personal relationships and individual lives, however, is predominantly cheerless in the short stories. Unhappiness and blighted lives are the norm. Characters are abandoned by others through death ("Hoffmeier's Antelope" and "Hotel") or through a loved one's choosing another ("The Hypochondriac" and "Chemistry"). Failure and fear mark narrators and other characters in all eleven stories. The Singletons' marriage is not happy in "Learning to Swim," and their son is afraid of the water. The shy woodland antelope can not be saved from extinction in "Hoffmeier's Antelope." In "Gabor" the narrator's father will always be disappointed—both in his own son and in Gabor, who has been acquired as a substitute. The doctor loses his wife and his health in "The Hypochondriac," and the young couple's ecstatic love breaks down into tension and boredom in "The Tunnel." The youths making the tunnel in this story succeed, but it is finally, in fact, a pointless achievement—in any real sense, it is a tunnel to nowhere. The narrator in "Hotel" is powerless to save his therapeutic guest house; in "Seraglio" the couple remain as silent and separate as ever. Little has changed in the drab lives of the protagonists at the end of "The Son." Knowledge has brought few gains. The grandfather is not saved in "Chemistry," and the narrator of "Cliffedge" remains tied to the spot where his brother has died—and loses his wife in the bargain. Longevity brings no nobility or insight to the Krepskis in "The Watch." The narrator finds his father peevish and cold. Only death brings any kind of relief.

Indeed, as in so many of Swift's novels, characters in the stories are trapped—in unhappy marriages, in jobs without perspectives, in sad relationships that cannot improve—with little hope of freedom. Mr. Singleton contemplates stepping off the high tower of a bridge as a way of attaining liberation in "Learning to Swim." Uncle Walter vanishes at the end of "Hoffmeier's Antelope," but his fate is surely extinction rather than escape. Only in "The Watch" does Krepski achieve something—by giving life to the Asian child—but escape from the destiny of his family means death. As has been suggested above, the tunnel in the story of that name really goes nowhere in particular and is not a real means of escape from anything. Motifs that are symptomatic of the characters' entrapment in the novels recur in the short stories. The mental institutions and hospitals that are a constant setting from *The Sweet-Shop Owner* through *Last Orders* find their echo in the zoo of "Hoffmeier's Antelope" and in the mental hospitals of "Hotel" and "Cliffedge." In these two stories, and in "The Hypochondriac," mental disturbance also produces an entrapment in fixed patterns of behavior, as well as literal institutionalization. In a review of *Learning to Swim,* Bryn Caless points to the deep sadness of Swift's vision of the world in his short stories. The reviewer argues, however, that he cannot accept that "such blighting is so universal or so unremitting" and suggests that most of the stories in *Learning to Swim* "are stark statements against which *The Waste Land* seems positively frivolous."[8]

This motif of entrapment, along with the dismal vision of the world it embodies, is reinforced by the doubling of characters and situations that recurs throughout Swift's short stories. This is not a matter of Gothic doppelgänger; rather, it is a generalization of individual short stories' despair, and a metaphor for the characters' hopeless entrapment. One observes not just the narrator's fate, but the similar lot of other characters too. Thus in "Hoffmeier's Antelope," Hoffmeier and Uncle Walter clearly parallel each other in their doomed mission to save the rare creature, but one could argue that Aunt Mary and the antelope, and Uncle Walter and the antelope, also reflect each other in their sorry fates. Gabor and the narrator in "Gabor" are echoes of each other, while the narrator in "The Hypochondriac" finds a kind of psychological doppelgänger in M. Father and son both turn out to be adopted in "The Son"; the tunneling youths ironically reflect Clancy and the narrator's bid for freedom in "The Tunnel"; and in "Cliffedge" the two brothers are linked together in a way that even death cannot disrupt. "Chemistry" establishes a multifaceted set of reflections—the narrator resembles his father in his mother's eyes; the mother resembles her mother in her father's; the mother begins to reject her father and her son, just as her mother abandoned her husband by dying. In "Seraglio" echoes and parallels become even more pervasive: the narrator is Mehmet the Conqueror in relation to his wife; she is the woman in the harem; the death of their unborn child haunts them as the savagery of the pillage of 1453 haunts Istanbul; the hotel manager is also called Mehmet; the wife's adultery with the porter—or her molestation by him—parallels the peculiar accident that the visitors see on the streets of the city, and perhaps even the power of the women in the seraglio that the narrator reads about in his guidebook (113); husband

and wife represent Asia and Europe, lying next to each other, not separate, but not quite touching (122–23).

One prominent aspect of Swift's novels—metafictional concerns—seems almost entirely lacking in these stories. This has nothing to do with the kind of text they are. The short story in the United States and Britain has proved a perfectly suitable vehicle for metafictional purposes.[9] The pervasive fascination with the role of texts on characters' lives and the high degree of self-referentiality (the text is full of devices that remind the reader it is a text) that can be found in *Shuttlecock* and *Waterland,* however, is absent in these short stories. Questions concerning knowledge are certainly present, as has been noted above, but clearly metafictional interests are marginal even in the texts where they might be observed. The war games that the narrator plays with Gabor, and which take precedent over his father's and Gabor's knowledge of real suffering in "Gabor," and the power of M's narratives of illness in "The Hypochondriac" echo metafictional concerns in a muted fashion. But the emphasis of the stories is elsewhere—on the psychological complexities of family relationships. The poetry that the narrator reads to Clancy in "The Tunnel" is an embodiment of the bright, evanescent, doomed moment of their love. No deeper point is being made about the relation of texts to reality. Only "Seraglio," with its complex reflections of character and situation—and, indeed, its density of metaphor (Asia-Europe, the seraglio, the rose and the massacre, the daggers and the empty hands)—may be said to be substantially drawing attention to itself as a text. Once again, however, this complex literariness of the story is primarily in the service of creating a delicate mood of care and cruelty—of love and despair—rather than suggesting anything about, for example, the relationship of text to reality.

The short stories in *Learning to Swim* are undoubtedly a minor part of Swift's overall output of fiction. Some can be criticized for being rather crude. For example, the final revelation in "The Son" seems a mechanical way to bring the story to an end. The conclusion of "The Watch," in which the narrator sacrifices near immortality to save a child, verges on the sentimental. But there is also much to admire about the stories. The metaphor of the tunnel in the story of that name is more ironic than is usually acknowledged, "Hotel" has an interesting inconclusive austerity about its ending, and "Learning to Swim" is a powerful dissection of the tensions of family life. A case can certainly be made for the complexity and subtlety of "Cliffedge" and "Seraglio," while the doomed, shy ungulate and the hapless Uncle Walter of "Hoffmeier's Antelope" are fine comic creations that humorously, and also very sadly, sum up a clear, if dispiriting, vision of the world. For most readers these stories are interesting, above all, because they show a major novelist working in another medium and because they echo the longer work in very clear ways. Yet the texts in *Learning to Swim* are of interest in themselves, although, primarily, they seem minor workshop experiments in preparation for the major achievements of the novels.

CHAPTER 5

The Uses of History
Waterland (1983)

Shuttlecock seems, in the final analysis, to be a relatively optimistic novel. The outcome of history, and of the scrutiny of the past, is in some kind of at least temporary balance or accommodation. Indeed, the novel ends on an epiphanic, Wordsworthian note.[1] *Waterland,* however, marks a return to the grim oppressiveness of history seen in *The Sweet-Shop Owner.* As Patrick Parrinder puts it, "Graham Swift is . . . [a] novelist who . . . is burdened by history, and for whom the central theme of modern life is our own historical self-consciousness."[2] Further, the epistemological unease which the principal characters feel in *Shuttlecock* is even more pronounced in the harassed, ineffectual, but perhaps all too eloquent narrator of *Waterland.* But this novel, too, performs a delicate balancing act as Tom Crick sets his awareness of history as a catalogue of brutalities against his appreciation of "civilization" (chap. 31), his sense of the futility of the pursuit of historical truth against his assertion of its necessity (even if one is finally left only with an enigma).[3]

Waterland has much in common with Swift's other novels. Those common motifs, figures, and concerns of the Swiftian novel recur throughout. It is a story of the Cricks and the Atkinsons over several generations; it has a social *mésalliance* (Tom's mother and father), a crippled war veteran, orphaned children born in the aftermath of war, and an asylum; its action is played out against the background of great historical events, in this case the Second World War and the threat of an even more destructive nuclear one; the narrator is fascinated by storytelling and memory; and finally, hints of a national dimension to the action continually intrude. It is perhaps the most exhaustive, complex treatment of the concerns that run throughout Swift's output.

The reception of *Waterland* has already been discussed in chapter 1 of this study. The novel has a very prominent position within Swift's work as a whole. It has always been very highly regarded by critics and scholars, and it has generated a substantial amount of academic interest. David Leon Higdon gives a useful summary of the novel's very positive standing and adds to it himself when he writes that "*Waterland* is a feast of riches bringing together absolute technical maturity . . . and a profound meditation on the uses of the past and the necessity of history. One can only hope that Swift can achieve such success in his novels yet to come."[4]

As is the case in all Swift's novels, history, in a variety of senses, is brought to the foreground in *Waterland*. This is emphasized by George P. Landow, while Michael Gorra declares that "the theme of *Waterland*—the inescapability of history—provides the motive for Mr. Swift's work as a whole."[5] Part of the novel's epigraph is the definition of the Latin word *historia*.

Historia, ae, f. 1. inquiry, investigation, learning. 2. a) a narrative of past events, history. b) any kind of narrative: account, tale, story.

The narrator himself is a history teacher, and much of the novel takes the form of an address to his history class. His narration is laced with historical references (to the French Revolution, to the growth of the British Empire, to the Second World War) and is full of speculations about, and reflections on, history itself and the activity of historical inquiry and teaching. The very organization of the story material of *Waterland* foregrounds history by its completely unchronological interweaving of past and present. For example, chapter 1 is set in 1943, and chapter 2 in 1979 or 1980, while chapter 3 starts with a brief account of the primeval geology of the Fens and continues with a history of land reclamation in the seventeenth century and the history of the Crick family up to 1922. Chapter 4 returns to 1979/80, and chapter 5 returns to 1943 (with interjections of the narrator from his position in 1979/80). The next three chapters alternate between the late 1970s and the 1940s, and chapter 9 gives a long account of the deeds of the Atkinson family from the late eighteenth century to the 1870s. And so it continues. Chapter 24 and several others are set in 1940. The final chapter ends not with the historically most recent setting, but in 1943. This element of the novel is further emphasized by frequent tense shifts (many events are recounted in a historic present, others in the more traditional past tenses) and by the persistent dating of events in the text (the reader almost always knows precisely the year in which something happens).

The novel also foregrounds history in a wide variety of ways. First, *Waterland* takes the form of both a personal history and a family history. It details the lives and experiences of Tom and Mary Crick, and also of their parents and their more distant forebears, the Cricks and the Atkinsons. Tom Crick tries, throughout, to give an account of how he and his wife came to be where and what they are at the moment. (She is a child kidnapper in an asylum, and he is a laid-off history teacher.) He also tries to give an account of his brother's death in 1943, a murder his brother committed in the same year, and because all these things are connected with each other and with the past, an account of the rise and fall of the Atkinson brewing family. Throughout, he sees himself and his family both as agents of history and yet also trapped in the pitiless grip of past events and their consequences. Gorra points out that all Swift's novels emphasize the "inescapability" of the past "by concentrating on families whose very structure provides a reminder of the past—families marked by death or divorce or perhaps, as in *Waterland,* by a retarded child."[6] Tom's brother Dick is the product of the incestuous love, the millennial ambitions of the last of the Atkinson line, and is himself the product of three generations of Georgian and Victorian businessmen. Mary's sterility is the product both of a botched abortion—the consequence of sexual curiosity and instilled guilt—and of fear, it is implied, of the powerful, murderous Dick. And over thirty years later the consequences of these actions in the past, themselves the consequences of previous events, push her into crime and bring her to the asylum. Tom Crick describes himself at one point as "a prisoner . . . of irreversibly historical events" (319–20). One of his last views of his brother is of Dick "riding, riding, his birthright on his back, the legacy of the Atkinsons on his back . . ." (327). The past—either of their own actions or the actions of others—lies like a dead weight on the principal characters of the novel.

The novels of George Eliot underlie *Waterland* in very specific ways. Despite the nonchronological organization of time in Swift's novel (which is, of course, a major qualification), so many components of the created world of the early Eliot novels, *Adam Bede* and *The Mill on the Floss,* are shared by *Waterland*. Many of these relate to the role of history in *Waterland*. The vision of characters bound by the consequences of their choices and the choices of others, trapped and bound by personal and family history (Michael Wood notes "a network of irrevocable deeds, a cage of consequences"), could scarcely be more Eliot-like.[7] Although this is an element—a moral determinism—which Eliot's novels share with the novels of Hardy or Moore or Gissing, or even with those of Lawrence, the presence of so many other echoes of Eliot's fiction make one want to see her figure brooding in the background. But certainly there are echoes of Hardy and Lawrence in *Waterland* as well. (It is interesting, incidentally, that Swift's readers are frequently prompted to make comparisons with Victorian writers—and not only with novelists; Landow makes extensive reference to Tennyson in his discussion of the autobiographical aspects of *Waterland*.)[8] As a piece of provincial, local history, *Waterland* also surely echoes Eliot in the early novels and in *Middlemarch*. For *Waterland* does not just deal with personal and family history, but with these as they are rooted in a specific locality (echoing Hardy's Wessex). Furthermore, Eliot's persistent device of referring local and personal events to those taking place on a wider historical stage, which she employs from *Adam Bede* through to *Daniel Deronda*, is quite apparent in *Waterland*. One might even find an echo of the persistent natural historical metaphors in that other novel of provincial life by water, Eliot's *The Mill on the Floss*, in Tom Crick's disquisition on the life of the eel (chap. 26).

History is also brought to the foreground by the way in which *Waterland* presents itself as, in part, a local history of the fictitious, but highly verisimilar Gildsey—the area of the Fens centered on the fictitious River Leem. Tom Crick explores local history at the same time that he gives his class the family history of the Cricks and the Atkinsons, and the two kinds of history are, in fact, closely intertwined. The Cricks' lives have been shaped by their work in the Fens; the Atkinsons have molded the nineteenth and part of the twentieth-century history of Gild-sey, and they have been shaped by it in their turn. For example, Crick (the history teacher) notes how the Atkinsons' success transforms them (74–75).

History, too, is foregrounded in the novel's constant reference to great events being played out far away from the Fens, the consequences of which are interwoven with local and personal fates. Much of the early history of Cricks and Atkinsons, and of the Fens themselves, is set against the Dutch wars, the Agricultural and Industrial Revolutions, the French Revolution (about which Tom Crick is supposedly giving lessons), and the growth of the British Empire. In 1917 Henry Crick and his brother find themselves in an ironically familiar, low-lying, muddy Flanders, where he sustains the physical and mental wounds that will incapacitate him, and where his brother dies (19–20). The later Crick family drama unfolds against the drone of Allied airplanes taking off to bomb German cities and against reports of the war in Europe. Each evening at six o'clock, Henry Crick listens to the radio. "A daily ritual. A daily homage to history," notes his son (134).[9] On one level, the historical events are obviously contrasted with the domestic, personal occurrences of the Fens. In chapter 5, Tom observes the sunrise on a July morning in 1943 and contrasts rural peace with world war (28).

But the contrast is disingenuous, and the peace of the scene is superficial, for Tom has been called out of bed to see Freddie Parr's body (murdered by Tom's brother Dick) being fished out of the canal. The first blows in a grisly tale of murder, fear, abortion, and suicide have been struck, and these actions themselves are the consequences of personal decisions and historical circumstances in the past (among others, Ernest Atkinson's distaste for his forbears' legacy, his despair at the course of late nineteenth and early twentieth-century British history, his love for his daughter, and his millennial ambitions). History—personal, local, national, and international—is present at this occasion. Later in the novel, the narrator explicitly links the grand historical event with the personal experience. As is so often the case in *Waterland,* the Allied bombers taking off for Germany form a sinister backdrop to Fenland happenings, such as Tom and Mary's going to the abortionist's cottage (299–300).

The narrator argues that, like Tom and Mary, the citizens of German cities are trapped in historical circumstances for which they are responsible, but which also seem grimly punitive in the price they exact. As Michael Wood argues, "History, for Swift, is the opposite of accident. . . . It is synonymous with guilt and blame, or at least with a burden that cannot be ditched or lightened."[10] Furthermore, the fate of those citizens of Hamburg and elsewhere anticipates the threatened apocalypse which hangs over the schoolchildren and citizens of London in the modern chapters of the novel. The fears of Price and his fellow students are closely linked to grand historical events, such as the arms race and the threat of nuclear destruction. As befits a historian, Tom Crick is always careful to see figures in both their national and their world context. He does this with Lewis, the headmaster, a product of the 1960s whose idealism has gone sour in the bleaker 1970s and 1980s (23). He also does it, very tellingly, at the moment of his father's death after a flood has destroyed the (carefully dated) buildings, waterways and landscapes of the Fens (340).

Chapter 26, "About the Eel," deals with another kind of history: natural history. But the connections with human history in its various forms are clear. The pursuit of the spawning grounds, the gradual tracing of the reproductive cycle of the eel becomes a model of the historian's activity, probing phenomena, seeking explanations, asking questions, constructing narratives. In chapter 10, entitled "About the Question Why," Tom Crick makes this connection explicit—natural history, political history, and personal history are all marked by causes and effects, and the study of these different kinds of history involves a pursuit of reasons, explanations, and an asking of questions. He declares to his class, "Another definition, children: Man, the animal which demands an explanation, the animal which asks Why" (106). To make the connection even more explicit between the kinds of history, the narrator counterpoints the scientists' pursuit of the elusive eel with contemporary world historical events.

Crick, as a historian, is also interested in the nature of the study of history, of history as an intellectual, academic, educational activity. Throughout the novel the narrator continually returns to the topic of what the study of history is, what the motives behind it are, and what its uses are. Early in the novel, we find him faced with his headmaster's decision to "cut back History," to remove it from the curriculum because it does not help to prepare pupils for the "real world" (21–23). The whole novel can be seen as Crick's attempt to demonstrate, despite everything that may be said against it, the necessity of history. It is important to stress from the outset that, although Crick seems to abandon the syllabus of his history class (the French Revolution gives way to family and Fenland history), neither traditional historical events nor historical method are abandoned. Quite the reverse, his "stories" seem to be a last desperate attempt to connect with his students and their world and concerns.

Crick's defense of history is complex. As will be seen shortly with regard to terms in *Waterland* such as "reality" and "nothing," Swift follows a very typical pattern with regard to "history."

He continually brings forward certain terms in his fiction ("pattern" and "role" in *The Sweet-Shop Owner*, "nature" in *Shuttlecock*) and plays with different senses and associations of these words. Christopher Driver remarks of *Waterland* that "As in the image structure of a poem or the tonal scheme of a symphony, words, phrases or sequences in the novel are simultaneously perceived as self-contained events and as transformations or modulations of earlier motifs. Ideas bleed into their neighbors." Other commentators, such as Hermione Lee and Wood, also remark on this pattern in Swift's fiction.[11] The best strategy here may be to look at how arguments about history are developed in specific contexts in the novel.

Crick finds himself in the position of having to defend history to his pupils, who fail to see the subject's relevance to "Now" (60). Crick's answer is to connect what he calls "the Here and Now" with History and history. At crucial points in a life, he argues—when a person's life changes, when one feels most caught up in the present—one has also been overtaken by history, by past events. His own impulse towards history comes most decisively when the events of 1943 push him toward finding explanations of the present in the past, trying to discover where the all-consuming "Here and Now" came from.[12] But it is not as simple as that. History is also a story, a "yarn" we use to fill up the empty spaces of our lives, a narrative that gives shape and meaning to the meaningless and the absurd (60–63). The intellectual paradox that is at the heart of the novel is here clearly raised. History is both necessary and a "yarn," both useful and pointless. Crick (and Swift) attempt to balance these two positions throughout the text. In chapter 10 Crick once more defends history to his pupils. The question concerns the usefulness of historical inquiry. Crick's defense is complex, and seemingly

paradoxical. The desire to explain—to know why—is something innate and healthy. The alternative is the idiocy of amnesia.
But the why's are endless, each answer suggesting another question. No explanation will ever do. And thus, Crick argues, history, by its constant asking why, constantly teaches us to probe,
to analyze, to be critical—never to settle for the glib fairytale or
the half-explanation, even though we may know there is no
final, all-encompassing explanation (106–9).

History, in Crick's terms, is no consoling story, no firm
explanation; it provides no certainty, only more questions, and
a disheartening sense of human destructiveness and folly. Later
he again defines, illustrates, and implicitly defends what he means
by history. "History:" he tells Price, "a lucky dip of meanings.
Events elude meaning, but we look for meanings. Another definition of Man: the animal who craves meaning—but knows—"
(140). A long, unanswered (unanswerable?) list of "why's" about
the French Revolution follows (141). In addition, as always in
this novel (and generally in Swift's work), there is a dark sense
of the massive destructiveness and viciousness of historical
events, especially at the hands of those animated by ideals and
illusions. This is surely part of what Crick means by realism—a
skepticism, a lack of trust in all the great narratives and yarns
spun in history. For him, history seems an almost circular process (like the one he will observe in the River Ouse in the next
chapter). "How it [history, in the sense of historical events]
repeats itself, how it goes back on itself, no matter how we try
to straighten it out. How it twists, turns. How it goes in circles
and brings us back to the same place" (142).[13]

Although Crick may express an uncertainty about the
explanations of history as an intellectual inquiry into the past,
he is in no doubt about the power of the past, the compelling

force of history in the present. Crick declares amnesia and lack of curiosity (traits possessed by Crick's brother Dick) are forms of idiocy. Nothing is just an accident. There are causes and explanations, however provisional they may be. All the "Now's" that seem so coercive, so all-consuming—Freddie Parr's body; Marie Antoinette's execution; the beating of Sarah Atkinson; Mary's abortion, sterility, and madness; Dick's idiocy and death; the mud of Flanders; and the bombing of German cities—have grown out of past actions and events. The past is forever returning—seizing, and affecting the present. Particularly emblematic of this, in a novel full of such metaphors, is the visit Tom and Mary pay to Martha Clay's cottage. "Children, have you ever stepped into another world? Have you ever turned a corner to where Now and Long Ago are the same and time seems to be going on in some other place?" (303). It is surely of considerable significance that Martha Clay is an abortionist and her cottage a place of horror. The text constantly reminds the reader (in action as well as in Tom Crick's comments) that the past—history—is inescapable and deeply operative in the present. "Ah, do not ghosts prove—even rumors, whispers, stories of ghosts—that the past clings, that we are always going back" (103).

"But man—let me offer you a definition—is the story-telling animal," Crick declares to his class ("About the Story-Telling Animal" [62]). The topic is raised continually with regard to history, which is itself a narrative, a yarn, and a story. Crick (and, behind him, the author of the text) deploys a whole panoply of ways of telling his story, of telling stories within the overarching text that is *Waterland*. One of the most marked features of *Waterland* (and something it has in common with a large number of other British novels in the 1980s) is genre mixture. It is one of the most composite texts of the decade in terms of genre.

The first chapter alone contains at least three of the genre markers that will run throughout the novel. It starts with references to fairytales, modulates to suggestions of a psychological novel of childhood development, and shifts at the end toward an indication that it may be a murder mystery.

The term "fairy-tale" is repeated throughout the novel in a variety of contexts, and in part, the narrator insists, what he is telling is a fairytale. "But we lived in a fairy-tale place. In a lock-keeper's cottage, by a river, in the middle of the Fens. Far away from the wide world" (1). "And since a fairy-tale must have a setting, a setting which, like the settings of all good fairy-tales, must be both palpable and unreal, let me tell you . . . About the Fens . . ." (8). Both the Clays—Martha and Bill—are figures from legend and fairytale (10–11). Freddie Parr tells stories about Bill Clay—"How he ate water-rats; hypnotized animals; how he was over a hundred; how he knew about the singing swans" (55). When Martha Clay finally makes her appearance in the novel, it is in a chapter entitled "About the Witch" (chap. 42), a title amply justified by her appearance and the appearance of her cottage.

The fairytale echoes in *Waterland* are hardly ever of a benign sort, but the narrator insists that this is generically appropriate. "So, children . . . these fairy-tales aren't all sweet and cosy (just dip into your Brothers Grimm . . .)" (298). After he strikes his wife and causes her to lose her wits, Thomas Atkinson behaves like a fairytale king. "He will offer a fortune to the man who will give him back his wife," the narrator tells his listeners, adding however, "but no man will claim it" (79). When Tom and Mary are reunited, they kiss, and the echo of fairytale is unmistakable. "It is not a kiss which revives drowned curiosity, which restores the girl who once lay in a ruined windmill" (121).

But the echoes are negative ones. This is not "Sleeping Beauty" or "Snow White," and the two lovers will not live happily ever after. In fact, the force that destroys their marriage—Mary's terrifying delusion that God will send her a child—is seen in the context of "fairy-land," an awful world of madness (148). (Mary's name obviously carries not only fairytale connotations, but also Biblical ones, which fuse ironically with her uncompleted prayer during her abortion and Dick's status as a mentally subnormal "Savior"). The fairytale elements almost always involve failure and destruction. The death of Tom's mother is brought about by a biting East Wind that is personified in the manner of legend or fairytale, in a passage that combines modern geography with ghoulish legend (271).

Fairytale is only one part of the genre kaleidoscope of *Waterland*. William H. Pritchard notes this when he remarks that the novel's "essence is discontinuity," and this variety gives the lie to Marion Glastonbury's mocking suggestion that *Waterland* exemplifies a kind of gloomily portentous novel "about feuds and forbidden passions through seven generations of a Norfolk rush-cutting community."[14] *Waterland* can scarcely be pinned down in this way. Chapters 3 and 15, "About the Fens" and "About the Ouse," take the form of geographical description. Chapter 9 is an extended piece of national, local, and family history, and throughout the novel there are sections which clearly echo historical studies (of the French Revolution especially). Chapter 26, "About the Eel," is an account of scientific investigation, a piece of natural historical writing. A number of other genres are echoed in a less prominent way—the encyclopedia entry in chapter 51, "About Phlegm"; the stage play (not strictly a genre, but a literary form containing multiple genres) or trial record found in brief passages of chapter 11 (110–12);

the newspaper reports of Mary's child-theft, quoted occasional-ly (chaps. 13 and 31).

At other points, the novel oscillates among genre markers of the psychological novel of childhood development and initiation, the love story or modern "romance," and the story of murder and detection (with strong Gothic elements in it). Crick's accounts of Tom's and Mary's relationship, of Freddie Parr's death, and of Dick's past and his involvement with the relationship and the death partake of all three genres. Several chapters involve the details of Tom and Mary's growing sexual awareness, and several chronicle Tom's growing up and the family relationships which surround that process, thus echoing the psychological novel of childhood. Tom and Mary's blighted life together can be read not just as a malign fairytale, but as a deviant "romance." Tom's establishment of his brother's guilt and his pursuit of his brother's secrets clearly and explicitly echo the detective or mystery story. Chapter 29 is entitled "Detective Work," and later, as he observes himself watching his brother Dick, Tom asks rhetorically, "Now what's turned this little brother into such an apprentice spy, into such a budding detective?" (245) Indeed, the narrator's approach to history and its study is reminiscent of the detective's investigation of a crime—"I used to ask you to liken the study of history to an inquest" (107).

The wide range of texts through which the story of *Waterland* is recounted is matched throughout the novel by a very explicit concern with storytelling and narrative and their relation to "reality." This is one of the major topics of *Waterland*, integral to the text as a whole, and not merely gaudy technique distracting from the human interest. The novel is full of storytellers of one kind or another. Tom's father and mother are such (2, 61–62). The Cricks are storytellers by nature and tradition, and in this they are to be distinguished from the Atkinsons who do things, who make history rather than tell about it (17). The Cricks transform the stuff of historical events into "the fabric of a wondrous tale," and it is a mark of the horror that he has been through that Henry Crick is unable for many years to tell tales of his experiences in Flanders (20). Tom Crick himself is a storyteller. Most obviously, he is the narrator of the story that is *Waterland,* but within that he is a storyteller, a history teacher who has abandoned his traditional narrative for folktales, legends, and family reminiscence. He is also a deeply self-conscious storyteller, perpetually concerned not just with the purposes, uses, and nature of history, but with the point and function of stories and their relation to reality.

Crick the narrator is an extremely sophisticated creation whose very nature and literary provenance raise the issue of the relation of narrative to reality. Just as the novel's determinism echoes George Eliot, so its narrator echoes the dominant narrational convention and technique of the great novels of the nineteenth century. Crick is as intrusive, opinionated, and generalizing as the narrator of *Middlemarch,* or of the omnisciently narrated half of *Bleak House,* or of *Tess of the D'Urbervilles.* But unlike the narrators of these texts, Crick is not, and cannot be, omniscient. His own narrative's claims to truthfulness are themselves undercut, objectified by the fact that he is a first-person narrator and by his own emphasis on the untrustworthiness of narratives. Thus the whole novel is marked by an irony and complexity typical of Swift's work. There seems no solid ground, no acceptable hierarchy of discourse, perhaps not even that of the text's implied author. Landow captures the complexity of the text in this respect when he writes: "On the one hand, *Waterland* seems a rigorously historicist presentation of selfhood; on the other, its self-conscious examination of the history that historicizes this self makes it appear that these narratives, like the historicism they support, are patently constructed, purely subjective patterns."[15]

As one might expect, reality is a complex term in *Waterland*. As is typical of Swift's fiction, the text plays with different meanings and associations of the word, bringing them into juxtaposition and finally into some kind of paradoxical balance. The novel operates with two connected meanings of reality. On one hand, reality is something that can be contrasted with legend, fairytale, and illusion. Imperial myths and yarns, ghost stories, narratives of progress, and delusions can all be contrasted with material facts and counter narratives of failure. The grand narrative of British glory and progress ends in the failures of the 1940s. Mary Crick's belief that God will give her a child can be set against the brute material facts of life, and against the historian/detective's retracing of cause and effect. The utopian aspirations of the French Revolution can be set against the reality of tyranny and bloodshed which the historical record exposes. However often Henry Crick closes his eyes, Freddie Parr's body is still floating in the lock. Ernest Atkinson's millenarian dream is set against the reality of his idiot grandson/son. But in all this, it should be noted that these illusions and these yarns have effects. They shape history, events, and actions just as reality does.

The second notion of reality with which the novel operates also involves contrast and paradox. "Reality's not strange," Crick declares to his class, "not unexpected. Reality doesn't reside in the sudden hallucination of events. Reality is uneventfulness, vacancy, flatness. Reality is that nothing happens" (40). Reality is thus the uneventfulness of hidden, dull lives—the lives of Cricks in the centuries before the union with the Atkinsons, the lives of Tom and Mary Crick prior to Mary's descent into madness. "They acquire regular habits, spiced with unspectacular variations. . . . They acquire regular habits and regular diversions"

(123). But reality is also—as Crick explicitly and implicitly indicates—a matter of event, of the here and now which overtakes people, which they seek out and wish upon themselves to relieve the flatness of their lives. This applies to the grand here and now of the French Revolution or the domestic, individual dramas of Freddie Parr's murder and Mary Crick's child-theft (40–41).

Finally Crick, narrator and history teacher, seems unsure of what reality is. He describes himself as "no longer sure what's real and what isn't" (41). His history lessons continually drift into legend, folktale, and myth. The wife he thought he knew turns out to be someone quite different. "Now tread carefully, history teacher. Maybe this isn't your province. Maybe this is where history dissolves, chronology goes backwards. That's your wife over there; you know, Mary, the one you thought you knew. But maybe this is unknown country" (265).

The novel's concern with storytelling—its metafictional concern—is closely related to the question of reality. Stories and narratives stand in complex relation to the already problematized issue of reality. The very panoply of different kinds of texts (fairytale, legend, detective story, psychological fiction, historical narrative) that the narrator feels he has to use to tell his story suggests both the elusiveness of reality and the necessity of employing a variety of different kinds of text to capture it. Both reality and the ability of texts to capture truth—the real—are hereby made highly problematic. But the position of *Waterland* on this issue is again quite complex. The text as a whole does provide some explanations (of Freddie Parr's murder, of Dick's death, and of Mary's madness). It can produce some texts that do seem to capture some aspects of the truth—the long chapter of Atkinson family history (chap. 9), and the account of scientific investigation of the eel's breeding cycle (chap. 26).

But even these successful texts are only partial expositions of reality, only partial explanations of the way things were and are. In this respect, the eel's story is representative. Crick concludes his account of the discovery of its life and breeding cycle with unanswered questions. The location of the eel's spawning ground in the Sargasso Sea is a hypothesis, a best guess. "Curiosity begets counter-curiosity, knowledge begets skepticism," Crick mutters. He lists the questions one is left with about the eel. "But even if we learn how, and what and where and when, will we ever know why?" asks the narrator. "Whywhy?" (204). Even the text that seems to explain most, is far from confident in its relationship to reality.

Waterland continually emphasizes this about stories, narratives, and accounts of reality. The novel abounds in storytellers telling tales whose relationship to reality is never simple and direct—tales which shape, form, or permit escapes from the real, rather than give access to it. The very beginning of the novel starts with words from a story, and it presents the reader with a storyteller (the narrator's father) and his variegated tales (2). Although Tom's mother also tells stories, tale telling is something that marks the Cricks rather than the Atkinsons (in this respect, it is worth noting that Dick is an Atkinson by blood, not a Crick). "While the Atkinsons made history," says the narrator, "the Cricks spun yarns" (17). They turn the events of history into "the fabric of a wondrous tale" (18). Henry Crick's response to the carnage of Flanders is to think "there is only reality, there are no stories left," and thus he is incapable of living in the world and must be taken into a "home for chronic neurasthenics" (20).

This is typical of the relationship the novel establishes between reality and narrative. Stories are a means of controlling, coping with, and evading the real; by no means do they give unmediated access to it, nor are they really meant to. Henry Crick "who once watched the wide world drowning in Flanders yet lived to tell the tale," will turn Freddie Parr's drowning into a tale one day too (33). Even non-narrative phrases, like Tom's and Mary's halting, childish "I love—I love—Love, love," are "those spell-binding words which make the empty world seem full" (52). Prompted by history-as-event to investigate history-as-subject, Tom Crick finds eventually, after forty years, that "history is a yarn" and that history as "the Grand Narrative" functions for the "Story-Telling Animal" as "the filler of vacuums, the dispeller of fears of the dark" (62).

He returns to this view of narrative later in the novel when, confronted by an event—the potentially disruptive here and now of sexual curiosity and development—he "escapes to his story-books" (207). It must be remembered that by "story-books" he means history. Stories of a variety of kinds are continually seen as an evasion of the truth. As he begins to feel his wife's madness, Crick thinks of himself "telling himself stories" to fend of misery (129–30). One of Ernest Atkinson's criticisms of his forebears is that they have "fed the people with dreams of inflated and no longer tenable grandeur" (16–61), and by 1947, the whole narrative of progress and national destiny has become, for both Tom and Henry Crick, an empty "yarn" (340). But the narrator (and the novel) is always ambivalent about stories and their function and value. Stories save Henry Crick from the scars of war (225–26).

Mary Crick's child-theft provides a final example of the narrator's complex attitude towards narrative and story. The "cheery prognosis" of the ward sister in charge of his now-confined and mad wife is a childish story, an evasion of the unbearable truth about his wife and, perhaps, about life in general.

"First it was a story—what our parents told us, at bedtime. Then it becomes real, then it becomes here and now. Then it becomes story again. Second childhood. Goodnight kisses . . ." (328). But Mary Crick is mad precisely because she cannot turn what she has done—what has happened—into a story (329).

Thus the treatment of narrative and story is complex in *Waterland* and involves several different positions and textual levels. First, there is the novel itself. As an overarching narrative—the product of a named author (Graham Swift)—it makes certain claims on the reader's attention; it is a text with a specific created world and a specific vision of that world. Second, that narrative, composed as it is of numerous sub-narratives and a kaleidoscope of genres, suggests that any narrative can, at best, give a partial and limited account of the truth (although it does provide narratives that seem to give better accounts than others do). Third, the narrator continually problematizes the relationship of story and reality, presenting narrative as, at once, an evasion of reality and a necessary means of dealing with the hideous absurdity and meaninglessness of historical events. Finally, and here the argument comes full circle, all the readers are left with is a text—a novel. As Tom Crick remarks: "First there is nothing; then there is happening; a state of emergency. And after the happening, only the telling of it" (329).

Epistemologically, the novel provides the reader with little solid ground, and, indeed, this metaphor is appropriate and fully implicit in *Waterland,* from the title page onwards. The Fens and the Fenlands—low-lying, shrinking, and empty—become, throughout the novel, a composite metaphor for emotional and psychological states and for the epistemological and existential conditions that give rise to them. They become a metaphor for the emptiness of human life, the inadequacy of human knowledge, and the oppressive absurdity of history. This metaphor is con-firmed throughout the novel. After his son's death, Jack Parr takes to drink. But his reasons are not only connected with Fred-die's drowning. The drinking also helps to dull his sense of the emptiness of the Fens (113–14).

This "intolerable geometry" of "emptiness" (113–14) is sure-ly a metaphor for all the human fates and experiences collected in *Waterland*—uncertainty, failure, lack of meaning, death, and madness. Tom speculates on what Mary experienced after her abortion when she locks herself away on her father's farm. Did ghosts visit her? Did she have religious experiences? Or is "the truth of those three years . . . that nothing, nothing at all oc-curred and that the future Mrs. Crick, gazing day after day from her farmhouse cell at the level fields, was only, wittingly or unwittingly, preparing herself for her later marriage—which would be a sort of fenland" (118)? Although he seems, at first, to have forgotten the awful absurdity of the war, the emptiness of the Fens recalls all too quickly, for Henry Crick, the mud of Flanders and all it represents in terms of death and madness. It gives him a "feeling of nothing" (223).

"Nothing"—like "reality" and "story"—is one of the key terms of *Waterland*. With its synonym "emptiness," it is repeat-ed throughout the text. What else is water, the narrator asks, "but a liquid form of Nothing"? And what are the Fens in their wateriness, "but a landscape which, of all landscapes, most ap-proximates to Nothing" (13)? Later we find Crick assuring his pupils that "Reality is uneventfulness, vacancy, flatness. Reality is that nothing happens" (40). (However, as was noted earlier, Crick's position is complex here, for events can occur, things can happen, or at least stories can be told, just as a womb—as Crick argues—can be filled, can bring forth something out of "an empty but fillable vessel" [42].) But the repetition of "nothing" and "emptiness" is insistent. It is an "empty world" which Tom and Mary make to "seem full" with words of adolescent love (52). Reality is "an empty space," Crick insists (61). Mary's marriage is described as a "fenland"; it is also "nothing"—a vacancy, an empty, purposeless space before she conjures her story of God and the child He will give her (118, 126–27).

Like Mary, characters continually strive against this nothingness. As Freddie Parr's father drinks, so the Atkinsons purvey beer "trying to assuage emptiness" (177). On a national-historical level, the Atkinsons' brewery attempts to give coherence and shape to the fluid emptiness of history. Its activities become emblematic of a national narrative of progress, which the narrator suggests is a confected tale to cover over the absurd emptiness of things (93). Tom Crick's irony and doubt are surely unmistakable when he discusses such matters. "All right, so it's all a struggle to preserve an artifice. It's all a struggle to make things not seem meaningless. It's all a fight against fear," Crick declares (241). Human activity becomes a long attempt to stave off a sense of meaninglessness, absurdity, and nothingness. We are "the animal who craves meaning—but knows" (140). Crick's position is reflected in his pupil Price's arguments. We are the seekers of "explanations," Price suggests, and we only look for explanations when things have gone very wrong, as a way of avoiding the truth (168–69).

One brief chapter succinctly sums up Crick's views. In chapter 36, which is appropriately entitled "About Nothing," he is talking to Price late at night in the pub, after his interview with the headmaster, Lewis. Price's concern about nuclear war is, Crick says, "the old, old feeling, that everything might amount to nothing"—a feeling that has been shared by many in the past

(269). In the next chapter, Crick returns to the same topic, the pointless absurdity of "History." "It's called terror, children. The feeling that all is nothing. There is your subject, your lesson for today" (270). For there is no Golden Age, no future; Napoleon leads his followers to a European bloodbath, just as the "yarn" of progress plays itself out in Flanders and bombed-out Hamburg. The future is the bloody residue of Mary's abortion (308).

The ambiguity of *Waterland* and its fragmentation over several genres are reflected in stylistic features of the novel. It is a mixture of the intensely articulate and the incomplete utterance, a text marked by an extraordinary skill with words and by the utter failure of words. Large parts of the novel are set in a formal language which is sophisticated in terms of vocabulary and syntax, educated, allusive, humorous, ironic, and at times very elaborate. Driver celebrates this distinctive style and finds it "infectious" in his review of *Waterland*.[16] Examples of this "*Waterland* style" abound. Note the sophisticated, educated, allusive vocabulary when Crick talks of the Dutch engineers who built the Fens and how they "dug subsidiary cuts, drains, lodes, dykes, eaus and ditches" (11). Note, too, the similar relishing of the sophisticated, the self-advertising lexis of Crick's description of himself as a "balding quinquagenarian who gabbles about the Ancien Régime, Rousseau, Diderot and the insolvency of the French Crown" (60). Chapter 26 ("About the Eel") prominently advertises the erudition of its narrator and his access to obscure knowledge, while the passage, quoted earlier, about the East Wind not only serves as a fairytale genre marker, but also serves to show the speaker's cosmopolitan grasp of European geography (271). Syntax, too, in *Waterland* is also appropriately complex and sophisticated. Note, for example, the very long and syntactically complex utterances which the narrator uses to tell of Freddie Parr's bruise, including one sentence which is nineteen lines long (34–35).

This example must stand for many others from throughout the text, but even a casual glance at Crick's speech reveals his fondness for the complex sentence, for the parenthetical insertion which add to the complexity of his style. The effect is clearly intended to indicate erudition, knowledge, sophistication, a way with words, and eloquence, all of which help to construct the central character and narrator. They also are clearly meant to be humorous as is seen, for example, in the account of the disturbances associated with the drinking of the special Coronation Ale in 1911—"With alarming frequency the women of the town were called upon to restrain displays of intemperance in their menfolk . . ." (172). The novel abounds in displays of verbal wit, stylistic juxtapositions, comic clashes of style and reference, word play, and elaborate parentheses. Crick is constructed as a talker, a prolific spender of words, and a man constantly advertising his own skill with language. Note the deliberate and comic clash of styles in his description of Dick. "And this impression—this pose—can lend Dick, in the eyes of others, a certain rugged pathos; can invest even him (for there's no getting away from it, Dick has an ugly mug) with a perverse appeal" (38). Here the narrator's irony—his elaborate and formal wrapping of his brother's simple-mindedness—is emphasized and counterpointed by his lapse into demotic language ("ugly mug"). When giving Mary's background, Crick cannot resist playing with the cliché of "mother's milk": "Thus it was not only mother's milk but Farmer Metcalf's milk which Dick and I drank when we were boys. And it was her father's milk—but, alas, never her mother's—that Mary Metcalf grew up on" (44). The elaborate irony of style is apparent, too, in the narrator's treatment of his father's sense of guilt at the coroner's hearing into Freddie Parr's death, in which grandiose vocabulary is used to talk about a relatively "simple" character (110). Crick is constituted as a clever speaker who is always willing to let us hear his cleverness. He cannot, for example, avoid even trivial cleverness: "For, indeed, after the razing of the brewery, no more Coronation Ale was ever seen (or drunk) again (with one exception)" (176). The first parenthesis is surely a minor, though revealing, example of his predilection to verbal play.

But if Crick is constituted throughout the novel as a figure of self-advertising verbal skill, his speech is also marked by alarming and recurrent failures of language. The Swiftian device of the incomplete utterance recurs frequently in *Waterland*. The incomplete chapter endings which run throughout the novel (chapters 2, 8, 14, passim) with their "let me tell you about" are not relevant here. After all, they are completed in the headings of the following chapters, and surely indicate a kid of novelistic and linguistic showmanship rather than the reverse. But genuinely incomplete utterances abound in the novel, and these seem to indicate points at which language fails Crick. "But why, we ask, did Louis's neck happen to be—? Because . . . And when we have gleaned that reason we will want to know, But why *that* reason? Because . . . And when we have that further reason, But why again—? Because . . . Why? . . . Because . . . Why? . . ." (107). Just as language seems to fail the narrator when considering historical events, the same thing happens in his own life as he considers his wife's slipping into madness. "The only important thing . . . If the truth be known, he is frightened. If the truth be known, he doesn't know what to think. He is telling himself stories. (How a girl and a boy once . . . How . . .)" (129–30). For a man of words, Crick very frequently cannot (dare not?) complete his sentences. Incomplete utterances abound: for example, in chapter 31 (235–36), chapter 38 (274), and chapter 44 (311–15). There are very many others.

These stylistic features of the text function in two major ways. First, they form part of the complexity and ambiguity of the novel. Linguistic virtuosity *is* possible despite the collapse of language in extremis. And, of course, vice-versa. Second, the movement between articulateness and its opposite connects with the novel's concern with the difficulty of grasping reality through any kind of discourse, and thus with the generic kaleidoscope of the novel (also itself a kind of virtuosity, a showmanship of the author, like Crick's with words) and its complex weighing of the concept of reality. It is part of the novel's richness and complexity.[17]

In keeping with its presentation of the collapse of its narrator's power of speech, the novel critically examines two closely connected narratives: a traditional account of nineteenth and twentieth-century British history familiar to anyone who has studied British history at school after the Second World War, and a narrative of progress. This is part of its scrutiny of the power of narrative (story and history) of any kind to grasp an elusive reality. The two narratives are of a particular kind, however, which permits their separate treatment, inasmuch as they (and their critical treatment) give *Waterland* its national-political dimension— a dimension which it shares, of course, with *The Sweet-Shop Owner* and *Shuttlecock*. Both are intimately connected, although the grand narrative of progress is obviously the property of nations and states besides Britain.

The narrative of British history that the novel presents is one that must be familiar to thousands of schoolchildren of Swift's generation and after, as it has been reworked in dozens of textbooks and is the stuff of state examinations throughout the United Kingdom. Glastonbury also points out that the motif of land-reclamation is an echo of a reference in Trevelyan's *English Social History*.[18] It is remarkable when one surveys *Waterland* as a whole to see how the text touches on most of the main stations and themes of the postwar British history syllabus—the starting point of the French Revolution and the Napoleonic Wars, industrialization, Empire, the First World War, the Second World War, and the new world of postwar Britain.[19] These form the substance and the background to Tom Crick's discussions of historical and personal events. He explicitly considers the French Revolution and Napoleon at various points throughout the text; his account of the rise and fall of the Atkinsons over four generations might be a representative summation of British industrial and imperial expansion; the carnage of Flanders is both agent and background to his parents' marriage; one is never allowed to forget a subsequent European war playing itself out as Tom and Mary, Dick and Freddie play out their sad childhood roles; both Tom and Mary go into the socially useful professions (teacher, social worker) that one would expect in socially reformist postwar Britain. If one leaves aside the desolation of the 1930s, then what the reader encounters is a potent, persuasive, and widely accepted narrative of British history. It is also, at heart, a progressive one, or one which has been so read. It is a history which, despite bloodshed and failure, ultimately points at a successful and promising resolution—a Britain of education, cohesion, improvement, and caring.

This is not, however, how it turns out. By the time Tom Crick starts to tell his stories, the progressive and hopeful postwar

Britain has become (in *Waterland*, at least) a place of public expenditure cuts, darkened by the threat of nuclear destruction and by attendant and widespread fear. Tom and Mary's marriage has declined into sterility, madness, and separation. It is noteworthy that the setting for their walks together, for Mary's revelation of her madness, and for Tom's own bleak future should be Greenwich Park and the meridian that represents Britain's imperial expansion and (literal) centrality in the world.[20] The novel points to the failure of this grand progressive narrative early on, in the figure of Lewis, Crick's headmaster—an educational idealist now forced to adapt to less hopeful, more threatening times—who is considering building a nuclear shelter for his family (chap. 4).

In this part of the novel, the reader should note Crick's dissent from the grand hopeful narrative—the reference to the cold war, his reluctance to leave the classroom for the world beyond it. At what point in his career Crick has come to this position is not clear, but he is certainly in full dissent by the beginning of the novel. As he touches on the main stations and themes of his history syllabus in his unorthodox lessons, he continually points to the failure of hope and the breaking of promise. The French Revolution leads to Napoleon and hundreds of thousands of deaths, and the rise of the Atkinsons brings loss and eventually ends in failure. The delusions of Empire are followed by the carnage of Flanders and bombed-out Hamburg. "What happened to that yarn our grandfathers spun us?" Crick has his father ask, as the old man lies dying in 1947 (340). At the end of chapter 47, Crick surveys his failed life and bleak future while in the setting of Greenwich Park (331). The national, imperial, and progressive associations of the setting are surely quite telling here. When Wood comments on what he sees as the "English" focus of Swift's fiction, it is surely passages like this that he has in mind.[21]

But it is not just a British narrative of progress that Crick is concerned to question; for him, the whole idea of progress is questionable. All our beliefs in progress, purpose, and utopia are dubious; they are narratives—stories—to fend off the nothingness, uncertainty, and malignity of things. "There are no compasses for journeying in time," he declares. Humans set off for utopia and organize "wars, butcheries, inquisitions, and other forms of barbarity." "Forward movements" have always brought "regression" (135). Crick goes on to list several such regressions. At a number of points in the text, Crick explicitly rejects the traditional understanding of progress (although one should note that he refuses to retreat into an easy pessimism). His final address to his school's pupils expresses this attitude (336).

Although both the narratives of progress (Britain's and the world's) are questioned, the narrator attempts to achieve a complex balance. As in the issue of the value of narratives and in the interplay of articulateness and the breakdown of language, the question of progress is complex. After dismissing the traditional notion of progress, Crick concludes the above passage by insisting paradoxically:

There's this thing called progress. But it doesn't progress. It doesn't go anywhere. Because as progress progresses the world can slip away. It's progress if you can stop the world slipping away. My humble model for progress is the reclamation of land. Which is repeatedly, never-endingly retrieving what is lost. A dogged and vigilant business. A dull yet valuable business. A hard inglorious business. But you shouldn't go mistaking the reclamation of land for the building of empires. (336)

The motif of land reclamation underlies the entire text. It is literally responsible for the novel's landscape, the product of generations of careful engineering with dykes and canals. Dick works on a dredger, perpetually laboring to prevent the Ouse from silting up. It is, however, difficult to judge whether Dick is to be associated more with the process of reclamation or with the silt that is its enemy. He after all embodies the "amnesiac mire" (245) that Crick sees as the enemy of such civilization and progress as there is.

Crick does believe in some kind of civilization and progress. He refuses to withdraw into a simple hopelessness. He is quite explicit about this (239–40). Perhaps he changed nothing as a teacher, but at least things have not got much worse. At least he fought to make his pupils a little different from their parents. Perhaps that is all progress and civilization are. These, at least, are his drunken musings (and the irony and self-irony are evident in the situating of Crick's arguments). In this endlessly hopeless but necessary process of defending some degree of progress, a process for which the motif of land reclamation is such a telling metaphor, history and the history teacher find their especial role. They struggle both against the folly of utopias and against the "amnesiac mire" of idiocy and forgetfulness. History "teaches us no short-cuts to Salvation, no recipe for a New World, only the dogged and patient art of making do" (108). History, land-reclamation, and the defense of some progress or some civilization become fused in Crick's long examination of his own and his country's history. History's attempt to find explanations for what cannot finally be explained—the land-reclaimer's continual battle against silt, the citizen's defense of what little progress has been made—become metaphors for one another and for the necessity of some kind of continued engagement with the malign and hostile world. There can be no withdrawal into forgetfulness or ignorance. These are represented in the text by idiocy, evasion, and death. Mary confined in the asylum, Sarah Atkinson's madness, drunkenness, and Ernest Atkinson's seclusion and suicide are understood but questioned by the narrator.

But lest the reader draw too much comfort from this conclusion, the text itself distances itself from Crick's judgments. After all, he is a particular and situated narrator, one with all the views (but finally none of the authority) of classic nineteenth-century omniscience. He too must narrate his history from a point of utter failure—Mary mad, himself dismissed. The last six chapters of the novel, with all the privilege of an ending, leave the reader with little in the way of consolation. Higdon comments extensively on the conclusion of *Waterland* from a theoretical perspective, as a balancing of the necessity of some kind of limit, or "closure"—in Higdon's terms—with the postmodern distrust of endings which seem to sum up and answer all questions.[22] Chapter 47 has Crick surveying a bleak future in Greenwich Park; chapter 48 presents the hypocrisies and evasions of the ceremony marking his retirement/dismissal. In chapter 49, he is allowed to speak of progress and civilization, but with what effect the reader does not know. In fact, is this what he does say to the school assembly? Does he indeed say anything at all? Chapter 50 gives Crick's father's death (as a result of the great flood of 1947 that undoes all the patient work of land-reclamation). Chapter 51 takes the form of a pastiche encyclopedia entry on the virtues, but also the demerits, of phlegm, while the final chapter depicts multiple failure and loss—of a life, of a brother and a son, of millenarian hopes, of the special beer—while in the background the reader observes the sinister flight of the bombers heading towards Germany. The final words of the novel are themselves ambiguous and sinister.

Stan Booth shuts off at last the bucket-ladder engine. The sudden dripping quiet strikes like a knell. "Someone best explain." We trip over empty bottles. Peer from the rails. Ribbons of mist. Obscurity. On the bank in the thickening dusk, in the will o' the wisp dusk, abandoned but vigilant, a motor cycle. (358)

The motifs and concerns of the novel achieve a grim summation here.

CHAPTER 6

Witnesses

Out of This World (1988)

Many features of Swift's fourth novel, *Out of This World,* are familiar from his earlier fiction: an attempt to give classical stature to contemporary fates; the interlacing of historical events with the domestic and the personal, and a consideration of the difficulty of escaping from history and assigned role; the presentation of problems concerning the recording of history, the power of memory, and the possibilities of knowledge; certain figures and settings—the damaged, heroic father, twentieth-century warfare, the asylum, Greece; that distinctively Swiftian narration, the isolated monologue to an absent listener; the narrator who mixes articulateness with reticence; the genre markers of the "family saga"; and the pressure of a national dimension in the text's events. When read together, Swift's novels set up elusive echoes of one another. A figure or a topic in one will be elaborated on or reduced to a minor role in subsequent texts. But, for all that, there are substantial shifts of emphasis in the four novels, not least in terms of the hopefulness or hopelessness of each of the novels' conclusions. *The Sweet-Shop Owner* and *Waterland* lie at the grimmer end of the scale, with *Shuttlecock* ending on a moment of balance, an epiphanic moment of happiness and insight. In this regard, *Out of This World* is closer to *Shuttlecock* than the others. Anna and Harry fall in love and dance in Nuremberg in 1946 (136); after a separation of ten years, Sophie will return to visit her father and celebrate his marriage at the novel's end (201–2). The created world of Swift's novels is a very nasty place, but sometimes there are glimpses of hope. Very much the heir of the nineteenth-century English novel, Swift's fiction is complex in its moral and social judgments.

Despite its partly optimistic ending, *Out of This World* has never been a favorite of critics. As was noted in chapter 1 of this book, Swift is frequently accused, with regard to *Out of This World,* of being overschematic in story material, too interested in ideas, and not sufficiently concerned to give his characters substantial life. Several critics, however, have seen important qualities in the novel. For example, Hermione Lee notes that women characters "are given strong voices for the first time in Swift's writing," and Anne Duchêne admires the novel's thematic organization and integration. "This is an extraordinarily closely laminated little story," she writes, "layer upon layer about violence and insufficient loving." Indeed, in the *New York Times Book Review,* Linda Gray Sexton speaks very highly of *Out of This World:* "Not a book the reader is likely to forget, *Out of This World* deserves to be ranked at the forefront of contemporary literature."[1]

The narration of *Out of This World* is largely carried by two voices, that of Harry Beech and that of his estranged daughter Sophie. Both Harry and his daughter are speaking in April 1982, ten years after the final event that drove them apart—the assassination of Robert Beech (father and grandfather) by an IRA car bomb. (Beech is chairman of the family firm B.M.C., an arms manufacturer "now virtually an agency of the Ministry of Defence.")[2] Both scrutinize their lives up till then. Beech recounts his relations with his father and his daughter, his father's own life, his (Harry's) decision not to enter the family firm, his marriage to Anna and her infidelity and death, his career as a war-photographer, his abandonment of photography after he finds himself photographing the burning remains of his father's car, and his new love affair with a woman half his age. Sophie considers many of the same characters and situations from her point of view—her abandonment by her father, her upbringing by her grandfather, her distaste for her father and all he represents, her marriage to the inoffensive Joe, her leaving Britain after her grandfather's death, and her subsequent life in New York. At two points in the text other narrators are allowed to speak—Joe, who is Sophie's husband (147–61), and, remarkably, the long-dead Anna, who was killed in a plane crash in Greece in 1953 (173–81).

The addressees of these monologues vary considerably. Many are not present, and thus the monologues are sent into a void. Indeed, when Harry speaks to Sophie, or to his father, or to Anna; when Sophie speaks to her children; or Anna herself speaks to her husband, the unavailability—the deafness—of the partners must be noted. It contributes toward the reader's sense of the sorrow and failure of the relationships. As Lee remarks, the "split narrative . . . enacts the dislocation it describes."[3] Joe seems to have a listener, Mario the bartender, but even here we cannot be certain how much is actually directed to someone present. Only Sophie has an audience there before her to any substantial extent. She is under analysis, and several of her monologues are addressed to Dr. Klein, her analyst. One section (33–34) is even a dramatic rendering of one of their exchanges.

But although all the narrators are to some degree speaking to themselves, within the text—if only there—some kind of dialogue is established. For example, the author's organization of the text on pages 78 and 79 allows Harry to put forward an argument answering Sophie's distaste for his photography. In a similar but opposite manner, the transition from Sophie's account of her affair with Joe in Greece allows this to be juxtaposed with Harry's account of his and Anna's meeting in Nuremberg twenty years earlier (132–33). Harry's account of his discovery that his father knew of Anna's affair with Frank is followed by the dead Anna's (impossible, of course) account of her life (173–81). The text allows its unhappy monologists to respond to each other, but only the text can do this, just as only the text can let Anna speak from the dead. The fragility—the artifice that permits some communication, some touching across the barriers of time and history—is surely emphasized here. Otherwise, the speakers are hopelessly isolated.

As in Swift's other novels, stylistic aspects of the narrators' monologues are worth noticing. The main narrators (Harry and Sophie) are articulate, eloquent, contemporary, and educated. They also possess some of the verbal playfulness and showmanship of the narrator of *Waterland*. A passage from the opening chapter of the novel ("That year, like the one before, was all Vietnam . . . didn't even think of me as another generation") establishes the main components of Harry's speech (12). One should note, here, the sophisticated vocabulary—"inane pitch," "parley," "mollify," "adrenalized and tensed," "denimed and bearded"—and the complex syntax of the second sentence ("That spring . . ."), and of the concluding one ("So the confused, angry kids . . ."). One should also note the rhetorically sophisticated parallelism: "Used to that feeling by then. Could bargain with it, parley with it, mollify it with whisky." The use of more informal vocabulary—"all Vietnam," "just far out, far out," "a big number to celebrate"—serves to emphasize, self-consciously, the sophistication of the rhetorical skill ("in the language of those days").

A later passage from one of Harry's monologues—the one describing the dying pilot of a Lancaster bomber—illustrates these features even better (105–6). This is clearly a stylistically (one is tempted to say rhetorically) sophisticated passage. The lexis is formal and educated ("posthumously," "compassionate concentration," "sacrilegious") as are the parentheses—"you do not think, I think, of heroism," "it would seem almost blasphemous to do so," and "assuming you were told the nature of the pilot's fatal wound." The elliptical and repetitive syntax is also rather formal—"to think of them all, impossible; to think of one, pointless." Above all, the pattern of parallelisms in the passage ("You wonder . . . ," "You think . . . ," etc.; "How it must . . ."; "Whether she . . .") indicates a conscious rhetorical skill and force. In fact, like the eloquence of Tom Crick in *Waterland*, Harry's way with words here is, perhaps, even a little suspect.

As with Tom Crick, there is a strong element of verbal play and linguistic self-consciousness in Harry's rhetoric. The parody, the wit, the exploiting of cliché and pun in the passage in which Harry reports press and TV reaction to his father's death are representative (90). The reader sees this verbal skill and self-conscious playfulness, too, when Harry searches for the deliberately inappropriate/appropriate word to describe Goering's defense in the Nuremberg trials ("Of the condemned, only Goering, whose defense had been—is this the right word?—so spirited " [104]), or when he points to the paradox of the photographer's injunction to "*act* naturally" (189). One also sees it in the deliberately convoluted syntax which Harry uses when he recalls assuring the proprietors of a Swiss pension that "the last thing, the very last thing my new wife was, was cold" (136).

Sophie, too, possesses this linguistic awareness and speaks very forcefully at times, although her lexis and syntax are not usually as sophisticated as Harry's. Her first lines illustrate this ("I guess I belong to the new world now, Doctor K. You see—I even say, "I guess" [15])—as does her short play with the word "fuck" later in the novel. But she, too, is capable of a quite sophisticated style; for example, talking of her children at one point, she employs a relatively complex vocabulary and syntax (75–76). Like Joe and Anna, however, Sophie speaks in a less formal, less complex style than Harry. He stands out very much as the man of words in the novel (paradoxically, since he is a photographer). But his discourse, like Sophie's, is marked by that common device of Swift's character presentation—the incomplete utterance. At certain crucial points—of evasion, of uncertainty, of fear, and when they are approaching the unspeakable—their eloquence fails them. Harry himself refers to this indirectly when he talks of the ability of photographs to show the unsayable, to show "the point at which the story breaks down. The point at which the narrative goes dumb" (92).

For example, from Harry's narration:

My one negligible wound in the cause of. (12)

And I never wished—So help me, I never, not for one moment, wished—(32)

And I thought: He can't actually change it. He can't come out of it, cast it aside. Not even now. Not even when—(72)

And though we haven't told anyone yet, and we haven't fixed a day, I was wondering, we were wondering—I was hoping—If, after all this time—? If—? (82)

This linguistic trait is even more marked in Sophie's speech. For example:

> Sweet, green visions. Oh to be in England now that—(Now, so it seems, they are off to fight the Argentines.) (15)

> And if he knew that I wanted—If he knew that, after all, I really wanted—Then I think he'd know too: that I don't—Haven't for years. Not any more. (98)

> I never went through this ritual. Because my mother—And my father—(139)

Once again, as in *Waterland,* words fail the otherwise eloquent, articulate narrators. History has surprises that defy language.

The organization of time in *Out of This World* clearly foregrounds history. There is an obsessive and precise dating of most episodes in the text. The novel is prefaced by the date April 1982, and its opening lines are: "I remember, in '69, three years before he died, when I was home for a brief while in the summer" (11). One of the key revelations of the text hinges on Harry's discovery that his father's act of heroism/suicide attempt took place *after* he had learned of his wife's death in childbirth (197). Dates are crucial throughout. The calendar tells Harry and Anna that she cannot be pregnant by him (168–69). The narrators very consciously tell their listeners when events occurred. Even the subsidiary narrations are no exception. Joe continually refers to time in his brief account of himself: "Nearly ten years now, but when I look out of my office window I still get that feeling I got when we first came here" (150); "When I was twelve years old, in '53" (151); "But by then it was all starting to happen with a Whoosh. Right through to the magic mid-Sixties"

(152); "Another photo from the wallet. Mum and Dad. Margate, Kent. August '61" (153); "I was a war baby. June 1941" (156). And even when he does not give the date of his conversations with Zoumbulakis and Karatsivas, the reader is quite clearly meant to understand that these conversations take place against the background of the Colonels' coup in Greece in 1967 and that this event is the foundation of Joe's fortunes (157–61). History is also very clearly brought to the foreground in the novel's utterly unchronological account of events. All the narrators organize their narrations associatively rather than in linear fashion, which is reminiscent of the temporal arrangement of *Waterland.* Thus he or she may move, for example, from the early 1980s back to the sixties, with an excursion to the First World War, a return to the 1970s, and then a reminiscence about Germany in the late 1940s.

This prominence of time and history is of crucial importance in *Out of This World,* for the novel is dominated by connected motifs of memory and the intrusiveness of history, and of attempts to escape and recover from history's malign force. Like *Waterland,* it is a novel of, by, and for historians. In the case of *Out of This World,* however, reviewers have commented with reservation on the way certain "ideas" dominate the text. For example, Gilbert argues that "Harry and Sophie are cardboard structures to provide the reader with a bird's eye view of our wars, of the ways in which those wars are represented, of the ways in which the media affect our sense of ourselves and our society in general" (36).[4]

Motifs of memory are very prominent. The novel is made up of a series of acts of memory, reminiscences within reminiscences, a painful scrutiny and laying bare of the past which has made the present. It is full of memorials, and it is full of characters that are trying to remember or expunge memories. The opening words of the text are quite simply "I remember" (11). All of the narrators—Harry, Sophie, Joe, and Anna—recall and relive the past. "I don't recall now where they had flown that night," Harry begins his anecdote about the dying Lancaster pilot, paradoxically signaling the act of memory to follow (104). "Küfergasse, *achtundzwanzig*," he intones to himself. "I still remember the names of the streets" (134). Sophie, indeed, is explicitly asked by her psychoanalyst to relive and retell her past (51, 53, 74); the others seem motivated by a desire to explain, to understand, even to excuse themselves. The references are numerous. Does Dr. K., too, have bad memories of "some mishap in middle Europe," Sophie wonders (16). Is America "made up of bottled-up bad memories, by people on the run," she asks (16). Memorials festoon Robert Beech's grave even ten years after his death (21), while Frank has a memorial bust of him commissioned (94), and Harry gives an account of the television obituaries after his assassination, which are composed of records of his past (89–92).

Sophie has managed for ten years to forget the past—she thanks her children for the respite from memory—but the effort has cost her too much, and now she must recall for her analyst all the painful horror and loss (75, 77). She insists there is no real escape from the past (109). Remembering haunts the novel and makes up its substance, and there seems no way out. Even when they look at Hyfield, the Beeches' family mansion, neither Sophie nor Harry can forget the source of the money that makes the beauty possible. Sophie urges her listener to "remember what all this is made of" (63); "Just remember what really grows in that orchard," mutters Harry (142). Joe's father can remember Queen Victoria's funeral, and in a moment during his family's

preparations for watching the 1953 coronation on television—
a moment that is almost comic, but not quite—he lets his family know that (155).

History, in two senses of the word, dominates character and
action throughout the text. First, quite simply and banally, the
past molds the present. Harry's present is the product of certain
actions taken by himself and others in the past—the loveless
relationship with his father, his wartime job, and his wife's infidelity. And the same can be said for Joe, for Anna, and for
Sophie. But in Sophie's case, as with the others, the past that has
shaped the present is one connected with, and shaped by, history in the broader sense of events of national or international
significance. For example, her grandfather does not simply die;
he is blown up by the IRA. Her father does not simply follow
any profession which obliges him to be absent for long periods
of time; he is a recorder of the world's wars and cruelties. History, in this second sense, continually intrudes on characters'
lives, shaping them, forming and deforming them. Like the
Bronze Age landscapes which Harry and his companions are
seeking in the novel's present, the characters of *Out of This
World* can all show the scars of a brutal twentieth century
(193–94). They are, each of them, as Anna says of herself, "one
of the world's walking wounded" (174).

Throughout the novel, the narrators are at pains to make
their absent listeners aware of the grand historical events playing
themselves out in the background. Harry's opening monologue
is a good example of this. The first moon landings, the Vietnam
War, and the political scene in the United States the previous year
all form the background to his memory of an evening spent with
his father. But the events are not merely background. Robert
Beech has made his fortune from twentieth-century technology

and warfare, both well represented by the war in Vietnam and the moon landings. The wonder of living to see men walk on the moon prompts his revelation (which the reader does not learn of until much later) of his possible attempted suicide in 1918, during another brutal war. Harry himself has been shaped by his experiences of war and destruction in, for example, Vietnam.

Indeed, throughout the novel the historical intrudes on characters' lives to shape and deform. This has been widely noted by reviewers. For example, Patrick Parrinder writes of *Out of This World,* "Graham Swift is . . . [a] novelist who . . . is burdened by history, and for whom the central theme of modern life is our own historical self-consciousness."[5] Robert Beech is one of the best examples of the effect of history on characters' lives. Maimed in the First World War and in charge of B.M.C. only because of his brothers' deaths in that war, his company's prosperity based on rearmament and the Second World War, he derives his money and status from supplying weapons of destruction to the twentieth century. Finally, he is assassinated by the IRA. Harry and Sophie are right to recall the source of Hyfield's beauty. Harry sees his father's collection of artificial limbs, which are increasingly less humanlike and increasingly efficient, as "like an index of the twentieth century" (200).

But not only Robert Beech has been shaped by history. Joe jokingly sees himself as a product of a dark night of desperation during the Blitz (156). More seriously, he very clearly establishes himself as a product of increasing prosperity and changing social values and habits in Britain in the 1960s, while his prosperity as a travel agent is founded on deals made with the backers of the Colonels' coup in Greece in 1967. Anna's marriage to Harry is an outcome of historical circumstance—the Nuremberg Trials—which brings them together, and also her own experiences of war in Greece, which, she suggests, have made her hard and calculating in her behavior (174). She never intended to return to Greece in 1946; did she marry Harry to achieve security and escape? Sophie's present and past unhappiness is shaped by her grandfather's murder and her father's reaction to it. Her whole attitude to Harry is also formed not just by his absences, but by the horrors of history that he brings back with him from the wars that are his career (78–79).

Harry himself is also a product of this century's brutal history (which Parrinder argues is, for Swift, "the historical century *par excellence*"), and his whole life is a rebellion against his father's status as an English hero.[6] "My father was a hero," he explains. "I didn't worship my father" (46). His whole life is a reverse image of his father's. He is a recorder of war rather than a war hero, a witness to the savagery of modern weaponry rather than a supplier of it. He is also someone clearly shaped—deformed—by his experiences of history. A witness to so much brutality, he automatically photographs the burning remains of his father's car—an action that, beyond all else, repels his daughter and drives her into exile. His whole life, too, is centered around what the novel sees as a major twentieth-century technological phenomenon—the photograph—just as his father's is centered around the technology of destruction. In his own eyes, he becomes as a photographer, not simply the recorder of the twentieth century, but somehow its motive force. Watching the first moon landings on television in 1969, he reflects:

The first rule of photography: that you must catch things unawares. That the camera doesn't manufacture. But that night was the first time perhaps that I thought: No, times have changed since then. The camera first, then the event.

The whole world is waiting just to get turned into film. And not just the world but the goddam moon as well. (13)

Again, while he is watching television pictures of the British Task Force sailing to the Falkland Islands, he muses:

And it goes without saying that a task force of cameras should accompany the Task Force to the Falklands. As if without them it could not take place.

When did it happen? That imperceptible inversion. As if the camera no longer recorded but conferred reality. As if the world were the lost property of the camera. As if the world wanted to be claimed and possessed by the camera. To translate itself, as if afraid it might otherwise vanish, into the new myth of its own authentic-synthetic photographic memory. (189)

As a photographer, he has become not just the recorder or even the victim of history, but its agent. This persistent interworking of character and history makes one question Linda Gray Sexton's judgement in the *New York Times Book Review* that the novel shows a world in which "families lose their members not to the age-old engines of warfare but rather to the modern engine of alienation."[7]

For the characters of the novel there seems to be no escape from memory, and no escape from history either. It is like the Parthenon in Athens, as Sophie sees it—an unignorable presence, despite all attempts to forget its existence (125); and what Sophie discovers when her grandfather is murdered is that "it's all one territory and everywhere, everywhere can be a target and there aren't any safe, separate places any more" (111). The motif of the impossibility of escaping from history is repeated through-out the novel. Hyfield is an important focus for such motifs. When Harry first speaks of it, it is to note that his father has put up barbed wire and alarms round it (11). Later we learn how his successor has turned it into a fortress, trying to lock out the threat of history (22). Despite its age and its beauty, however—despite Robert Beech's precautions—historical events intrude on it. The IRA bomb is waiting for him under his car, precisely at a moment of domestic happiness (and even national celebration), on April 23, 1972—St. George's Day (68).

Of course, the sanctuary has always been one based on for-getting. As Sophie and Harry remind the reader, it is maintained by arms making and all that entails (63, 142). Its safety—its insu-lation from twentieth-century horrors—has, in any case, always been illusory. Sophie comes to prefer the unvarnished threat and violence of New York to the illusion of security (17).

There is no doubt that the created world of *Out of This World* is one of death, violence, monstrosity, and absurdity, and that these are what the text means by historical events. The car-nage of the First World War, the fate of the Lancaster pilot Harry photographs, the mass bombing to which that pilot has been a party, the actions chronicled at the Nuremberg Trials, the Greek civil war, Oran, the Congo, Vietnam, the bomb that kills Robert Beech—these are history, and this is what the characters seek, unsuccessfully in each case, to insulate themselves against. Sophie is terrified when she accompanies her father to Fleet Street. "Everything from the world comes here," he says. She is ap-palled by the men, the telephones, and the machines (52). The hideous world of violence intrudes on Hyfield and on her feel-ings for her father when she finds one of his photographs (78). There is no safety with her children in the New World, for memories return and the children start to play with toy guns (73, 75, 85).

When Sophie is born, Harry wishes to protect her against the world, but, paradoxically, he brings that world's cruelty into her life (31). It is his photographing of her grandfather's burning car, almost more than the murder itself, that makes Sophie realize there is no escape from history anywhere (111–12). Joe, too, would like to keep history at bay, to shut the door on horror, to stand "sentry" to happiness (137, 150), but he can no more do this than Sophie or Harry can. Anna can escape from the horrors around her in wartime Greece by dreaming of a fabulous, paradisiacal England, but even she emphasizes her luck in surviving and acknowledges elsewhere the scars of the war on her life and personality (175, 177, 174). Harry sees this attempt to hide—to protect oneself from history's barbarism and absurdity—as widespread. Late in the novel, he thinks of his Uncle Edward, who was killed in France in 1915. Did his classical education, Harry wonders—"that other world" of noble phrases, deeds, and myths—help him to bear the horrors of the western front (187)?

History's cruelties and stupidities seem to repeat themselves. While Harry, who is based in his picturesque rural "retreat" from history, is looking for Bronze Age field patterns, what should he see but the British Ministry of Defence installations which dot the countryside? But, as his companion points out, perhaps this should not be surprising. Much of the legacy of the Bronze Age is in the form of military structures and technology (194). In the present of a novel that chronicles many of the twentieth century's brutalities, the British Army is moving to fight the Argentineans for control of the Falkland Islands (185). There seems no end to the cycle of war and destruction. "There's no decline or progress, just monstrous repetition," Lee notes.[8]

But Swift's view of the power of history is complex, and characters are not trapped in a maze of failed escapes and death. In a review of *Waterland*, Michael Wood points out that "Much of Swift's earlier fiction is concerned with flimsy or paradoxical chances of freedom."[9] While *Waterland* can hardly be said to grant the Cricks any escape from the grim oppressiveness of history, *Out of This World* marks a cautious return to an earlier, already cautious, optimism in this matter. The characters can, for example, conceive of other possibilities, the might-have-beens that would have made at least their own lives different. Harry tells us he might have acceded to his father's wish that he work for B.M.C.—for love of Anna, and perhaps for love of his father (22, 145). Harry, too, can at least imagine that his father could have given him a redoubled love after his mother's death, instead of ignoring him (29). Sophie can picture a world where Uncle Edward does not die and in which she and her grandfather visit him (123–24), and Harry can envisage a world in which the Trojan War is called off—a world that, like Sophie's, would be a sensible antithesis to the one he knows is real (186–87).

But these are all hypothetical possibilities and imaginings, themselves even a kind of refuge from an awful reality. Swift does, however, allow his characters (as in *Shuttlecock,* although not in his other novels) some escape, some recovery. In many ways, Nuremberg is the focal point for this aspect of the novel— the possibility of escape and recovery from history. Nuremberg is representative of many of the novel's motifs of destruction and death. Subject to mass bombing, it is also the site of the Nuremberg Trials and their chronicle of human depravity. But Nuremberg is also where Harry dances with Anna. "To be happy in Nuremberg! To fall in love in Nuremberg! In that city of guilt and grief and retribution, to think of only one face, one pair of eyes, one body," Harry exclaims (133), before going on to describe, ecstatically and with passion, the couples in a dance hall in 1946 (136). In a place that represents a century gone mad, Anna and Harry fall in love and dance. This sums up in a single motif the possibility of at least temporary escape from history's madness, of rescuing something of value from the ruins.

The pattern is repeated elsewhere in the novel. Harry is given another chance for happiness with his young assistant Jenny. "She's out of this world," he declares ecstatically (36). She makes him almost believe that "the rest of the world doesn't matter. The world revolves round that tinier and tinier figure, as it revolves round a cottage in a tiny village in Wiltshire, where she has taken up residence. That I am home, home" (39). "She makes me feel—," he tells us later in the novel, "hell, she makes me feel that I'm half my age, that everything is possible. . . . She makes me feel that the world is never so black with memories, so grey with age, that it cannot be re-colored with the magic paint-box of the heart" (141). The whole situation is dealt with in complex fashion. Jenny is "out of this world"—beautiful, a wonderful chance for Harry—but she is also not of this world, and therefore she provides for Harry an escape, a refuge in a world where we have been told there are no such safe places. Notice, too, the ambiguity of "the magic paint-box of the heart." Is there not a hint of childishness and sentimentality here? There is certainly more than a suggestion of touching up the truth Harry has spent his life trying to bring to the world's attention in his photographs. But there is an escape, and Harry's relationship with Jenny makes him write to Sophie asking her to come (140). At the novel's conclusion, Sophie is flying to Britain with her children. There will be some reconciliation. Perhaps the novel suggests that, just as the lizards which Joe so admires can grow a lost tail, so people can recover from the awful events of their past (156–57). Perhaps Sophie's words about the healing of scars are meant less ironically than they sound. Swift himself acknowledges the optimism of *Out of This World*. "It could be called a more hopeful book than *Waterland*," he suggests in a brief article in the magazine *Bomb* from 1988.[10]

The very end of the novel shows Harry as a young boy about to take off in an airplane, for once being indulged by his father. Of all the recurrent airplane motifs in the text, it is striking (but also highly ambiguous) that the novel should end with this positive flight experience—pointing as it does to reconciliation, freedom, and hope. The passage contrasts the mud of the western front, still in his father's mind, with Harry's escape into the air. "And I was being lifted up and away, out of this world, out of the age of mud, out of that brown, obscure age, into the age of air" (207). Of course, the age of the air will shortly be that of the bombing raids on Hamburg and Nuremberg, and of air strikes in Vietnam. This is noted by Parrinder who also argues that Harry's "final position . . . is somewhat equivocal . . . . We are not going to get out of this world, with its accumulations of images and memories and deposits of mud, as easily as all that."[11] But for the moment, the novel holds this knowledge in suspension, and Harry is allowed to step momentarily "out of this world." Sophie captures the novel's balance here as she imagines herself traveling back to England—also by airplane—to be reconciled with her father (145). But, of course, Harry's flight in 1928 (ten years after 1918) led to no final reconciliation with his father. Why should Sophie's, which also takes place ten years after an albeit more localized act of violence?

If history is foregrounded in *Out of This World*, so too are the problems of knowing and understanding that history. This concern is familiar from Swift's previous novels—especially *Shuttlecock* and *Waterland*—and, in many ways, his fourth novel is reworking this aspect of the earlier texts. Questions of knowledge and understanding are raised throughout the text. One should note, first, that the novel presents the reader with two central mysteries that it unravels with a considerable amount of traditional suspense. Early on, it is hinted that Robert Beech made some crucial decision in 1918 (29), but the nature of that decision—to commit suicide—is not revealed until near the novel's end. The same can be said about the number of teasing references to Harry's having done something terrible at the time of his father's death (41–42, 84, 94). The nature of his act is not made clear until well on in the novel. There is also a considerable amount of mystery about the characters and the motives for their actions. (This was something one can note, too, regarding *The Sweet-Shop Owner.*) Almost as a rejection of the nineteenth-century British novels that underlie so much of Swift's fiction, the narrators reveal via hints, and they leave more mysteries than they solve. Why does Harry take up photography? Why does he say no to B.M.C.? Why does he become a war photographer? Why does Anna commit adultery? Why does Harry write to Sophie asking her to come to England? Why does Sophie marry Joe? Why the enormous psychological disturbance, the random sexual encounters, and the necessity to visit Dr. Klein? Why does Robert take on the chairmanship of B.M.C., and why does he build it up as he does? At times, answers to these questions are hinted at, but they must remain surmises on little evidence. One may either judge this to be a strength or weakness of the novel; however, it can certainly be seen to emphasize questions of knowledge and understanding.

The element of genre mixture in *Out of This World* also surely functions—as it does in *Waterland*—to foreground problems of giving an account of things. Here, too, the text merges family saga, historical novel, psychological novel, fairytale, Greek legend, television obituary and interview, and essay (on photography) in order to emphasize those same questions of how much one can know and how one understands events. Indeed, it is important to note the prevalence of references to illusion and falsehood in the novel. Joe makes no secret of the fact that he sells illusions of England—dreams of a fantastic nature—to his American clientele (16, 58, 153). Sophie wonders if this has not become part of his own nature now (77). Hyfield itself is a prime example of an illusory, "historical," and charming England. But both Sophie and Harry see it clearly as such—as illusion, and a dangerous one at that—for they urge us to remember on what the beauty is founded, and the event that takes place in its grounds. Robert Beech, the victim of that act of violence, is himself part illusion, part falsehood. One of his arms is artificial, it must be remembered. His act of heroism and the foundation of his later fortune and esteem may well have been quite the reverse—an attempt to commit suicide. When Harry visits him in the hospital after his first heart attack, the son at least sees the father as playing out a role (and as being trapped within it) as the patriotic arms manufacturer and patriarch of B.M.C. on his deathbed (71). Sophie is well aware of the charms and illusions of memory. When she talks of England near the end of the novel, she addresses this directly. "What's it like? It's where you come from in a way, it's where you *were,* but of course you won't remember it. And maybe it's no longer the way I remember it. Or rather, the way I remember it is like it never was" (191). Nuremberg itself becomes a metaphor for illusion and distorted memory. Harry points out that the medieval city, which was destroyed during the Second World War, has been reconstructed, though it is "not real, of course" (103).

Harry sees photography as a way of fighting against illusion and forgetting. "Seeing is believing," he declares, "and certain things must be seen to have been done. Without the camera the world might start to disbelieve" (107). For him, the camera shows "only unaccomodatable fact," "the point at which the story breaks down. The point at which narrative goes dumb" (92). It shows the public the facts of wars, of concentration camps, the ordinariness of Nazi criminals (102). Originally, he saw the camera as a means of banishing "myths and legends," allowing us to "see ourselves clearly only as what we are" (187). He has come increasingly to question this however. "But I think the world cannot bear to be only what it is," he remarks (187). The photograph itself can lend itself to illusion and evasion. His photograph of the dying Lancaster pilot has "a perverse formality and poise," has become an aesthetic object. It also, as Harry points out in a passage already cited, omits an enormous amount of salient detail (105–7). Harry's sequence of pictures of a grenade-throwing marine in Vietnam are distorted by the journals and its viewers (119–20).

Photography even comes to be seen by him as an evasion—of loss, of horror, of simply too much emotion (122)—and as an escape from the realities he would have his viewers confront. He points out that it has, in his view, become increasingly difficult "to distinguish the real from the fake, or the world on the screen from the world off it" (188). The camera itself has become the agent of a modern myth. It is "as if the camera no longer recorded but conferred reality. . . . As if it were a kind of comfort that every random, crazy thing that gets done should be monitored by some all-seeing, unfeeling, inhuman eye" (189). It is as if, he might say, the camera had replaced, in its own twentieth-century way, the God the century has difficulty believing in.

But despite the problems of photography—of recording, of telling the truth—Harry insists on the necessity of bearing witness. (One is reminded here of Tom Crick's insistence on the importance of the historian's trade.) "Someone has to be a witness," he declares (49).

> Dear Sophie. Someone has to be a witness, someone has to see. And tell? And tell? Tell me, Sophie, can it be a kindness not to tell what you see? And a blessing to be blind? And the best aid to human happiness that has ever been invented is a blanket made of soft, white lies? (163)

He, like Dr. Klein (26, 98, 102), must bear witness, must remind others of "unaccomodatable fact," must prompt and correct memory. Sophie's whole progress towards mental disturbance indicates, in the novel's world, the cost of forgetting. The novel's epigraph—"What the eye sees not, the heart rues not"—must, at the very least, be seen to be ambiguous, and is probably, in the last analysis, meant ironically.

There is no tailing off of Swift's ambitions in his final novel of the 1980s. *Out of This World* is replete with the kind of references to twentieth-century British experience that make one want to read the action as having a national-political dimension (as is the case with regard to the three previous novels also). Lee writes of Swift's novels that they depict "secret family pasts that come to stand for a national history."[12] The repeated references to how characters view England, the status of Robert Beech as a national icon, and the motifs of Harry flying high above the English countryside force this aspect on the reader. But the novel is also, like Swift's other texts, remarkably ambitious in its attempt to go beyond the parochial and to touch on a whole century of European history. Here again, the use of settings (Greece, Nuremberg), and the use of experiences beyond the British (Anna's, for example) push the novel in this direction. These and the novel's complex treatment of history and of knowing add to the richness of the text. In its conciseness, its scope, and its integration of character, experience, history, and intellectual concerns, *Out of This World* is a remarkable performance, a quite unjustly underrated novel.

CHAPTER 7

Against Transience

Ever After (1992)

Swift's fifth novel continues his line of unhappy monologists that began with Prentis in *Shuttlecock*. "These are, I should warn you," begins Bill Unwin, the novel's narrator, "the words of a dead man."[1] Unwin is not literally dead—although he has recently tried to commit suicide—but he is deeply damaged emotionally. He tells three main complex and interweaving stories in the course of the novel. As befits a narrator in a state close to despair, the chronology of Unwin's narration is anything but linear. Unwin moves freely among the different time settings of his stories, just as Tom Crick does in *Waterland* or Harry Beech does in *Out of This World*. Indeed, the reader must work hard to reconstruct, in retrospect, the chronological sequence of events.

The first story is that of his mother Sylvia and her affair with a young American in Paris in 1945 and 1946. Unwin's father commits suicide in 1946, and for much of the novel the reader and Bill are given to understand that this is a result of his wife's adultery. Later in the novel, it is revealed, however, that there may also have been political motives behind Colonel Unwin's suicide (204–5). Slightly earlier it has also been revealed that Unwin may, in fact, not be Colonel Unwin's son, but rather the product of an earlier affair his mother had with a locomotive driver (168–69). At the moment from which Unwin is narrating his stories, his mother has recently died, as, too, has her lover and subsequent husband, Sam.

The second strand of the story material concerns Unwin himself—his life in the shadow of his mother's adultery (to which, as a child, he is accomplice and witness) and his father's suicide, and his complex relationship with mother and stepfather. The latter becomes a millionaire industrialist, supplying the postwar world with plastic goods. Coming from a line of professional and social failures on his mother's side (31–34), Unwin leads a life that is a mixture of drabness and glory. He spends some thirty years married to the glamorous Ruth, a brilliantly successful actress. For much of that time, he is nominally her manager, though, in fact, his duties as such are minimal, and he is really only her "secretary-cum-minder" (123). He gives up a far from flourishing academic career to be with his wife, to be a shadowy, slightly comic figure against her splendor (81–82). Shortly before his mother's and stepfather's deaths, Ruth is diagnosed as having lung cancer (Unwin's mother will die of throat cancer), and within a year she commits suicide. Unwin returns to his academic life, to a bogus fellowship—with only a few modest duties which Unwin, after a fifteen year absence from university life, is scarcely qualified to perform—at an ancient (Oxford or Cambridge) college, which has been financed by his wealthy stepfather.

It is in this college setting that the third main strand of the novel's story material appears. Unwin's mother possesses the journal of a distant ancestor, Matthew Pearce, and his farewell letter to his estranged wife Elizabeth. Written between the 1840s and the 1860s, the journal mainly documents Pearce's loss of traditional religious faith, the impact of Lyell's and Darwin's writings on him, and the eventual break with his wife, children and in-laws occasioned by his turning from mid-nineteenth-century Christian orthodoxy.[2] This journal is an important historical-cultural document, charting as it does the impact of nineteenth-century thought on the life of an individual. Despite jealousy and hostility from one colleague, Unwin decides to edit the journal with a view to publishing it. He becomes involved in the messy personal lives of his younger colleague, Potter, and Potter's wife Katherine. He is almost seduced by Katherine, who is, perhaps, trying to get the Pearce manuscript from him for her husband, though Unwin is unsure about this. It is this final failure—his life is so drab that he cannot even manage to have an affair with an attractive and willing woman—coming on top of the three deaths of wife, mother, and stepfather, that finally pushes Unwin toward suicide. And even in that, he fails.

Ever After has attracted some negative criticism, some of which has to do with Swift's choice of Unwin as a narrator and protagonist. In the *Observer*, James Saynor notes that the "problem with writing about life as a mess and an anticlimax is how to make it narratively at all interesting."[3] The critic suggests that only occasionally (in the Paris episodes and in those connected with Pearce's loss of faith) does the reader escape "the stifling skeleton-cupboard of Bill's self-encounter session." In the *New York Review of Books,* Hilary Mantel calls Unwin "not the most promising company for the duration of a sizable novel." While she admires Swift's rigorous sticking to the point of view of his narrator, she argues that the novel lacks "energy" and that "Always, the main problem is Unwin himself," for "Unwin is a bore." Both Saynor and Mantel insist that the novel has too much meditation and reflection, and too few lively events, to be successful. Mantel concludes her review by saying: "*Ever After* may have deeply advanced Swift as a thinker, but sadly it has not advanced him as a novelist."[4]

Several critics acknowledge the richness of the novel's material, but Kirsty Milne in *New Statesman and Society* finds this a source of concern. She argues that there are "fledgling novels struggling to get out" of Swift's texts, complex stories to which he does not give full weight. This commentator also insists that the strands of the story material do not cohere. "Past and present co-exist without interaction, like two static pools," she claims. "Bill Unwin's obsession with his father . . . finds no answering echo in the life of Matthew Pearce."[5] The charge of incoherence is also laid by Stephen Wall in the *London Review of Books*. "In the end," he writes, "the different areas of narrative interest in *Ever After* disperse rather than concentrate attention. Although its varying strands are conscientiously knitted together . . . , they don't seem significantly to cohere."[6] Lorna Sage, in the *Times Literary Supplement*, does not agree. "*Ever After*," she writes, "is structured as a palimpsest—the present's nightmare of bereavement intercut with that of Swift's imaginary Victorian. . . . In both times what's being lost, in essence, is a sense of individual value."[7] The anonymous reviewer in the *Economist*, however, gives the novel its most unstinting praise, comparing it favorably to *Waterland*, and judging it as "light and deft," an exploration of the "teasing possibilities of the monologue . . . to the full."[8]

Like several of Swift's novels (*Shuttlecock*, *Out of This World*, and *Last Orders*), *Ever After* is made up of a double narration. The majority of the text is narrated by Bill Unwin, but he quotes extensively from another's text (just as Prentis does in *Shuttlecock*), so that the narrator of the quoted texts comes to assume something of the status of a narrator in his own right. One should note, however, that as with Prentis's father, Matthew Pearce, Unwin's distant ancestor, only speaks in fragments and only when the main narrator permits him to do so. In fact, he is completely subordinate to Unwin, and has no autonomy at all (unlike Sophie in *Out of This World,* for example). Therefore, Unwin's is really the central narrational voice in the text. As a narrator, he is a marked continuation of the kind of narrator established in most of Swift's earlier fiction (only *The Sweet-Shop Owner* is different in this respect). Unwin is a highly self-referential, self-scrutinizing narrator, various features of whose makeup foreground very clearly the act of narration and the nature of fictional (or indeed any other kind of) narration.

First, he is a narrator who is prone to comment on his own qualities as a narrator, especially those of his prose style or of specific components that he introduces in the text. For example, on the novel's second page, he notes in a parenthesis that he has "slipped into the insidious 'we'" when talking about his fellow academics. Two pages later, he comments further on his own writing (6). Here the focus on the stylistic aspects of his narration and their relation to his identity clearly foregrounds the act of narration. This foregrounding is evident elsewhere as well. For example, Unwin corrects himself on occasion, suggesting that he may have earlier misled the reader. "All this she told me in the early stages of her illness—not, if I have given that impression, on that final gilded evening" (34). Later in the text, he again comments on his style, in this case in a letter he has just written. "The language we use! The postures we adopt! A little ingratiating mimicry of those whom (we think) we are dealing with? Or is this stuff me?—the professional blather . . . the palpable signs of fogeydom" (188). In a self-scrutinizing fashion, he also comments on his own focus as a narrator. "I read up on Brunel; but I do not research my own father," he writes. "I summon up Matthew, but I do not know my own father" (219). And towards the end of the novel, he self-consciously notes and emphasizes the relevance of the name of the hotel (it connects with the Hamlet motifs in the text) in which he and Ruth spend their first night together. "He selects a hotel. Are names significant? It is called the Denmark Hotel" (272).

Second and above all, however, the narrator constantly draws attention to himself and to the act of narration by emphasizing how much he is surmising, guessing and inventing in the text. Indeed, this becomes an extraordinarily prominent motif in the last two-thirds (and more) of the text. He introduces his summary of the Potters' married life thus: "A brief history of the Potters, Michael and Katherine. Part fact and part surmise, just like my reconstruction of the life of Matthew Pearce. Just, if it comes to it, like my reassembly, here in this afterworld, of my own life" (88). The element of imaginative invention in Unwin's presentation of his ancestor, Pearce, is, indeed, heavily emphasized. "I imagine, I invent," Unwin insists (138). "I see him" (139); "I conjure him up, I invent him" (155). "You have to picture the scene" (197); "I imagine some white-fronted villa, a gravel sweep, a backdrop of dark, shielding trees" (231).

One should notice that Unwin questions not only the veracity of his own narrative, but also that of his subject, Pearce himself. His memory, too, may have been "subject to a degree of narrative licence" (100). Pearce's whole account of his first meeting with his future wife clearly signals its invented nature (114–18). It begins with "The scene. . . ," and goes on, after a mass of verisimilar details, to remark that "Matthew would have been impressed by the improvements to the workshop," through the perfect conditional ("would have"), suggesting invention and surmise. The use of the present tense in the narration of the ensuing scene further emphasizes its made-up quality by deviating from the traditional past tenses of narrative.

Unwin does not emphasize the invention that lies behind narrative exclusively in relation to the distant past. Even more recent events, some indeed very recent, are clearly presented as reconstructions via imagination. For example, with regard to his wife's relationship with her parents, the narrator writes: "I picture Ruth as a young girl quarreling with her mother, and Bob trying, rather ineffectually, to keep the peace" (124). When he discovers Gabriella's perfume bottle in Potter's car, Unwin, too, reconstructs a whole imagined scene he has not actually witnessed (175–76).

Even with regard to parts of his own life, Unwin suggests that the narration is not wholly true. After recounting a trip and a meal on his mother's birthday (which just happens to be on the day before the first atomic bomb is dropped—a coincidence to which the narrator himself alludes), he remarks that "The past, they say, is a foreign country, and I fictionalize (perhaps) these memories of that afternoon" (243). Constantly, the reader encounters a highly self-conscious, self-referential, and self-doubting narrator.

Linguistic aspects of Unwin's narration further foreground the act of narration and reinforce the reader's sense of Unwin's at least partial untrustworthiness. Unwin's lexis and syntax is, quite simply, flauntingly self-advertising. Like the narrators in *Waterland* and *Out of This World,* Unwin employs a variety of English that is remarkably sophisticated and knowing. The very beginning of the novel establishes a distinctive voice. It is one with a highly sophisticated style. The vocabulary is particularly so: "induced senescence"; "the lean and slippered pantaloon"; the whole list of possible donnish personae ("the crusty and cantankerous . . . wide-eyed, latter-day infant"—whereby the alliterative effects in the list make it seem even more sophisticated and clever); "rare birds" (depending for its effect on the Latin original, "rares aves"); "worthy of living enshrinement." The passage's syntax is equally elaborate and sophisticated. Complex sentences abound, as do parenthetical phrases and clauses. See, for example, the last sentence of the third paragraph ("By seventy or eighty . . ."), which embodies all these aspects. The elevated sophistication of lexis and syntax is highlighted, however, by a slippage into the informal and colloquial which, in the context of these particular utterances, becomes itself a sign of knowledgeable sophistication. Examples of such a stylistic shift downward include "sexy young studs of academe," "their no longer galloping careers," "there's no reason . . . why they shouldn't go on for decades," and "Potter, by the way, is pushing forty-eight" (3–4).

This stylistic configuration, in which all aspects suggest a witty sophistication, occurs throughout the text. One more example must stand for many. In chapter 7 Unwin writes of his wife Ruth's first singing engagement in a Soho nightclub (82). Once again, in this passage, the elevation—the rhetorical questions, the unusual vocabulary ("sugared lubricity"), the parallelism of subordinate clauses mostly without main clauses ("how" and "as if") and of phrases ("not the real thing . . . substance of love")—is coupled with slippage into the colloquial ("smoochy," "gooey," "and when were they going to get on with it"). The final effect of these colloquialisms must be to suggest, paradoxically, the speaker's own witty, sophisticated competence with language.

Examples of such language occur on virtually every page of the novel. In addition, Unwin shows himself as a narrator particularly fond of inserting parenthetical statements into his utterances, commenting on or amplifying or making more complicated what he is saying. Once again, two examples must stand for dozens. The passage beginning "The Notebooks . . ." and running to "into his media style" (54) contains six parenthetical interruptions, four within parentheses themselves, and two others: "whatever the College planned" and "anticipatorily perhaps" (the last being a parenthesis within a parenthesis). This feature appears even more prominent when one considers that there are approximately seventeen such parenthetical insertions (counting only those contained formally within parentheses) in the last three pages of chapter 4, from which the above excerpt is taken (54–56). A brief paragraph from later in the novel (111) is also shaped by parenthetical interruption—almost half of the passage is a parenthesis which contains a sub-parenthesis within itself ("they bred hard, these Victorians, and with reason"). As with the narration's other stylistic features, this element constantly draws attention to the act of narration itself. The narrator constantly interrupts the narrative to expand, comment on, be ironical about, and question what he is saying. The reader is constantly jolted into an awareness of the narrator's voice, just as the narrator's constant references to guessing and imagining draw the reader's attention in a similar fashion.

Two other related stylistic features of the narration function in the same way—the presence of numerous questions, and (as in several of Swift's other texts) incomplete utterances. Consider the last two paragraphs of chapter 4 (55–56) or much later paragraphs from chapter 18 ("Did his fears permit . . ." [233]), both of which are full of questions—direct and indirect. A few citations must do justice to the enormous prominence of this stylistic feature of Unwin's narration. The other, expected by those who know Swift's earlier novels, is the incomplete utterance. Just as in *Waterland* or *Out of This World,* the narrator of *Ever After* seems frequently unable or unwilling to complete his sentences. They trail off frequently into dots or dashes. For example: "So when Sam came up with his little arrangement for me . . ." (76); "a look which, even as she cradled her mug of sweet tea, made you feel as if you were out on an adventure . . ." (80); "the first time she shed her clothes for me; the first time my bare palms pressed her bare breasts; the first time . . ." (83); "Alas, poor ichthyosaur . . ." (155); "The more he strove, not being my father, to become my father, the more I resurrected, like a shield, my real—" (160); "my mother barely eight months dead: 'the funeral baked meats . . .'" (166); "Sam, I've got to tell you . . . Sam, did you ever know what my father—I mean, my—I mean what he did . . . ? Sam, will you take a look at this . . . ?" (207). Unwin not only continually poses questions, he constantly leaves sentences unfinished or trailing off into vague unspoken, hinted-at endings.

As in Swift's earlier novels, the functions of such stylistic features—sophistication, frequent parentheses, questions and incomplete utterances—are, first, to foreground the act of narration, and, second, to make the narrator seem less than wholly trustworthy. The whole narration is done in such a strangely prominent and distinctive style that one is continually brought up against the very material—the words, phrases, syntax—of the text. Also, one realizes as one reads that this is a narrator using the language of sophistication and authority, who is nonetheless deeply hesitant and uncertain. He asks questions, which he rarely answers; he lets his sentences end in vague, indefinite dots and dashes. Just as the narrator's self-referentiality raised issues of his reliability—of the reliability of any narrative—so his voice raises similar questions.

There is, as one might expect, a certain amount of genre variety in *Ever After*. Although it is not nearly as marked as in *Waterland*, it is still a quite prominent feature of the text. The novel as a whole is, it is suggested, a long, written monologue. (Unwin indicates this when, having been interrupted by Katherine Potter, he puts away "these pages" and then adds "I am writing this—days later" [87].) It is partly a memoir of his life, a recollection of childhood and young adult life, and also a partial account of a marriage. It, however, mixes elements of memoir with accounts of more recent events—all the events after Ruth's suicide, and Unwin's relationship with the Potters. These later events and the earlier ones have strong elements of psychological fiction in them. They recount the narrator's complex relationship with mother, father and stepfather, his sad, maimed life after his wife's suicide, and his failed relationship with Katherine. The incidents involving the Potters often recall social satire, or that usually satirical sub-genre of the social-psychological novel—the campus novel. This is particularly true of the section of chapter 14 in which Potter maniacally drives with Unwin in his car in order to scare him into relinquishing the Pearce manuscripts (174–82). Here the text achieves quite substantial comic-satirical effects, especially when the hapless Potter calls out in a frenzied manner, "The spiritual crisis of the mid-nineteenth century is my subject!" (177). Chapter 21, with its account of Katherine Potter's failed seduction of Unwin, also belongs within this genre, although it clearly is more firmly rooted within more purely psychological fiction.

The text, too, must be classed as a kind of story of detection, as Unwin explores his father's past, trying to uncover the reasons for his suicide. But, in genre terms, one of the major elements in the novel is Matthew Pearce's diary and letter. The letter makes up the whole of chapter 5, while Unwin's narration is interlaced with extracts, often quite long ones, from Pearce's mid-nineteenth-century journal. As a result of this, the text takes on a further genre coloration, that of historical fiction. This element is also strongly present in the scenes of reconstruction that Unwin conjures up in, for example, chapters 9 and 15.

These are substantial shifts in genre, though they are less extreme than those of *Waterland*, and—as in Swift's previous novels—they serve to foreground textuality and to suggest the problems of giving account of events and of the past. *Ever After*, however, signals its fictionality even more markedly through intertextuality. More so than any one of Swift's previous novels, *Ever After* is deeply and constantly literary. The range of intertextual reference is quite considerable. It extends from *La Bohème* (three times: 15, 23, 264) to *Anthony and Cleopatra* (131–32). There are numerous quotations from Sir Walter Raleigh, a putative ancestor of Unwin's (77, 246–47), references to *A Midsummer Night's Dream* (85) and *Love's Labor's Lost* (245), and an allusion John Donne ("O Mayflower Road! O my America, my new-found-land!" [264]). Even where there is no direct quotation, the text often draws on literary or artistic reference. For example, in a description of Katherine Potter, the reader learns that a "light breeze . . . wreathes her hair about her face and flutters her thin dress against her body with almost sentient, Botticellian tenderness" (96). Earlier in the same chapter, Katherine is described, in very literary terms, as the lady in a medieval romance (88). These are only a small selection of the literary and artistic allusions that recur throughout the text. One constantly has a sense of a novel that is permeated by, and constantly seen in reference to, other literary texts.[9]

References to one text in particular, however, are remarkably prominent in *Ever After*. A casual examination will note at least twenty references to *Hamlet* in the course of the novel as a whole. They start to occur from the very first pages of the novel.

"I will only say, for the time being," declares Unwin, "that for a large part of my life, ever since my old English master, Tubby Baxter, made us read the play, I have imagined myself—surreptitiously, presumptuously, appropriately, perversely—as Hamlet" (7). The next page contains a further evocation of the "doleful but charismatic Renaissance protagonist who has somehow got under all our skins" (8), and makes a direct correlation between Unwin's family and Hamlet's—"For Claudius, read Sam Ellison" (8). The first chapter ends with yet another reference to the play, when Unwin speaks of his "forty years' vicarious habitation of Elsinore as my second home" (13–14). The references continue throughout the novel. Unwin uses them with regard to Matthew Pearce, to his intellectual difficulties and to his family: "What was Darwin to him? What is Matthew to me? 'What's Hecuba to him or he to Hecuba?'"(154); "Alas, poor ichthyosaur . . ." (155); and "I see a graveyard scene. Not Hamlet juggling a jester's skull" (155). About Elizabeth Pearce's second marriage, Unwin asks, "What was she supposed to have done? An Ophelia routine? Talked to the flowers?" (226). When he decides to suggest that some personal-sexual motives may underlie the Pearce family's fate, Unwin does so via a reference to *Hamlet* (235).

Indeed, the allusions to Shakespeare's play hardly stop in the course of the novel. For example, his stepfather's possible embarrassment is related by Unwin to the scandal of Claudius's and Gertrude's marriage (166). Later, in chapter 13, Unwin boldly announces: "I am Bill Unwin (there, I declare myself!). I am Hamlet the Dane" (172). At times, the allusions to *Hamlet* can become quite dense and extensive. For example, when he thinks of the causes of his father's suicide, Unwin's prose becomes permeated by echoes of Shakespeare's play (206). As has been noted earlier, Ruth and Unwin's first night together is spent in the Denmark Hotel (272).

The functions of such intertextuality are multiple. They exist, on one level, to contribute to one's sense of Unwin's character—withdrawn, literary, afraid of life ("And what I became was—bookish" [64]). Further, *Hamlet* is closely relevant to the motifs of decay, chaos and death which play such an important role in the novel. But another function of the constant (and they really are very frequent) allusions to *Hamlet* and other texts (including a visual one—a Botticelli painting) is to foreground fictionality. *Ever After* becomes through these references a very obviously literary-artistic entity, a text premised on an earlier text and shot through with constant allusions to, and quotations from, that text and others. As with so many other features of the novel, genre and intertextuality become highly self-referential elements in the text.[10]

As in all his novels, in *Ever After* Swift shows a fascination with history—both history as event and history as account. Historical events form the background, and, at times, the foreground of the novel's action. Private lives are linked with public events. The narrator spends some of his early years in Paris, where his father is involved in various (unspecified) activities connected with the end of the war (chap. 2). His father, the reader learns later, may have killed himself because of his distaste for his involvement in the development of the atomic bomb (204–5). Unwin's mother celebrates her birthday on the eve of the dropping of the first atomic bomb (243). Technological change of a more mundane kind haunts the narrator's imagination. He writes of his childhood interest in train spotting in a way that dwells on technological development and transformation (as well as continuity of a kind). He sees the landscape like a "vista" from "a children's encyclopedia" illustrating different forms of transport and different kinds of technology, as a "living palimpsest" of water mill, road, rail, and canal (213).

In addition, Unwin's stepfather Sam Ellison makes his fortune (a fortune which will provide Unwin eventually with his scholarly sinecure) from plastics, the material of future commercial development. "It's the stuff that's gonna mould the future. I mean, literally. Anything from a coffee cup to an artificial leg, to the sock that goes on it," Sam remarks (19). The growth of the mining of tin and the eventual collapse of the industry provide the background for some of the events in Matthew Pearce's life (231–32), as do technological developments, railway and bridge building, centered on the figure of Brunel (215–19).[11] Most importantly of all, however, at least for Pearce, Darwin's theories and their publication form a major historical watershed in the novel. One of the readings of Pearce's life provided by Unwin suggests that it is the former's loss of faith occasioned by Darwin's *The Origin of Species* that brings about the collapse of his marriage and his death.

Much of the history-as-event that is observed in this novel is a matter of destruction and transience. The atom bomb destroys; the great trains of the thirties and forties pass into oblivion; plastic becomes a substitute for hundreds of other materials; the tin boom comes and then fades. Further, Darwin is, according to Unwin, all about transience (249–50). These are all part of a prominent line of motifs of transience in the text. There are numerous deaths—Unwin's father, mother and stepfather, Unwin's wife, Pearce's drowning, the death of Pearce's son Felix. From the start of the novel, we are aware that Unwin has attempted to kill himself, and that he sees himself as, in a sense, a dead man. Unwin feels his cloistered college threatened by some unnamed ruffian outside its walls (4). The glorious Paris of his childhood has vanished (15). "Fuel, fire, ash," Unwin intones when he thinks of his own dying wife and of the dying Brunel (126, 216). Watching his wife smoking cigarette after cigarette (the habit that will lead to her cancer and suicide), Unwin reflects: "It was at such times, rather than in the darkness of theatres, that the truth of something would come to me: that people are fuel. They are consumed. Some, for some reason, more quickly, more brightly, more readily than others. But they are burnt, used. Fuel, fire, ash" (122). Along with the Pearce notebooks, it is a clock, that symbol of passing time and the transience of all things, which is passed from generation to generation in Unwin's family (51–54). As in *The Sweet-Shop Owner,* the created world of *Ever After* is replete with motifs of transience, destruction, and death. History—in the sense of great events—is part of this. Indeed, all event, all occurrence becomes a matter of destruction in the novel—"fuel, fire, ash," as Unwin notes.

In common with Swift's earlier novels, *Ever After* is also concerned with history as account. The problems and difficulties of giving an account of events are a major focus of this novel, as they are of *Waterland* and *Out of This World.* The narrator's emphasis on the role of invention and surmise in any record of events has already been noted. The novel's convoluted chronology (typical of Swift's fiction) further develops this. Through it the reader is made aware of the selective, organizing nature of any narrative (the chronological order of events is not followed, but, rather, a different, and subjective order is imposed on them). The chronology of *Ever After* is indeed far from linear. Chapter 1 starts in the novel's present, after Unwin's suicide attempt, and his wife's and stepfather's deaths. Chapter 2 goes back in time to Paris in the late 1940s, and to Unwin's childhood experiences there. Chapter 3 leaps forward forty years to Unwin's mother's death, and also provides background details concerning his mother's family and her marriage to his father. Chapter 4 returns to the novel's present and Unwin's life in a venerable Oxford or Cambridge college. Chapter 5 is made up of Matthew Pearce's last letter to his wife Elizabeth from 1869, and chapter 6 recounts Unwin's childhood act of revenge on his new stepfather. Chapter 7 takes the reader to 1957 and Unwin's first meeting with his future wife. And so it goes on. The narrative continues in this nonlinear fashion throughout, moving erratically between past and present. The novel's conclusion maintains this pattern. Chapter 18 provides a long account of the Pearces' life before and after their separation in 1860. Chapter 19 relates (largely) an outing Unwin makes with his mother to Aldermaston in 1945. Chapter 20 consists of reflections on mortality, and chapter 21 gives an account of the hours just before Unwin's attempt at suicide. But chapter 22 returns to 1957 and ends with the young Unwin and Ruth in bed together for the first time. Clearly such a chronology is multifunctional—the past is interwoven with the present; past and present echo one another to universalize the novel's concerns—but one such function is surely to emphasize the act of telling, the act of making a narrative, through selection and organization.

Motifs of not knowing and crucial, unexpected silences further reinforce this aspect of the novel. The former are very prominent in the text. "We see what we choose to see, we see what we think we see," Unwin remarks about human beings and their perceptions and memories in general, and about his own in particular (15). His mother's adultery in Paris is something he both sees and does not quite see (19–20). The principal figures that surround him seem to be enigmas. Unwin describes his father as "inscrutable," as "open to interpretation" (26). His ineffably ambiguous mother sings "Who is Sil-via. . . ?" (37, 42) (her name is Sylvia), and he reflects that, as a half-knowing child, he perhaps knows her better than anyone else does, better than even her husband. Of his glamorous and successful wife, Unwin says, "She was everybody's. But the thing is, she would always come back to me. Me. I don't know why, but she did. Always. A dullness for her brightness? A nobody for her somebody?" (121). Despite all his reconstruction of Pearce's life and emotional and intellectual conflicts, Unwin feels compelled to say of his subject (twice in close succession), "I don't understand him" (143). If Sam is to be believed, Unwin spends most of his life not knowing his real father (168–69). He certainly ends up quite unclear as to the motives for his nominal father's suicide—moral, political or personal (208–9). "And how do I know? And why should I believe it?" he asks (187).

The novel relentlessly generalizes problems of knowing and understanding. Chapter 13 begins with a speculation on innocence, on knowing and not knowing. Is it better to be "innocent" of the truth, to live "happy in . . . worldly credulity," or better to know the truth as Matthew Pearce sets out to do (171)? Matthew Pearce and his father-in-law have their final confrontation while wearing beekeeper's masks, thus hiding their faces from each other, making themselves unknown, obscure (192). While speculating on his true father, the engine driver, Unwin talks of him thus: "My nameless, engine-driving, killed-in-the-war father. And why should I, when I never got to know the living, breathing man whom I took to be—? What difference does it make? The true or the false" (219). Unwin's dilemma about

Matthew Pearce is the same as his dilemma concerning his "other," nominal father. He does not know the motives for his behavior. "And while we're about it, we may as well ask the big question: which came first—the failed marriage or the ideological anguish? . . . So, have I got it all wrong? I invent. I imagine" (226). He has questions, too, about Elizabeth Pearce. "So what are we supposed to believe? That from 1854 until 1860 Elizabeth held out, the mystified, forbearing, loyal, loving wife, until it was all up? And then, and only then—?" (225). The questions remain even after Pearce's separation from Elizabeth. "And what, in the end, would he [Pearce's father-in-law] have judged to have been worse? His son-in-law's defection to the forces of godlessness? Or his daughter's rush . . . into the arms of Mammon, that false god that it was his duty to denounce in his sermons?" (233). We seem to be dealing with a narrator who knows less and less, the more he examines his, or Pearce's, past.

There are also remarkable silences at the heart of *Ever After,* which Unwin's questions and uncertainties surround. (This presence of silences over crucial matters is true, too, of *The Sweet-Shop Owner* and *Waterland.*) The whole issue of Unwin's mother's relationship with his "true" father—the mysterious, dead train-driver on the Great-Western line—is finally a complete enigma, an area of the narrator's history which remains quite unilluminated throughout the text. Is he even factual, one wants to ask, or is he an invention of Unwin's stepfather? In any case, he exists simply as an absence, a silence. The same is true of Unwin's nominal father's suicide. Why did he do it—for personal or moral reasons, because of his wife's adultery, his son's illegitimacy, or because he had become increasingly disturbed by the diplomatic work in which he was involved? Questions and silences. The same is true of the narrator's life with his wife—the glamorous, successful Ruth (parallels with Crick's silences in *Waterland,* about his married life with Mary, are quite insistent). One is given plenty of detail about the beginning of the relationship, and certainly some detail about its conclusion. But the central portion of several decades of marriage and intimacy are scarcely touched upon at all. Again, there is silence where one might expect detail. Something similar is true of Pearce's relationship with his wife Elizabeth. One witnesses Pearce's intellectual and emotional conflicts, and the beginning of their relationship (invented, as he acknowledges, by Unwin), but one learns nothing of the central years of their marriage. Unwin draws attention to this himself by his surmises and speculations, by his questions. At the end of the novel, the author has relentlessly problematized the whole issue of giving a narrative account. Unwin's account leaves too much unanswered—is too reticent and uncertain—and thus becomes, to some degree, suspect.

As has been suggested above, one of Unwin's key silences concerns his relationship with his wife Ruth. Are there things he is not telling the reader? Is she an adulteress? At the end of chapter 10, Unwin insists that between their first meeting and Ruth's death, there was quite simply "Happiness. . . . Happiness ever after" (132). But he has just compared her to Shakespeare's Cleopatra, not the most chaste of women. Throughout the novel, he gives teasing hints that all is not fidelity in their marriage. He witnesses her "inconstancy" on stage, seducing and being seduced (121). Of a kiss between her and an actor friend, he insists: "It wasn't what you think. No, it wasn't what you think" (122). Is he protesting a little too much? "*Così fan tutte,*" he says of other women (Pearce's wife, his own mother), and then continues: "And Ruth. And Ruth? No, I don't believe that she ever—But suppose, suppose" (227). Toward the novel's end, he asks himself the following unanswered (and now unanswerable) question: "And can I really believe that in all this turning into other people, in all this promiscuity of personae, up there before the lights, she never, ever—?"(269).[12]

The reader must similarly wonder. *Ever After* is partly organized around parallels. Pearce loves his mother more than his father (59), just as Unwin does. Potter is an adulterer (90), just as Sylvia Unwin is. Brunel is marked by self-consuming glamor and energy, as Ruth is (141, 217). Pearce is a paleontologist; Unwin sees himself as being one in a figurative sense (197). Thus, the presence of at least three probable adulteresses in the novel is, perhaps, meant to make one speculate about Ruth (just as Unwin himself does). Elizabeth Pearce, Unwin reflects, was probably having an affair with an admirer and future husband before the collapse of her marriage with Matthew (195, 222, 225, 234). Unwin's great-grandmother, Alice, most likely (Unwin again speculates) also had her "Latin lover" before the break-up of her marriage (229–30). It is scarcely surprising that the narrator wonders about Ruth as well (227), although it is finally his lack of knowledge that he stresses. For him, Ruth is "a woman who for nineteen years of her life inhabited the undiscovered country of my complete ignorance of her" (267). He is talking here of the period before their romance and marriage, but the same terms ("complete ignorance") seem to apply to their life together as well.

The question of knowledge and ignorance in the text is further underlined by the prominence of motifs of illusion. The self-referentiality of the narration, the open inventing of scenes and motives, and the highly foregrounded intertextuality which were noted above are part of this concern with the limits of knowing. Narrative is unreliable—at best it is a guess, a surmise, an invention—and the created world of the text is permeated by things that are not what they seem, that are lies and convenient fictions. It is hard to exaggerate the degree to which Swift weaves these motifs through the substance of the novel. Relentlessly, the text probes the question of what is real and what is—somehow—not. Motifs of illusion are present from the opening pages. Unwin reflects on the college in which he has found refuge that the walls are "artificial and implausible, like a painstakingly contrived film set" (4). In chapter 2, the Paris of Unwin's childhood is an illusion brought to life. The city is a realization of an opera set. "It had never struck me before that reality and Romance could so poignantly collude with each other; so that ever afterwards I saw Paris as a palpable network of 'scenes,' down to the subtle lighting of a smokey-blue winter's morning, or the blush of a spring evening, the incarnation of something already imagined" (15). Paris, a "fairy-tale city" (63), is associated for the young Unwin with, if not exactly illusion, then frivolity and decoration—what he calls "the highest aim of civilization," that is "the useless: ballerinas, café chatter, Puccini operas, Elizabethan sonnets, silk underwear, parfumerie, patisserie, chandeliers, the magic hush when the lights go down in an auditorium" (22–23).

When Unwin talks of his wife and her skills and her glamour, it is also in terms of illusion. "Glamour, I know, having lived with Ruth, is only a kind of dressing, a trick, a concoction, the promise of something else. . . . It is as desirable and meaningless as money" (48). They first meet in "a tinselly temple of illusion, a den of late-night delights, called the Blue Moon Club in Soho" (78). Their love is a type of illusion, like all "Romantic love," which Unwin calls a "made-up thing. A concoction of the poets" (121) (earlier he had included romantic love among all the decorative, useless things for which Paris stands [22–23]). Certainly, their first night together is spent under an assumed name (274). Ruth's roles, too, are all a matter of illusion (121). Indeed, the whole business of theater and acting is seen in this way (267).

There is a constant generalization of this motif of illusion. For example, Unwin talks about literature as—in comparison to "the real world"—"a more reliable world in so far as it does not hide that its premise is illusion" (75). Sam Ellison produces plastic goods that are often "substitoots" for the real thing (19, 158–59). Indeed, as Unwin wryly remarks, his death while having intercourse with a prostitute might be seen as a pursuit of a substitute for his dead wife (158). Unwin himself talks of his own life as a "fiction" (171), as does Pearce (195). The latter's journals are, according to him, "the record of his life as a fiction: 'the beginning of my make-belief'" (195). The quotation from Raleigh's poem—"Our mothers' wombes the tiring houses be/ Where we are drest for this short Comedy" (247)—emphasizes the generalization of this sequence of motifs. All human life becomes a play—an illusion—and any account or record, any version or shaping, even more so.

Illusion is absolutely necessary, however, in the created world of *Ever After*. This is a world of transience, death, chaos, and betrayal. In such a world, Unwin asserts the importance of illusions, of fictions, of lies. That is all there is to set against the grim consuming fires of this world. Most memorably this occurs when Unwin stands over his wife's dead body. Deeply grieving and under no illusions as to the finality of her death and their separation, Unwin nevertheless insists on the validity, on the importance, and on the necessity of an illusion in the face of a highly generalized destructive force (131–32). Here the insistence on the fictional, illusory conclusion—"happy ever after"—is meant to achieve a kind of paradoxically impressive dignity. In the face of the world's transience, the narrator asserts the importance of human love. "*Amor Vincit Omnia*" is the paradoxical, ambiguous inscription on the family clock that Unwin and Ruth receive from Sylvia Unwin (52).

The narrator also insists on the importance of texts, even though they are shot through with fiction and surmise and can scarcely provide a reliable account of reality, even though their promises are also largely illusory. "Happy ever after" belongs to fiction, to narrative. Unwin does come to some kind of understanding (or understandings) of Pearce through his reconstructions. Literary texts provide a framework for his version of his own life. One of the reasons for Unwin's disfavor in his College is that he insists that the literary text is something beautiful that can stand, for a moment, as something consolatory. "They [the words of a fifteenth-century lyric] catch up and speak to us in their eloquence and equilibrium, and just for a little moment . . . the obvious is luminous, darkness is matched with light and life is reconciled with death" (77). Like Crick in *Waterland* and Harry Beech in *Out of This World,* Unwin insists on the necessity of the flawed, the partial, the untrustworthy, and the illusory that is also beautiful and saving. That is surely why the novel finishes where it does, with Unwin and Ruth in bed together for the first time in a night of love (one permeated with suggestions of artificiality and the stage) (275–76).

Of course, this section and the novel does end with a *memento mori,* the reminder of Unwin's father's suicide, which foreshadows Ruth's own, and indeed all the other deaths in the novel; but it is placed against the glorious fiction of the young lovers' night, no matter how transitory that night and that glory may finally turn out to be. Like so much of Swift's fiction, *Ever After* focuses on chaos, death and flux, but also insists on what might be set against that—a night of love, a written text—even as the fragility and deceits of these are also emphasized.

CHAPTER 8

A Narrow World? (II)
Last Orders (1996)

Graham Swift's sixth novel is prefaced by two epigraphs that neatly sum up the concerns, the milieu, and the powerful paradoxes of the text. The first comes from Sir Thomas Browne's grandiloquent meditation on funerals, *Urn Burial* (1658). The quotation reads: "But man is a Noble Animal, splendid in ashes and pompous in the grave." The second epigraph quotes the author (John A. Glover-Kind) of a popular music hall song first published in 1907: "I do like to be beside the seaside." Browne's sentence is impressive, archaic, and sonorous, touching on last things; Glover-Kind's song captures a fun-seeking, saucy, seedy, lower-class world of Edwardian and 1930s seaside resorts. *Last Orders* embraces both intellectual and social worlds. It is a complex meditation on grand, universal matters; it is set in a lower-class world of nonstandard dialect, mundane work in shops and offices, and trips to the seaside. The title of the novel itself embodies this paradox. "Last orders" are the final drinks one can obtain in a British pub before it closes. "Last orders" also suggest last things, death, mortality, and the ineluctable passage of time.

The novel's story material is both simple and complicated. On April 2, 1990, four friends—three older, one younger—set out from the "Coach and Horses" public house in Bermondsey in South London.[1] Their aim is to scatter the ashes of their recently dead friend, Jack Dodds, according to his last wishes, in the sea by the Southern English resort of Margate. The four men are Ray Johnson (an insurance clerk), Vic Tucker (an undertaker), Lenny Tate (a fruit and vegetable stall owner), and Vince Dodds (a used car salesman). Jack Dodds himself was a master butcher with his own shop. Ray, Vic, and Lenny are contemporaries of the dead Jack, men in their sixties; Vince is Jack's adopted son, and is in his forties. As they travel in one of Vince's luxurious used cars, a royal blue Mercedes, the complexities of their lives and their present situations and relationships begin to emerge. Why is Jack's wife Amy not with them? Why is there tension between Vince and Lenny? In an interweaving chain of monologues, the characters—those present on the outing, and those who have not come—tell their stories. It is very difficult to summarize the complexly interlacing chains of disappointments and failures. Jack and his wife Amy have a mentally deficient daughter, who has spent fifty years in an institution. Ray has had a brief affair in the 1960s with Amy. Vince loathes his adoptive father and has rejected his wishes that he follow him into the butchery business. In the early 1960s Vince impregnates Lenny's daughter Sally. She has an abortion (financed by Ray's skills as a gambler on horse racing), and has since had a disastrous life. Around the same time, Ray's wife Carol leaves him, and his daughter Susie goes to Australia. Over the years father and daughter lose contact with each other. After five years in the British Army in the 1960s, Vince sets up his own used car business, marries Mandy—a runaway from Blackburn in the North of England, whom Jack has found in a café near the meat market in Smithfield and taken home as a substitute daughter—and now he has his own daughter, Kath, who is the part-time mistress of one of his rich Arab clients. In fifty years, Jack never visits his mentally handicapped daughter June. For fifty years Amy continues to do so, twice a week, almost without fail. On the day of the trip to Margate, Amy is traveling by bus to the asylum where the daughter, who has never recognized her, lives.

The trip to Margate itself is bedeviled with complications. "We can do detours," says Vince (115), and the company meanders toward Margate. They stop in Rochester for lunch and drinks (107–16). Then they make—at Vic's request—a detour to the British naval war memorial at Chatham (119–22, 139–42). They stop in the Kentish countryside, where Vince decides on his own initiative to scatter some of Jack's ashes and brawls with the outraged Lenny in a muddy field (144–51, 180–81). They make another halt in Canterbury and visit the cathedral (192–94, 195–207, 225–26). It is a disheveled and weary group that finally arrives in a gray, windy and eventually rainy Margate to fulfil their friend's last wishes.

Swift won the Booker Prize for *Last Orders* in 1996, and a motion picture—with an extremely distinguished cast of actors —was subsequently made by Fred Schepisi and first shown in 2002. The novel received the usual highly respectful reviews that accompany the publication of one of Swift's fictions. In the *London Review of Books,* Gaby Wood notes the continuities of the novel with Swift's earlier work, and this topic is also discussed by Adrian Poole in the *Guardian Weekly.* Indeed, Wood sees the novel as a return to the characters and milieu of *The Sweet-Shop Owner.* The text's intricate narration—multiple monologues—is widely discussed by critics, usually with approval. For example, in the *Sewanee Review,* Gary Davenport worries about the "forbiddingly intricate multiple narrative" of *Last Orders,* and suggests that the novel seems "like the work of the fresh graduate of a creative writing program who wants above all else to strut his stuff." He concludes, however, that "this novel could probably not have been written any other way, and of course that is the ultimate justification of technique."

Critics praise Swift's fusion of personal and national memory and history in the novel (Wood and Reynolds), while others comment favorably on his deployment of strong female characters and voices—something they see as unusual in his fiction (Poole and Reynolds). The eminent Irish novelist John Banville provides a perceptive and positive review of *Last Orders* in the *New York Review of Books*. He praises Swift's sensitive and detailed portrayal of the lives of "ordinary" and humble characters. "He is never patronizing to his characters, never smarter than they, and firmly eschews cheap effects, so that, although they may be 'small' people, they take on an almost mythic stature in Swift's presentation of them, of their minor triumphs and abiding sorrows, and their capacity for endurance." Banville, too, writes with approval of Swift's "strong" female voices, and finds Swift to be a writer who celebrates an England that is admirable and decent. "Book for book," Banville declares, "Swift is surely one of England's finest living novelists" (8). This praise is echoed by both Reynolds and Poole. Indeed, at the end of his review, Poole declares: "I think *Last Orders* will come to be seen as Swift's best novel. So far."[2]

In his review Banville wonders whether "the plot of *Last Orders* is extremely intricate or if it is just that the manner of its exposition makes it seem so."[3] Certainly the narrational technique in *Last Orders* is complex and striking. The novel is narrated by a group of characters via their monologues. The narrators are the four male friends who make the trip to Margate—Ray, Vic, Lenny, and Vince—and Amy (Jack's wife) and Mandy (Vince's wife). In addition, at the novel's end the dead Jack also delivers a brief monologue, which is largely made up of the words of his dead father (285). Despite the fact that critics have described the women's voices in this novel as "strong," they speak much less than the male characters. Mandy has only one monologue, although it is a long one (153–64), and Amy herself only speaks five times. Male voices predominate, especially that of Ray. The novel is divided into seventy-five short chapters (some are only half a page long) in which various characters speak to the reader. Each chapter is headed with the name of the speaker, except for seventeen chapters that have place names as their headings, but which are spoken by Ray. The latter character is, thus, the main narrator, giving twenty-two monologues under his own name, plus the seventeen with place names. He is, however, far from alone. Vince delivers twelve monologues, and Lenny and Vic give eight apiece.

The characters' monologues fall into three (usually overlapping) kinds: narrative monologues that give accounts of events; interior monologues that show elements of stream of consciousness technique; and reflective, non-narrative monologues that tease out the implications of events or make generalizations about life. Many individual monologues have features of all three groups—for example, Vince's monologue between pages 71 and 73 provides reflections on automobiles and also an account of his attempt to sell one to Hussein, with occasional eruptions of his immediate thoughts and feelings that are reminiscent of stream of consciousness technique. But usually one type of monologue is dominant. For example, in the opening chapter, Ray relates what happens in the "Coach and Horses" as he waits for his friends to arrive (1–5). In one of Vince's monologues (93–97) and in Vic's wartime memory (123–26), however, the narrative element is limited, and the ebb and flow of the speaker's feelings are given, at times in a relatively unsystematic

way. This is particularly evident in Amy's wide-ranging monologue toward the end of the novel (274–78) in which memories,
immediate impressions, accounts of actions, and worries and
reflections merge together to give the reader a sense of the
motions of Amy's mind as she travels, probably for the last time,
to visit June in her asylum. In addition, a number of monologues
have more reflective and speculative aspects. In them characters
muse over questions that have been thrown up by memories of
the past or by immediate experience. For example, Lenny does
so on the matter of duty and family reconciliation (131–33), and
Vince offers his hymn to the automobile (71–72). One can find
strong reflective elements in Lenny's monologue on his daughter's abortion and his own feelings for Amy (208–10), and in
Jack's, in which he recounts his father's words on "wastage" in
the butcher's trade (285). In Canterbury Cathedral, Ray, too,
muses on time and the future (207), while earlier he has given
the reader an unusually headed chapter—"Ray's Rules"—in
which his principles for betting on horses are presented as a
guide to life (202).

"The accent is flat London vernacular," notes Banville of
the speech of the characters in *Last Orders,* and Swift himself
has discussed his attempt to capture the "colloquial language"
he sees as appropriate for his characters.[4] They certainly speak
a nonstandard dialect of English, one that suggests the real
speech of lower-class South London. Ray sets the linguistic tone
from the novel's first sentence—"It aint like your regular sort of
day" (1). "Aint" is certainly nonstandard, while "your regular
sort of day" sounds very informal. The double negatives that are
so much part of various demotic dialects in English are very
prominent in characters' utterances. Again on the novel's first
page, Ray reflects, "I never meant to make no joke of it." The

characters' grammar is informal throughout the novel. "Even then it don't move," notes Ray of the clock in "The Coach and Horses" (9); "So I didn't say nothing," recalls Vince (93); "We troop back across the field, not saying nothing," Ray says after the brawl in Wick's Field (180). The tense shifts—the movements between past and present tenses that are associated with verbal, informal narratives—also appear in the characters' monologues. Once again this is established early in the novel when Ray gives an account of a conversation with Lenny (6–7). Another example is Vic's recollection of the moment when Jack tells him he is going to retire (80–81).

Syntax and vocabulary are also notably informal. For example, Amy's memories of hop picking in the 1930s are marked by sentence fragments and run-on sentences (234). The vocabulary, too, is colloquial: "tash" for mustache; "used to crack his face" for smile; "pushing it" for lucky; "at the crack" for early in the morning; "ma and pa" for mother and father; and "chuffed" for pleased (234). One can also note that recurrent linguistic aspect of Swift's texts—incomplete utterances. As in his other novels, they abound in *Last Orders*. For example, Ray says of Jack and dying: "like he aint stopped being himself, just because"(152). "What hard-nosed," says Amy of women, leaving out the "tricksies" (deceitful females) she has used earlier (239). "This is where. Here, in the garden of," she declares a page later, omitting "June was conceived" and "England" (240). This linguistic feature runs through most of the characters' monologues, and examples can be found throughout the novel. While such incomplete utterances mark linguistic breakdown in Swift's earlier novels—such as *Waterland* and *Out of This World*—in *Last Orders* they seem, rather, to mark the essentially spoken and highly informal nature of the monologues of the lower-class South Londoners that are the novel's central characters.

One might wonder if the voices of the characters are too similar to each other. There are differences. Vic, the undertaker, is at times capable of utterances that are much more correct in terms of standard English than are those of his companions. Examples of this are his memories of the war (123–26) and his general reflection on death (143). But even here, the vocabulary is far from formal, and the syntax is marked by fragments and run-ons, or by compound rather than complex syntax (links between clauses with "and" rather than subordinating conjunctions—often a marker of informal speech). Characters speak a very homogeneous language in *Last Orders*. Banville wonders whether this is a failure on Swift's part.[5] This seems unlikely. Rather Swift is suggesting that there is, indeed, a similarity of language among his characters. They think in very similar ways about things and express their thoughts in a relatively homogeneous language. There is a kind of linguistic community among these figures, just as there are shared experiences and stories among them.

Last Orders is, thus, made up of a series of interweaving monologues by a group of South London characters speaking a suitably informal, lower-class English. Their different narrations move freely through time, and the story material of the novel only emerges gradually via highly disordered and digressive accounts and memories. "We can do detours," says Vince (115), and the narrative itself is composed of radical detours and digressions. The framework for the novel—the present from which it starts, to which it constantly returns, and in which it ends—is the April day in 1990 when the four companions set off to scatter Jack's ashes at Margate. From the novel's second chapter, however, the text moves freely backward and forward in time, oscillating between that present in 1990 and various points in the past. The reader can distinguish several recurrent past time settings—the 1930s, the Second World War and the immediate postwar period, the 1960s, and the late 1980s (largely centered on Jack's illness). There are minor settings in other periods, for example Vince's childhood in the 1950s and early 1960s (93–97), but the novel restricts itself largely to those principal settings. Individual monologues move among time levels. Ray shifts, for example, between the late 1980s and the 1960s within a single chapter (26–28), and Lenny, too, moves from the late 1940s or early 1950s to the 1960s in one reminiscence (40–45). Most of the characters, however, recall specific single periods: Amy remembers the late 1930s (234–41, 252–55); Lenny and Ray the 1960s (66–70, 51–60); Vic the 1940s (125–26); Vince the 1960s (102–6). These memories are not ordered in any linear sequence within the novel, but rather they interweave. The reader can move from the novel's present (71–73, 74–77) to 1989 with some movement into an unspecified past (78–86), to the 1940s in Egypt (87–92), and then to Vince's childhood in the early 1950s (93–97)—all within a few pages.

The temporal organization of the novel has certain consequences. Many details of characters' lives, experiences, and relationships emerge only gradually in the course of the novel. Indeed, there is a degree of old-fashioned suspense about the novel. As the reader goes through the text, questions insistently come up. What is peculiar about Vince's position within the Dodds family (6–7, 25)? Why is Amy not with the four men on their way to Margate (2, 29)? Who is June (15)? Why is Ray reluctant to speak of wives (21)? What is Ray's business with Vince about a yard (39)? What should (or should not) Vic tell

Jack? What was he a witness to (the answer is Amy's adultery with Ray) (85)? What has happened to the money Vince lent Jack in the hospital (128, 134–35, 184)? Slowly, as the novel proceeds, answers emerge. The reader is allowed to build up a sequence of events, just as they reconstruct a chronological time line in the course of reading the text. This is very appropriate to a novel about the force of past actions over the present and about the secrets and half-hidden stories that underlie the characters' lives. It also brings the reader slowly into the community of shared experiences and knowledge. The reader has to put it all together like a jigsaw puzzle and play an active role in understanding the text.

An important aspect of the novel's time settings is their selectivity. One should note that they omit large stretches of the principal characters' lives. Very little of the novel takes place in the 1950s or the 1970s and early 1980s, for example. There are three possible reasons for this. First, in *Last Orders* Swift is not writing an unselective chronicle, nor are the character-narrators interested in telling everything about their lives from birth to death. Second, as is the case in *Waterland* and *Ever After,* silence about certain long stretches of time may suggest a reluctance on the part of characters to discuss or even to remember certain parts of their lives. For example, there is very little indeed about Vince's childhood in the Dodds' family, nor are Jack's reactions to Vince's presence on his return from the war presented. Vince's relationship with Lenny's daughter Sally also largely remains without comment on Vince's part. Third, the novel's passing over certain long stretches of time suggests something about the characters' lives—the sameness, the repetition, the featureless oblivion into which passing time sucks everyday existence. The fact that the reader learns so little about Jack's daily work in the shop, of his fifty years of marriage with Amy, or of Ray's years of work in the insurance agency, is harrowing in its implications. As Jack's father has told him, it is "wastage" that is the problem in butchery, and perhaps in life (285).

If the novel moves freely through time, it is, in comparison, limited in terms of spatial settings. The characters go places, but, in a sense, they take Bermondsey with them. The settings are also often drab and unglamorous—small businesses, a South London pub, a scrap yard, an automobile showroom, a hospital ward. Amy travels as far as the asylum in which June is kept. Ray goes to race meetings. Jack and Ray go to Egypt with the British Army in the 1940s. The Dodds go to Margate in the 1930s (252–55) and the 1950s (40–43). The four companions take Jack's ashes to Margate via Rochester, Chatham, and Canterbury. But all these journeys are scarcely journeys from Bermondsey. Amy travels alone on the bus, except when Ray takes her in his camper van. The fact that Ray travels with a kind of home on wheels is striking. He makes little connection with the world outside his home district. When he travels to Egypt, it is with the British Army, and there he meets Jack, who is from Bermondsey too (88). The journey to Margate is made in a small, if contentious, group of close acquaintances. For much of the journey, the four men are enclosed in the Mercedes; the only person they talk to is a barmaid in Rochester (110). The characters that leave Bermondsey—Carol, who leaves Ray; Ray's daughter Susie, who goes to Australia; Lenny's daughter Sally, married to a criminal and living elsewhere in London—appear lost to the real world of the novel. Even June, in her distant asylum, is powerful as an absence in the world of the novel.

The novel's settings are limited and local, even when they seem not to be. They are firmly rooted in a mundane, contemporary world of bus routes and motorways: "We drive out and join up with the M2, Junction 3, Dover 48, then he really puts his foot down" (141); "He takes the slip road for the exit coming up, not saying a word. Junction 6, Ashford, Faversham" (144); "She'd get a 188 to the Elephant, then a 44, and sometimes she'd have to change again in Tooting" (171). When the four central characters arrive in Margate, their destination is shabby and run-down (289). "It aint much. It aint much to write home about" mutters Ray (281).

The only substantial exception to this drab urban world is Amy's recollection of hop picking in Kent ("the garden of England") in 1938 (234–41). Here there is a temporary sense of freedom ("of being set loose" [234]) in a world of growth and vegetation. There are even gypsies in the background, whom Amy envies for their vitality and permanent mobility (235). But this semi-idyll, like occasional escapes to sunny beaches (239), is limited. Amy goes back to Bermondsey—after all, she chooses Jack from Bermondsey, not Romany Jim, as a lover—and the restrictions of her role as wife and mother.

The novel's social milieu is similarly unglamorous and local. The characters are almost without exception drawn from a narrow, drab, South London, lower-class world. Critics have commented on the smallness, the ordinariness, and the seeming insignificance of such characters, and have indicated how Swift in *Last Orders* returns to the small world of William Chapman in *The Sweet-Shop Owner.*[6] All the main characters in *Last Orders* belong to a lower-middle-class and working-class environment of small shops and offices. Socially, however, they are not an entirely homogenous group. Vic, the undertaker, is clearly financially, as well as personally, much more successful than his friends (48, 74–75). Vince wears flashy clothes and drives luxurious cars (17–18). He buys coffee in an up-market shop in

Rochester (109); Lenny has never risen above owning a fruit and vegetable stall (40, 176–77). Some of the social mobility is generational, as in Vince's case, but it also has to do with profession and diligence, as in Vic's. Despite their differences, however, it is striking that the characters form a community. They share experiences—the war, certain kinds of work, certain kinds of recreation; they share a language; their lives intersect and interweave with each other's; they share friendships; they know each other's secrets, or at least some of them. Four of them travel together to scatter their friend's ashes. Despite their tensions, they remain together and complete their task.[7]

These characters may be from a socially humble milieu, but they are complex figures. "It's anyone's guess what each of us is thinking," says Ray (77). *Last Orders* shows that its lower-class subjects have rich and complex emotional lives. One is constantly aware of the tensions and intricacies of the characters' feelings, dreams, and desires. For example, the reader detects Lenny's gnawing distaste for Vince, and his own sense of failure (7, 176–77). Jack's paternal and yet lustful feelings for his daughter-in-law are made apparent (8). In the car on the way to Margate, Ray feels envy of Vic; he wants to hold Jack's ashes (18, 30, 46). Amy copes, and yet does not, with Jack's death; she wants Vince to hug her "right there in front of Mandy, like I'm her new husband" (33). Ray's wife Carol is jealous of her daughter's youth (59). Vic knows about Ray and Amy's affair, but tells no one (77, 81, 85). Does Jack know? Ray thinks he does (223, 224, 283), and Ray, in any case, is haunted by a sense of guilt (247–48, 279). The ambivalence of Vince's attitude toward his adoptive father—defiance, admiration, pity—adds depth to his character (32–36, 136–37, 159). The novel's narrational technique and narrative organization contribute toward the reader's sense of character complexity. Vic says that an undertaker has the privilege of seeing people "stripped bare" of their "everyday concerns," exposed and revealed for what they are (78). This captures the way that *Last Orders* allows its characters to reveal the depths, conflicts, and intricacies within them. The protagonists tell their own stories, and they reveal the truth about themselves and others gradually. The novel's vision of human life is one in which mundane surfaces hide intricate and conflict-ridden emotional lives, and in which the truth of what people are needs to be carefully teased out from hints and half revelations.

The social setting of *Last Orders* puts the novel in a long and respectable tradition of British fiction that takes lower-class and working-class life very seriously indeed. George Eliot's *Adam Bede* (1859), with its programmatic chapter 17 containing a defense of its humble subject matter, is a key text in this tradition, as are Thomas Hardy's two last novels, *Tess of the d'Urbervilles* (1891) and *Jude the Obscure* (1896). D. H. Lawrence's fiction, especially *Sons and Lovers* (1913), is also surely a presence behind *Last Orders*. In addition, Swift's concern with lower-class life echoes the 1950s fiction of Alan Sillitoe—for example, *Saturday Night and Sunday Morning* (1958). In its deployment of lower-class speech, *Last Orders,* further, refers back to Henry Green's great novel of working-class life and speech, *Living* (1929). *Last Orders* has another contemporary, nonliterary intertextual reference, however—to British television soap operas of working-class life, especially the very successful BBC series *Eastenders*. The novel's South London lower-class setting of pubs, shops, and small businesses, the characters' language, the novel's story material (adultery, illegitimacy, confused and conflict-ridden family relationships) are the very stuff of

Eastenders. Last Orders is a serious, mainstream novel, and a Booker Prize winner; yet it draws on a repertoire of motifs and characters from popular entertainment. The paradoxes of the novel's epigraphs, noted above, are present on another level here.

But the intertextual references in *Last Orders* are even more complex than that. For this novel of humble South London life and a journey to the seaside is permeated with references to canonical literary texts. As in any novel of lower-class London life, echoes of Dickens' fiction are inevitable, and this is true as well of the geography of Kent that plays such an important role in *Last Orders*.[8] One should also note that the novel's climax— the scattering of Jack's ashes—takes place in Margate. In Book III of T. S. Eliot's *The Waste Land* (1922) the river Thames declares: "On Margate Sands. / I can connect / Nothing with nothing. / The broken fingernails of dirty hands. / My humble people who expect / Nothing." Eliot's poem is also echoed in the very title of Swift's novel. The monologue that concludes Book 2 of *The Waste Land* is constantly interrupted by the landlord of a pub calling "HURRY UP PLEASE ITS TIME" (indicating that the time for last orders has passed). The monologue in question is given by a working-class London woman, talking of adultery and abortion, and reference to it, as to the "broken fingernails of dirty hands" in Swift's novel (Vince's, for example—see page 159) is clear.[9] Further, the four companions and the other narrators in the novel tell their stories within the framework of a journey that takes in Canterbury Cathedral and starts in early April. Echoes of Chaucer's *Canterbury Tales* (which begins, "Whan that Aprille with hise shoures sote") are obvious.

Intertextual reference in *Last Orders* is not just limited, however, to highly regarded British texts, but also extends to the literature of the United States. Allusions to William Faulkner's *As I Lay Dying* (1930) have been noted by several commentators. The central element in the story material of the two novels is certainly similar. In *Last Orders* four men make a detour-beset journey to scatter their dead friend's ashes; in *As I Lay Dying* members of the Bundren family make a long and difficult journey to bury their dead wife and mother. Both novels are narrated in monologues by a variety of relatively poor and ill-educated characters who speak a marked nonstandard dialect. The differences between the novels, however, are also striking. Jack's ashes are not Addie's decaying corpse; the Bundrens' journey is much longer and the difficulties they have to overcome are quite different from the day-trip to Margate. Faulkner's novel also seems to lack the epiphanic reconciliation of the conclusion of *Last Orders*.[10]

The functions of such intertextuality are twofold. First, as with the novel's epigraph from Sir Thomas Browne, the allusions to canonical literature of a very high status—Chaucer, T. S. Eliot, Faulkner—dignify the lower-class milieu and characters. These are characters, the text insist, whose doings, sufferings, failures, and successes can be seen in relation to major texts from the tradition of English-language literature. Second, the intertextuality in *Last Orders* suggests that there is, at some level, a culture that is shared between past and present, between the poorly educated and high art. The modern pilgrims retrace the literary steps of Chaucer's storytellers; they face death and the universe on Margate sands; their acts parallel (with variation) those of the Bundrens. It must be stressed, however, that they themselves seem largely unconscious of this. Indeed, at the only point when the four central characters consciously look at a product of high traditional culture—Canterbury Cathedral—

their responses to it are ambiguous. Although they are able to relate the great church to their own lives in terms of being impressed or being driven toward introspection (194, 195, 196–97, 200–201, 203–5, 206, 207, 225–26), Ray feels the cathedral is "looking down at you, saying, I'm Canterbury Cathedral, who the hell are you?" (194). Because the characters of *Last Orders* seem unaware of the literary models they are echoing, however, one must conclude that the culture is not truly shared, but only one that is perceived by the informed reader of Swift's novel.[11]

These allusions to an august literary tradition are made against a background of a very mundane here and now of pubs, motorway junctions, and lower-class speech, and against a background of the small-scale pleasures of lower-class urban life such as a sexually suggestive exchange with a pretty nurse (117–18), a day at the races (231), a pub filling up with customers and a popular song in the background (12), sunshine, a fancy car, companions, and beer. This striking mixture of the prestigious and the seemingly trivial is very typical of *Last Orders*. Its characters, in their far from illustrious context, grapple with some centrally human existential concerns. These fall into two main groups—those involving human relationships (personal or social), and those involving the major (connected) determinants of human existence, time, and death.

Last Orders is about the complexities of living with other people. This can be seen on a personal level in the novel's fascination with parent-child relationships. Such relationships are deeply flawed in *Last Orders*. At the center of the novel is Jack's damaged connection with June and Vince. In fifty years Jack has never visited his mentally retarded daughter. He all but denies her existence. He has tried to find a substitute for her in Vince, but has failed to make him into the master-butcher he would like him to be (45, 96–97). In a conscious act of rebellion, Vince joins the British Army and, on his return to civilian life, starts his business as a mechanic and used car salesman—in defiance of his adoptive father's wishes (66–69). There are certainly more successful parent-child relationships in the novel—Ray's with his father, for example (37), or Vic's with his father and sons (78, 83, 125–26)—but Ray, Lenny, and Vince all have complex and finally disappointing ones with their daughters. Ray's daughter Susie goes to Australia and they lose contact with one another (281–82). Lenny is alienated from his daughter Sally, who is married to a criminal and now a semi-prostitute (204). Vince feels as if he "pimps for his own daughter," using her to sell cars to Hussein (72–73, 166–68), while Jack's attempts to find another daughter in Mandy and to use her to make Vince bend to his will, both go awry (67–68, 158–60). Jack himself has been forced by his father (according to Ray and Lenny) to become a butcher contrary to his own aspirations (45, 86).

As one can see from the above, the characters in *Last Orders* also wrestle with the issue that vexes so many characters in Swift's novels, that of role and identity. "I'm a butcher, Raysy. That's what I am," declares Jack (221). But the matter is not nearly as simple as that, not for Jack, nor for the other characters in *Last Orders*. They are well aware that who they are is shaped and determined by their decisions and by those of others, and that their identity is, to an extent, arbitrary and illusory. Vince states this clearly: "And I see them all hanging up before me, like clothes on a rack, all the jobs, tinker, tailor, soldier, and you have to pick one and then you have to pretend for the rest of your life that that's what you *are*" (96). Vic, too, recognizes the moment when his future as an undertaker was determined. His father proposes that he help lay out his dead grandfather.

"So later I said, 'Yes, all right.' Your life cut out for you, your chances altered. And then it was too late to have any other foolish notions, like running away to sea" (126). Jack has been shaped by his father's wish that he be a butcher and his own acquiescence in that wish, and also by his failure to see other possibilities. At least, that is what Lenny says of him. "He didn't know nothing better, like most of us, than to stick like glue to what he knew, like there was an order sent down from High Command that he couldn't ever be nothing else but a butcher" (132). Ray wanted to be a jockey, but follows his father's suggestions and his sense of what is possible for him in his time and his place, to become an "office boy" (37–39).

The constraints seem less determining for a younger generation, however. Mandy has rebelled against her prurient Blackburn background and has run off to London (158–59); Vince has chosen not to be Jack's successor in the butcher's shop (159). "Why d'you think I took off in the first place? Why d'you think I joined up? Because I wasn't going to be no Vince Dodds. I wasn't going to be no butcher's boy" (159). The ambiguity and flexibility of his identity is well captured in the name on his kitbag, "V. I. Dodds," and one of his tattoos, "V. I. P." (Vince's real parents were called Pritchett) (157, 159). He also calls his business Dodds Motors (249). But even Mandy and Vince see themselves fixed in specific roles, once certain steps and certain decisions have been made. "It's never how you picture it," says Mandy. "Mrs Vincent Dodds, Mrs Dodds Autos" (161). Vince, too, finds himself playing the role of the used car salesman, buttering up a client he does not like, prostituting his daughter in order to sell cars (72–73, 166–68).

The characters of *Last Orders* are deeply aware of their roles as roles—as identities assumed and maintained—although others might have been possible. Vic realizes in the garden of the asylum that he could easily be mistaken for an inmate (215). Lenny knows the changes in his identity that the birth of his daughter brings (177). Looking at Jack in hospital, Ray feels that he is seeing not Jack the butcher, not Jack the drinking companion, and not Jack the soldier, but someone else—"the man himself, his own man, private Jack" (183). Vince has a more harrowing perception of the illusory nature of identity. Looking at Jack's dead body, he reflects: "He aint Jack Dodds, no more than I'm Vince Dodds. Because nobody aint nobody" (199). Earlier Amy has asked Ray "You think Jack knows who he is?" To Ray's reply—"Never met anyone more sure about it"—Amy responds ambiguously (172). She herself, after fifty years, is unsure of who her husband really was (274–75).

"All the wrong choices," muses Amy (254). She, too, has made choices that fix her in a specific role, that of June's mother—the woman on the 188 and 44 bus on her way to an asylum twice a week to see a daughter who does not recognize her and who will never acknowledge her existence (171–72). Toward the end of the novel she sums up her life and Jack's in terms of the roles they have chosen and become trapped in (229).

For roles in life seem to become traps for several of the characters: Ray, the little man, Jack's companion, the bet-maker, "Lucky" Johnson; Lenny, the failed, old pugilist; Vic, the smooth undertaker; Jack, the bluff master-butcher; Amy, the devoted mother. The figure of June, who has been institutionalized from a very early age, embodies this motif in the novel. Amy sees June stuck immovably, mentally and physically (173). Vic reflects about the inmates of such places that, when he comes to take charge of their remains, it is a matter of "taking them out of one box just to put them in another. As if there was never any choice in the first place" (212). Even as Jack lies on his death bed, Ray sees him as a "puppet," as if he is being controlled by forces outside himself, trapped in a specific role (223).

As in all Swift's novels, the characters in *Last Orders* have to come to terms with major historical events and processes. Ray describes himself in Libya and Egypt during the Second World War as a "small man at big history" (90). Mostly the protagonists (as is typically the case for the characters in Swift's other novels too) encounter history through war and its consequences. Lenny has never been successful—either in business or in boxing—because of the war, which has resulted in the death of his father, a lack of savings in 1945, and an interrupted sporting career (40, 44, 178–79). Vince has been bounced into the Dodds' life because his parents died in a V-1 attack on London in 1944 (42–43, 158). Ray and Jack—like Lenny—survive the war in North Africa (87–92, 182). Indeed, it provides them with opportunities for sexual experience and for friendship, and makes them appreciate how easy it is to die. Vic has gone through the war in the Royal Navy, and his encounters with the hostility of the elements, the fragility of human life, and the chances of war, have shaped his mind and attitudes (123–26). In the 1960s, Vince, too, meets history—in the British Army in Aden in the 1960s (69, 165). His life—his trade, his racism—has been partially formed by that brush with history too. Among the female characters, only Amy speaks of the war. She, too, has faced the chance of violent death in the bombing of London, but it is rather the separation from Jack—the forced drawing together of her and June that war brings—which have consequences for her life (239).

History in *Last Orders* is not just a matter of war, however. Mandy and Vince live through the cultural and social changes of the 1960s in Britain. The climate of the times gives them the inspiration and the opportunity partly to determine their own lives (105, 161). Jack, Amy, Lenny, Vic, and Ray have never had any such possibility. Amy's and Jack's only escapes from their determined lives have been hop picking in Kent, or (paradoxically) the freedom that the war offers male soldiers. In addition, in the course of their journey to Margate, the four male protagonists move through a landscape redolent of history. The episode in which they visit the naval war memorial at Chatham is one point in which they are consciously connected with, and respond in varying way to, the history of their country (119–43). But they are aware of other parts of history as they travel toward their destination. In Blackheath, they reflect that there were once highwaymen there (31), while in Rochester they walk through old-fashioned streets, and Ray can imagine a stagecoach turning into the "Bull Hotel" (108–9). Here one should note, however, that Ray's sense of the history of the place he is observing is relatively superficial. He gets his idea of the stagecoach from an image on a Christmas card (109). His response to the old street is also rather ambiguous. "It looks like a high street in a picture book, like you shouldn't be here, walking in it, or like it shouldn't be here itself, with the traffic belting along the A2 close by. Except it was here first" (108–9). It is also striking that his companions make no comment on the historical aspects of Rochester.

The four protagonists come into contact with the distant past most thoroughly in Canterbury Cathedral. Here they all do respond to history in some way. Vince buys a guidebook and reads it to the others—an act that his companions find amusing and self-important (196). Lenny is at first dismissive and then reflects on duty (195, 204). Vic ponders on the leveling force of death (196–97, 206). Ray is moved to think of last things and guilt (200–201). All of them in some way—the older ones more substantially—are prompted to reflection by their encounter with fourteen centuries of history. Indeed, it is here that Lenny comes to an insight about the nature of historical change and the arbitrariness of many rules. His daughter's illegal abortion would have been legal a few years later. In the 1940s the British fight to control the North African desert; in the late 1960s they withdraw from Aden (204).

How profound is the conscious engagement of the characters in *Last Orders* with history? Certainly Canterbury Cathedral means something to them, but their interest in it is relatively superficial. It is war that has shaped them most closely and that gives rise to many of their reflections. The protagonists of all Swift's other novels are enormously aware of history and its impact on their lives and the lives of others. They are even engaged with it as a subject or an intellectual issue. In his set of lower-class South Londoners, Swift shows characters altered and formed by historical events, but whose sense of the role of history in human life is largely limited to what directly impinges on them. These are far from stupid men and women, but their perspective on history is quite different from that of Tom Crick in *Waterland* or Harry Beech in *Out of This World,* for example.

They are, however, extremely reflective. Throughout their monologues they frequently speculate on and think about a wide variety of aspects of human existence. Some reflections are relatively mundane, however acute they are—for example, Vince's discussion of the importance and admirable nature of automobiles (25, 73, 105) or Ray's review of all the urinals he has used (112). However materialist and even trivial such reflections may seem, they show an inclination to generalized reflection on the part of characters that is quite striking and that is often applied to deeper matters—for example, Ray's sense that "what a man does and how he lives in his head are two different things" (38), or Lenny's perception that "every generation wants the next one to make it all come better" (43) and his insistence on the importance of "duty" (132). Further, the characters speculate on some quite profound matters concerning the relationship between the body and identity. Ray wonders whether Jack's ashes are, perhaps, mixed up with someone else's (4). Do they have Jack in the jar? Vic, who should know something of such matters, insists that Jack, once dead, is "none the wiser" about what his friends are doing (29–30), and he argues strongly for death as a great equalizer (143). Vince, too, reflects on mortality and identity as he looks at Jack's wasting body (34), and he comes to a searingly materialist conclusion about death (199).

Banville suggests that the characters' observations on existential issues may be commonplace or even banal at times.[12] This seems unfair. The language is not sophisticated and formal, but the observations are the stuff of human reflections on such issues for centuries. Indeed, the language in which they are expressed gives Vince's comment on Jack's death ("nobody aint nobody" [199]) an austere vigor. In addition, what Swift is trying to do is to show relatively poorly educated characters addressing difficult issues that affect them deeply, and it seems churlish to patronize them for the attempt.

Swift's narrators do not restrict their speculations to matters of this world. They engage in a substantial amount of metaphysical reflection too. In their own words, they wonder about the immortality of the soul. From early on in the car journey to Margate—from when Vince asks Lenny, "So you think he [Jack] does know? You think he can see us?" (31), through a range of observations and exchanges, to Ray's sense of the insubstantiality of human existence ("you don't make a blip" [128])—the four companions constantly worry over the metaphysical endurance of identity. They also worry about whether there is any God or plan to the universe. When Vince walks in the fields of Wick's farm with Jack, he has a sense that "the view's all far-off and little and it's though we're far-off and little too and someone could be looking at us like we're looking at the view" (65). Ray thinks regarding life that "there aren't no odds given and you can't see no larger mathematics" (127), while Amy fights against her sense that June's disability is some kind of "punishment" (202) and, like Ray (202), finally settles for a view of life as "All a gamble" (268). Ray, at times, even comes close to the language of traditional metaphysical discourse (presumably unconsciously) in his evocation of "the sea, the sea" as a symbol of the infinity of things (262, 273), and also in his description of his companions "holding their hands out cupped and tight like they've each got little birds to set free" (293), as if Jack's ashes have been transformed into that traditional symbol of the soul, a small bird.[13]

As so often in Swift's fiction, the characters in *Last Orders* must come to terms with passing time and with death. (Compare *The Sweet-Shop Owner* and *Ever After* in this respect.) In *Last Orders* the characters are, whether they fully realize it or not, obsessed by transience. The title itself emphasizes this, as do the characters' reflections on the body and identity and on the immortality of the soul. Clocks appear constantly throughout the novel (1, 83, 239, 257, 259, 286). The monument in Chatham is not just a *memento mori,* but is, in effect, a giant sundial, a sign not just of mortality, but of passing time too (139). The companions carry one of the ultimate symbols of human transience with them to Margate—their friend's ashes (16, 283). When they finally scatter the ashes, they are "like smoke" (294). The substantial Jack has become insubstantial. In the background, as they scatter what is left of their friend, are the remains of the once solid jetty (292). The dead Jack sums it all up in his dead father's words. "Jack boy, it's all down to wastage. . . . You got to keep a constant eye on wastage, constant. What you've got to understand is the nature of goods. Which is perishable" (284).

In the face of such transience, the journey to Margate assumes considerable importance. Why do the companions go there? Most of them are certain Jack is dead and gone and cannot care about whether they fulfil his last wish. Jack is not even special in any way, Vic reflects (143). Death comes to all. But, like the monument at Chatham, what they are attempting is, in Ray's words, an "effort at dignity" (122). Vic, who knows death and transience best, insists that "decency and respect with regard to the final disposal, everyone deserves that" (212). In the final moments of the novel, it appears that the four companions have achieved just that. At last reconciled with each other, if only temporarily, they have devised a kind of ritual whereby Jack can have appropriate respect shown to him. Ray's language starts to take on an impressive repetitive quality as he reports the scattering of the ashes, even though it is an impressiveness mixed with the mundane detail that he knows "in the end I'm going to have to hold up the jar and bang it like you do when you get to the bottom of a box of cornflakes" (294–95).

Last Orders is a dark and serious novel in which a group of socially humble, poorly educated characters try to make sense of their lives and the questions those lives raise. These are concerns that are the stuff of traditional literature and human speculation.

Their accounts, their questioning, and their answers are expressed in a highly nonstandard English, but are nonetheless often moving and powerful. Their very attempts to tell and to answer difficult aspects of life are worthy of respect as an "effort at dignity." One ignores part of the specific quality of *Last Orders,* however, if one dwells on the serious and the darkly problematic. It is also a novel that celebrates the small-scale pleasures of urban life—the pub, the pretty girl, the handsome young man, the good car. It is a novel, too, with many jokes. Characters make puns. Amy does so (252, 253, 254). Ray and Vince's exchange about the Margate Pier is pure music hall patter (270–71). Ray's winning horse is ridden by a jockey called Gary Irons ("Heavy name for a jockey," muses Ray [259]). On his deathbed Jack dryly comments that "It's something I aint go to do now, make a living" (221). He has already told the surgeon that they are in closely related professions (27, 28). Ray gets nearest to being a jockey on a camel in Egypt in the 1940s (90), and, most memorably, completely mishears the kindly Egyptian prostitute on two occasions (91–92). It is in its fusion of Sir Thomas Browne (*Urn Burial*) and John A. Glover-Kind ("Oh, I do like to be beside the seaside!"), and in its combination of motifs of transience and existential speculation with popular humor, that *Last Orders* achieves a quite specific quality all of its own.

But is it metafictional? This question is relevant because, apart from *The Sweet-Shop Owner,* the rest of Swift's fiction is. On the surface, *Last Orders* seems quite without the literature-oriented concerns of the earlier novels. But this is not entirely so. The characters' monologues represent a highly conventional device, and may function to alert the reader to the high degree of artifice that underlies any literary discourse. They are not written down but are meant to be the reflections and memories of characters that the reader can overhear. This kind of monologue is highly artificial and a matter of convention. But the most strikingly metafictional aspect of the novel is its deep intertextuality. *Last Orders* is a tissue of reworkings of other texts. One is invited to see that this is an observation that one can extend to many other novels.

Finally, one can suggest that *Last Orders*—in a true postmodern, metafictional manner—plays a game with the reader in terms of its intertextual references. The discussion of intertextuality in *Last Orders,* earlier in this chapter, did not mention that Swift's novel can be seen as referring not just to *Eastenders,* and to the works of Dickens, T. S. Eliot, Chaucer, and Faulkner, but also, in a more covert way, to the British Romantic poet William Wordsworth's collection of poems, *Lyrical Ballads* (1798/1802), and especially to the Preface to the 1802 edition. No critic or commentator has noted that in the choice of language and social milieu, and in the placing of central human existential concerns in a drab, lower-class setting, Swift echoes Wordsworth's arguments about what poetry should do. In a letter to Charles James Fox from January 14, 1801, Wordsworth writes that he has composed *Lyrical Ballads* "with a view to shew that men who do not wear fine cloaths can feel deeply."[14] This is certainly the agenda that underlies *Last Orders.*

Such echoes of Wordsworthian poetics serve, like those to Faulkner's fiction, to dignify and universalize the fates of a group of lower-class South Londoners. These allusions are different, however, from those to Chaucer and Faulkner, inasmuch as they have not been noted by critics. Are they a trick that Swift plays on his readers? Some commentators have argued that the central figures in *Last Orders* are unaware of the cultural signposts that their journey takes them past. Ray and the others do not read Chaucer or Faulkner, and, thus, the informed reader feels superior to them.[15] But if such covert allusions to Wordsworth exist, then even the partially informed reader's position is shown to be inadequate. The reader has no right to feel superior to the characters of *Last Orders,* and cannot be at ease. Who knows what other layers of intertextual reference have been missed? Ray and company, perhaps, have the last laugh.

CHAPTER 9

The Narrow Way
The Light of Day (2003)

The Light of Day has divided critics, not in what they observe as its principal features, but rather in their evaluation and interpretation of those features. In the *International Herald Tribune* Michiko Kakutani, while identifying the novel's relation to detective fiction (especially to that of Dashiell Hammett), its focus on time, secrets, and "the deeply buried emotions lurking beneath the effluvia of daily life," and while praising it for being "meticulously crafted," nevertheless argues that "there is something lugubrious and solipsistic about its delivery." She finds the mind of the narrator "a highly claustrophobic place to be," and thinks that the text provides too much space to his reflections, thus "turning what might have been a slender, elegant book into a puffy, self-important volume." She sums up the novel with the judgment that it is marked "with such labored and ceremonious gravity that the reader finishes the novel wishing it were a good forty pages shorter." In the *New York Times Book Review* Anthony Quinn makes similar observations and complaints concerning *The Light of Day*. After discussing the novel's narration and narrative organization, the recurrence of key motifs throughout the text, the "broken connections" that bedevil characters' relationships with each other, and the echoes of Graham Greene's *The End of the Affair* (1951) that permeate Swift's novel, the reviewer bemoans its "want of dramatic urgency." The "pivotal scene" of the novel, presenting an act of murder, "falls mysteriously flat"; the novel, as a whole, is "somewhat under-powered"; and, with all due respect to Swift's craft and "scrupulous technique," "the [reader's] pulse never quickens." D. J. Taylor makes similar observations and judgments in the *Times Literary Supplement*. He, too, finds Swift's later fiction, including *The Light of Day*, "claustrophobic." He points to the limitation of range of setting and of characters' emotional circumstances in Swift's fiction, but especially in his latest novel. He describes it as "a kind of boiled-down version of more amply framed earlier books. Chief among *The Light of Day*'s characteristics is its oddly desiccated feel—material stretched beyond its natural limit, characters reduced to a rudimentary minimum, prose pruned savagely back." Taylor concludes by observing that "this is a very difficult book to read."[1]

Clearly these critics, for all their respect for Swift's work, are disappointed by certain features of *The Light of Day*: its restriction to one point of view and its geographical and social limits; the nature of the narrator and his particular, seemingly unostentatious language; the lack of the exciting events that one might expect in a piece of detective fiction; and its failure to explore its characters in detail. Other critics, however, while noting very similar features of the text, evaluate these differently. The distinguished novelist, Anita Desai, writing in the *New York Review of Books*, also points to the shrinking "canvas" of Swift's fiction after *Waterland*, and demonstrates that he has "pared down" his language in his latest novel. She argues that the characters of *The Light of Day* are unglamorously everyday, and compares it to a small "suburban garden" with poor soil that Swift, the author, has carefully cultivated and now asks the reader to inspect. However, Desai, after rhetorically asking "how to read" *The Light of Day*, goes on to argue that Swift compels the reader to acknowledge that the grand themes of tragedy are played out in the "tawdry lives littered throughout a tawdry world" depicted in the novel. This is the argument that James Wood sets out in the *London Review of Books*. "Out of this apparently limited material and apparently limited style," he writes, "Swift coaxes a novel of solemn depths." Rather than echoes of Hammett and Greene, Wood sees references to Samuel Beckett in *The Light of Day*. Above all, Wood praises Swift's courage in choosing to present an unglamorous suburban world and his novel's "commitment to ordinary speech" in its principal character's monologues. Wood finds the seeming "grey" of George's language full of subtle linguistic effects, and even a "fugitive lyricism." Indeed, he suggests that the novel is "an investigation into cliché," and its uses, ambiguities, and even strengths.[2]

The story material of *The Light of Day*, for all its echoes of detective fiction (a genre notorious for its complications of plot), could scarcely be simpler. The narrator, George Webb, is a disgraced policeman, dismissed from the Metropolitan Police (in 1989) for attempting to frame a suspect (who he was sure was guilty). His wife leaves him as a result of this, although his relationship with his previously rebellious daughter flourishes after his fall. George takes up gourmet cooking to maintain his spirits, and also sets up (in Wimbledon in South London) as a private detective specializing in matrimonial cases. His job is to investigate possible adultery, usually on behalf of female clients. In the course of his work he sometimes has sex with the women who hire him, and it is in this way that he acquires his assistant, the resourceful Rita. In 1995 he is asked by Sarah Nash, a college lecturer in her forties, to make sure that her husband and his lover really do part, as they have promised to do. Sarah has been aware of the affair for some time, and, indeed, has consented to its continuation. The woman in question is a Croatian refugee in her twenties, Kristina Lazic, who—now that the war between Croatia and Serbia is over—wishes to return to her home in the Balkans. Sarah's husband, Bob, a successful gynecologist in his mid-forties, has promised to deliver her to Heathrow, put her on a flight to Geneva, and then come home to Sarah. George watches the lovers part at the airport and follows Bob. On the way back to Sarah, Bob appears to attempt suicide, but he eventually reaches their home in Wimbledon. Although Sarah has prepared a fine meal for her husband, recalling one they ate many years ago when they first fell in love, immediately on his return she stabs him to death with a kitchen knife. She is now serving a life sentence (perhaps, however, it will only be one of ten years), and George visits her twice a month. Sarah has encouraged him to start writing and he brings his work for her scrutiny and advice. The novel's present is November 20, 1997, the second anniversary of the murder, a visiting day at Sarah's prison. She has asked George to visit her dead husband's grave on the way to see her. The text follows George through this day from morning to late afternoon, as he recalls the events of two years ago and earlier, including some connected with his wife, daughter, and parents.

In its story material and characters *The Light of Day* is clearly reminiscent of detective fiction. The ex-cop private eye, his murky past, his glamorous assistant, the beautiful client in difficulties, the violent crime—these are basic elements of the genre, familiar from novels by Dashiell Hammett or Raymond Chandler, and their British counterparts.[3] But there are very clear differences between *The Light of Day* and most detective fiction. George Webb is certainly not the glamorous Sam Spade.

The novel's central act of violence (and one of only two—the other is the stabbing of Mr. Patel [chap. 28]) is recounted by George at second hand, to the extent that at least one critic confesses to having missed exactly what happens.[4] The story material itself lacks the complications of that of most detective thrillers. George is disgraced through a very simple error of judgment (chap. 30); Bob Nash confesses his adultery to Sarah without great pressure or intrigue on her part (chap. 15); the lovers really do part at Heathrow (chap. 43); the Nash case itself (Sarah's murdering her husband) seems on the surface, and perhaps is, very straightforward (it certainly appears so the police inspector investigating it).[5] The degree of suspense in the novel is really quite small. Although the fact that Sarah has murdered her husband is spelled out only on page 187, the reader can scarcely miss earlier hints that this is so.

Thus, *The Light of Day* is a deviant detective story, and in the *Guardian* John O'Mahoney describes it as "an inverted police thriller."[6] However, it does certainly echo that genre, and more specifically particular texts related to detective fiction. It is surprising, and probably coincidental, that George's waiting for Sarah in *The Light of Day* recalls Sam Spade's promise (possibly ironic) to Brigid O'Shaughnessy toward the end of Hammett's *The Maltese Falcon* (1929) (chap. 20). However, more relevantly, critics have pointed to Greene's *The End of the Affair* as an intertext for Swift's novel. There are certainly reminiscences of Greene's novel in Swift's—a heroine named Sarah, the South London Common setting, the interview between client and private detective (bk. 1, chap. 2), the correlation of detective and novelist (bk. 1, chap. 3), and the obsessive protagonist/narrator. Quinn, however, points out that Swift's novel is not marked by Greene's "tormented Roman Catholicism."[7] It certainly lacks the overt concern with belief and the miraculous of the earlier text. *The Light of Day* also echoes Elizabeth Bowen's *The Heat of the Day* (1948) in both its title and in its obsessive, cliché-using detective figure, Harrison, who loves and stalks the protagonist, Stella Rodney (like Sarah Nash, the social superior of her detective-suitor).[8]

The principal functions of these reminiscences of the detective story genre and of specific texts are double, but connected. First, by placing his novel within a genre that tends to deal in plot complications and violent and lurid action, and then doing everything possible to filter out those elements, Swift is surely offering a vision of human life, driven by grand passion certainly, liable to tip into violence at times, but bound within a drabber, more even course than the detective thriller genre would usually suggest. Second, by echoing Bowen's and Greene's novels, Swift indicates that the real interest of *The Light of Day* lies not in the detective-story framework, but in its psychological portraiture, in its examination of the uncertainty of knowledge (which is a major concern of both earlier novels), and, perhaps—and here the echoes of Greene are particularly important—in its consideration of what might provide a source of transcendence in a fallen world. A third function of the echo of the detective thriller in *The Light of Day* is that it reinforces Swift's respect for a demotic and democratic tradition that has run through his fiction from *The Sweet-Shop Owner* to *Last Orders*, and which is part of his vision of the world. Not only have some of Swift's protagonists been from socially humble circumstances, but also he has constantly placed his novels in relation to popular genres, such as the family saga in *Waterland*, the spy novel in *Shuttlecock*, and the television soap opera in *Last Orders*.

The Light of Day most radically diverges from the norms of the detective story genre in its narrative, that is, in the organization of its story material. George himself, as a first-person narrator, is not an unusual narrator for a piece of crime fiction (Chandler's Philip Marlowe tells his own stories). But the manner in which he tells his story is.[9] The overall movement of the narrative of *The Light of Day* is logical and chronological, inasmuch as most events are presented in that order, and George does proceed from the morning of November 20, 1997, at the novel's start to late afternoon of the same day at its end. However, the novel interweaves chapters set in 1997 with ones set in 1995, and, indeed, some set considerably earlier. This is marked by a change in tenses. The 1997 chapters are usually narrated in present tenses, while those set earlier are predominantly, although not entirely, told in past tenses. There is no mechanical ordering of chapters throughout the whole novel, although there are extended sequences in which chapters set in 1997 alternate with those set in 1995, for example with the first eight chapters. Some chapters go back even further than 1995. For example, chapter 12 returns to the early 1980s; chapters 18, 24, 28, and 30 to 1989; and chapters 20, 31, and 63 to the 1960s and the 1940s. By and large, events are recounted in chronological order within individual chapters, and the 1995 chapters, for example, move toward the climactic moment of Bob's death. (One clear deviation from this sequencing is in chapter 2 where George asks Sarah about her husband [9]. In chapter 4 the reader is given the dialogue that precedes his question [21]. There is another in chapter 44 where the reader is with Sarah at eight o'clock on the evening of November 20, 1995, before Bob's return from Heathrow has been narrated [222–25]).

Such a narrative organization is certainly not typical of most crime fiction. It is, however, not unexpected for readers of Swift's other novels. Within an overall forward movement, his narrators—from those of *The Sweet-Shop Owner* to those of

Last Orders—constantly interweave past and present. Tom Crick in *Waterland* is even more radical, in that he narrates events in reverse sequence in the novel's concluding chapters. The functions of such a narrative organization in *The Light of Day* do not differ from those in Swift's earlier fiction. It highlights, and, indeed, embodies, the power of the past over the present, and the rootedness of narrators and characters in past trauma.[10] It also emphasizes, as it does in *Waterland*, that narratives are constructed things, not simple retellings of past events but accounts shaped by particular narrators. Kakutani takes this interpretation further when she points out that it is also one of Swift's concerns in *The Light of Day* "to explore the ways in which people try to construct narratives of their lives," a concern made evident by the text's organization.[11]

Despite the intricate interweaving of past and present, the attentive reader is never lost (or so it seems) in *The Light of Day*. George (and Swift) provides clear temporal signposts throughout the novel. "I note these things exactly," George declares at one point (168). The novel proper is preceded by a date, "1997." Like a good detective, George meticulously records dates and times. Bob's death and Kristina's departure take place on November 20, 1995 (6, 23, 27, passim). Sarah comes to see George in late October, 1995 (16, 38). Kristina comes to Britain "five years ago" in late 1992.[12] She becomes an asylum seeker in late 1993 (45). George is dismissed from the police in 1989 (84), and Rachel, whom he meets in 1968 (120), leaves him in the same year. George's parents meet in 1946 (106), George is born in 1947 (106), and his family moves to Chislehurst in 1952 (107). His father dies in April, 1986 (162), and his mother three years later, just before George is dismissed from the police (165).

The reader is also provided with times of day, especially relating to November 20, 1995, and 1997. In 1997 George comes to the office shortly before eight-thirty (4), he promises Rita not to leave the office before ten, and plans to be back by five-thirty (7). In fact, he gets back to the office at "almost twenty to six" (319). In between, he has constantly supplied the time of day as he visits Bob's grave and then goes to the prison to see Sarah. In recounting the events of November 20, 1995, George also gives the readers the hour at which things happen. He arrives outside Bob and Kristina's Fulham flat "at four o'clock" (167), and at five-fifteen the lovers go to their car (168). Kristina passes into the departures lounge at six forty-eight (213). Bob returns to the Fulham flat and stays there until "nearly eight o'clock" (242). He reaches home at eight thirty-five (262). Sarah calls the police at eight forty-six (263). The detail with which both days in November are documented is insistent.

The reader would expect this of an ex-policeman. But the obsessive recording of days, years, and hours has other functions besides verisimilitude. Once again the past is made vividly present. George is constantly aware as he makes his way through November 20, 1997, where he was at that time on the same day in 1995. "Half past three. . . . On this day, two years ago, I hadn't even arrived yet outside the Fulham flat" he notes (208). He continually sees the present year in relation to other years too: to 1989, to 1968, to 1960 (when he caddies for his father on Chislehurst golf course [105]). The trauma of 1995 draws in the rest of his life.[13] The meticulous noting of times, however, also comes to be seen as a desperate attempt to give credibility to a story that has deep uncertainties and gaps in it. It is both a strategy, on George's part, to prevent doubt, and yet, paradoxically, in its obsessiveness starts to cast doubt on his account. (This will be discussed in detail later in the chapter).

A striking feature of the time settings of *The Light of Day* is that the times documented so carefully are almost all signposts of a personal history, and not those of a nation or even a locality. Kristina's being stranded in Britain, her dependent status, and her decision to return to Croatia, are exceptions. Her life, and those of the Nashes and George, are shaped by the grand historical and political events of the Balkan wars of the 1990s. However, even the historical personages of the exiled Napoleon III and the Empress Eugénie (who appear in the novel because they, too, lived in Chislehurst and Sarah is translating a biography of the Empress) are dealt with by George and Sarah primarily as private figures, one of whom outlives the other by many years (312–15). The large historical forces of war, technological and intellectual change, and social transformation that formed and deformed the lives of characters in *Shuttlecock*, *Waterland*, *Out of This World*, *Ever After*, and *Last Orders* are largely absent in *The Light of Day* (as they were in *The Sweet-Shop Owner*, too).[14] One of the clearest signs of this is the central date in the novel, November 20. This places the novel firmly in the dark of autumn, although, in fact, in 1997 the day is particularly sunny. However, beyond this, the day appears to be a date quite without relevant historical or social resonance. It is simply a day that is of enormous importance for the central characters of the novel, but bears no wider cultural or political significance—a personal anniversary, not a date for others to remember. Indeed, for all the meticulous noting of years, days, and hours, *The Light of Day* is paradoxically timeless. Political, social, and cultural signposts are lacking in the novel. George, Sarah, Bob, Kristina, and Rita pursue their lives in a world that seems indifferent to a wider society. A sign of this is that Bob and Kristina are replaying the liaison between George's father and Carol Freeman in 1960 (chaps. 20, 25). The central story material of *The Light of Day*, Swifts suggests, could happen at any time.

If time is predominantly personal in its significance, place setting is profoundly local, without, as Taylor remarks, much reference beyond the confines of a few South London postal districts.[15] These are Chislehurst and Wimbledon, with excursions north of the Thames to Fulham and Heathrow. This is not such a restricted (or really suburban) area, as some commentators suggest, but takes in a substantial swathe of a very large city. Nevertheless, this setting is presented in the kind of small-scale, meticulous, if limited, detail that might be expected from the narrator. He continually informs the reader of the route he takes in his car from one of the "points on our map" (167) to another. For example, in chapter 5, George travels to Beecham Close, the street Sarah used to live on. "From Wimbledon's lower end (my end) to the snooty Village on the hill. Past Worple Road. Then at Woodside I turn right, and then left into St. Mary's Road" (25). One can follow most of this route in a *London A–Z* (Beecham Close is fictional; the other streets are not), as one can trace Bob's journey back from Heathrow: "at the exit for the North Circular—the first option for Wimbledon, via Kew Bridge—he carried straight on, and when he took the Hammersmith exit he didn't take the second option—via Hammersmith bridge—but continued round the Hammersmith roundabout and took the Fulham turn" (239). There are many examples of such detail, routes given with what Taylor calls "cab-driver accuracy."[16] In addition, George supplies a specific kind of local detail to his settings. "I turn into the cemetery," he says. "It's past an Asda superstore" (71). Later he describes the area near Sarah's prison. "A street of houses. . . . Left at the end, then right. Then I emerge into shops and traffic and crowds. Safeway, Argos, Marks and Spencer" (186). These are mundane details indeed, although—as will be argued below—this is not all George notes about his environment. However, place setting in *The Light of Day* is local, limited, and rendered with a particular kind of meticulous, material observation.

But these are not the only "points on your map" (185) in the novel. What is for George "this safe familiar world" (267) of (largely) South London high streets and side streets has connections with a wider world—both literally and in George's imagination. "This international world," George muses in chapter 38 (187). Croatia and the murderous history and politics of the Balkans do impinge on Beecham Close, the Nashes' "leafy, looked after," well-off street (25). Wimbledon may seem far from Dubrovnik, far from Geneva, George reflects (143), but it is not entirely so. Perhaps in Geneva Kristina has forgotten Bob, just as the people who have bought the Nashes' house have forgotten the murder that took place there. In the former Yugoslavia, murders have also taken place. "Streets in Dubrovnik. In Croatian villages. Walls, yards, squares. It happened here" (272). If Kristina has, indeed, gone back to Croatia, will she, too, be like a detective, trying to find out exactly how her brother and her parents died? "All the pools of blood. Forget Wimbledon, forget Beecham Close" (284). Although George stresses why Kristina might never think of South London again, he also establishes a connection between the two. He even talks of Kristina and Bob's walking through "the battle-zone" of Heathrow airport (212). "All's fair in love and war" is the novel's epigraph (thus linking Wimbledon [love] and Croatia [war]), and George himself makes connections between what happens in Beecham Close and what takes place in the distant Balkans (144). It is difficult to know what to make of this. It seems inappropriate to correlate a single murder, however unfortunate for all concerned, with the appalling death toll and brutality of the Balkan wars of the 1990s. One should note, of course, that it is not Swift who makes this correlation, but George. Perhaps this is one more sign that the reader is meant to have a certain distance toward the narrator of *The Light of Day*. This aside, however, the local quality and the mundane detail of the novel's setting are clear. A story of passion, betrayal, murder, and devotion is played out in a context of relatively unglamorous high streets, golf courses, and chain stores.

Critics have seen the characters of the novel as mundane too. Kakutani calls their lives "humdrum." Desai calls them "people from the only too familiar world that we might bump into on a golf course or in the supermarket or at the airport: flawed and fallible, common and, dare we say it, boring."[17] They are certainly a socially restricted group of characters: white, lower-middle-class (for example, George and his parents) to solidly urban upper-middle-class (Sarah and Bob). The novel presents few social extremes, except for the two working-class criminals George deals with in chapters 28 and 30. The only non-white characters are the Patels (chaps. 28, 30). In this respect, critics' concerns that Swift provides socially and ethnically limited fare in his fiction are justified. Further, the female characters are seen in a restricted fashion. George describes his ex-wife Rachel as a "brave, tough-minded bitch" (120). The same might be said of Kristina—who manipulates her way into her benefactor's bed, gets her qualifications, and clears off back to Croatia—or of Rita, or even of Sarah, whom Rita, at least, considers a "nasty piece of work" (296). But to what extent are the characters "common" and "boring"? A corrupt, obsessional ex-policeman? A beautiful murderess? A man who risks his marriage and loses his life for a grand passion? A Croatian refugee whose family has been murdered and who survives as an asylum seeker in the U.K.? The redoubtable Rita, who beards her own husband in his love-nest (chap. 52)? A respectable middle-class high-street photographer who has an affair with the lady from the realtor's opposite? These characters are surely "boring" and "humdrum" only by rather exacting standards. If they are indeed "common," then it is surely in the sense that many people could find (and doubtless have found) themselves in George's, Sarah's, or Kristina's situations.

The characters are, however, almost all fragmentary and dealt with in a restricted fashion, for they are all seen through George's eyes and presented as they are relevant to him and his concerns. The reader knows very little about Bob. Why did he really fall in love with Kristina? George does not know what has become of Kristina after she leaves Heathrow, nor, in fact, why she takes up with Bob. The motives behind his father's adultery are never given; he does not really know what his mother thinks of her husband after his death; the reasons for Rachel's leaving are never supplied, except very speculatively; and George tells the reader very little about Rita's marriage or even her life after coming to work for him. As frequently in Swift's fiction (compare *The Sweet-Shop Owner* and *Waterland*, for example), mysteries, unanswered questions, and silences run throughout *The Light of Day*. (Indeed, George's language is literally full of question marks).

This opacity of character is a result of Swift's narrational strategy and his choice of narrator. George has, or chooses to have, a very limited perspective on the characters around him. He dominates the novel—his is the only voice the reader ever hears directly, the only point of view encountered. His voice is distinctive and has been commented on by the majority of reviewers.[18] As opposed to the intermittently magniloquent, linguistically showy narrators of *Waterland*, *Out of This World*, and *Ever After*, with George, Swift continues the line of less obviously sophisticated narrators that he develops in *Last Orders*. George speaks largely in very short sentences, with a relatively informal vocabulary. He also produces many fragments and, when his sentences are of any length, they are often run-on ones. The first page of the novel provides an excellent example of George's language. Wood writes of "the even grey" of George's voice, but praises it as demonstrating "the novel's commitment to ordinary speech," a commitment that reveals the falseness of many characters' language in other fictions. He also writes extensively on George's use of clichés, such as "memory lanes," "I knew the ropes," and "working flat out," among others.[19]

However, George's language is not as drab, limited, and unliterary as the above description might suggest. Presumably under Sarah's influence, the ex-policeman is now interested in words (139, 177, 216, 226), and works with them in two striking ways. First, throughout the novel he produces descriptions of people and things that are precisely detailed and vivid. For example, he describes some of his first impressions of Sarah thus: "She had eyes that seemed to shift—under a slight frost—from black to brown, to ripple. Tortoiseshell. The hair was the same. Black, you'd say, but when the sunlight from the window caught it you saw it was deep brown" (17). There are many examples of this. Later George notes: "The sun picks out bursts of frozen fire. Rowan berries, pyracanthas. Virginia creepers in flame" (28). Another example comes when he describes the road as he drives: "The sun is almost straight ahead, so everything in front has a glint, a metal sheen, like some great glistening slide" (70). He describes the world in this way throughout the novel. As he waits to enter Sarah's prison, he observes that "while we shiver in the shadows, the brickwork up above glows like the crust of a just-baked loaf" (193). As he leaves the jail, he tells the reader what he sees: "The sun has dipped behind the rooftops. There's a red bloom low in the sky. Up above, it fades to pink, then gas-flame blue. A slice of moon. A vapour trail, thin and twinkly as a needle. Another bitter night coming, the air hard as glass" (251). These descriptions recall imagist poems ("gumshoe haiku," Quinn calls them) and run through the drabness of George's prose like bright threads.[20]

George also plays with language in a self-conscious way. He does not only use cliché; he draws attention to the ambiguities and conceptual oddities that underlie both cliché and, indeed, any use of language. Sometimes he draws the reader's attention to these slippages and absurdities of vocabulary and phrase; at other times he leaves the reader to detect them for him/herself. Thus, for example, George remembers Sarah's looking at him. "She's reading my face like a book," he thinks. However, he cannot leave the cliché at that. "But that's just an expression. I didn't read faces like books (I didn't read many books), I read faces like faces" (10). Later he reflects on his being seen as a "corrupt" policeman. He then looks at the graveyard he is standing in: "And this place, when you think about it, must be riddled with corruption" (183). Immediately afterwards, by a peculiar but comprehensible chain of thought, he thinks of the work of a policeman. "A dirty job sometimes. Things you have to clean up. A filthy job sometimes—and the police were sometimes just the Filth," he says to himself, playing with the literal meaning of a slang term for the police (183). It is not only George who does this. Toward the end of the novel, Sarah puzzles over the literal and figurative meanings of the phrase "I can't live without her" (226–27, 229). Despite his assertion, Bob did live at one time without Kristina, although, in fact, because he was murdered soon after her departure, he did not live long without her. George also engages in this same wordplay (233).

Frequently George lets the puns stand by themselves without comment. When he learns that Bob is a gynecologist, he muses that that would surely make him a "safe" husband, since he "sees other women every day" (10), punning on the double meaning of "see someone," that is, to visually inspect and to have an affair with. The ambiguity of the term "private eye" provides George with lots of opportunities for wordplay. He is also a "private belly" (he cooks for himself) and a "private ear" (he listens to his clients' woes) (29, 38). When he confesses that he knows little of Croatia, he cannot resist the joke that "my field was domestic affairs" (that is, matrimonial cases) (44). The lewd innuendoes of his language are very marked at times. The gynecologist is a kind of "private investigator," and the private eye, also an investigator of private matters, should perhaps introduce himself as "Dick" (47–48). George, whose last name is Webb, reaches a high point with his punning when he talks of his clients' joining with him in "a little web of deceit" (53). Thus he continues throughout the novel, constantly playing with the ambiguities and absurdities of language. Even *in extremis*, with Bob's body lying between him and Sarah, he cannot resist the punning cliché: "If I hadn't felt it before, I felt it now. A stab to the heart" (292)—not a literal one, as Bob received, but a figurative one—the realization that he is in love.

This makes George a much more complex and odder character than critics have acknowledged. There are other features of his character that at best suggest a psychological intricacy, and at worst a kind of pathology. He is certainly able to appreciate complexity in others. See, for example, his evenhanded analysis of the relations of exploitation, gratitude, dependence, and benevolence in the Nashes' taking in Kristina (45–46). Both the reader and George are aware that in the early stages of their relationship he manipulates Sarah in order to see her again (53, 140). His own feelings toward Bob (both while he is still alive as well as when he is dead) are a peculiar mixture of jealousy, loathing, and a desire that he get back to Sarah. "Look what you've done, look what you've done to her," he says over the dead husband's grave. "Look what you did—letting her go and do *that* to you" (73). On the anniversary of the murder George looks at his own feelings: "*I* should feel hurt today. The absurdest things: I'm jealous of the man she killed. I want him out of her life. And he is. But today he has visiting rights. It's his day, I can't deny it" (234). While he is trailing Bob and Kristina, and later Bob alone, George is savagely torn between wanting Bob not to come home and knowing that that is what Sarah wants. As he watches the lovers drive into the airport and feels "in [his] bones" that they intend to separate, he says: "Part of me—my bones only?—must have rejoiced. The rest of me begging to be wrong" (191). But he rejoices only when he is sure that Bob is really on his way back to Sarah (267, 270), although he knows that Bob is a "man who'd forgotten who he was" (214), a "lost soul" (231) and a "ghost" (243, 248, 300), someone who tries to commit suicide on the way home and who, instead of going directly home, goes first to his lover's apartment (chap. 48).

George is also a deeply obsessive character, a lost soul himself who has condemned himself to live permanently in the shadow of the events of two years previously.[21] What would his ex-wife Rachel think of him now, George muses in 1997: "That I've lost it altogether, passed way beyond the bounds" (70). This is clearly what Rita thinks (chaps. 1, 64). She calls his behavior "this nonsense" (307). "I think Rita thinks I'm mad," he tells Sarah (236). Many readers might not consider Rita's response to be unfounded. "I hardly knew her. I'd met her three times," George says of his relationship with Sarah (291). Yet he is prepared to devote the next eight, or ten, or more, years to her (124). His immediate fascination with Sarah's knees is a striking example of George's fetishistic enchantment by a woman he scarcely knows (11, 19, 58, 92, 94). His devotion to her contains moving, if slightly pathological, aspects. After Sarah is imprisoned, George takes charge of her property, including the bag she carries at their first meeting: "I have that shoulder-bag— along with all the other things. In my safe keeping. And, yes, it's like a pet. I've stroked it, talked to it" (27). When Rachel leaves him, he imagines following her, spying on her, watching her with another man, and he imagines doing the same with Sarah (141). George even wants to be imprisoned with her (191); he feels he should have been in her bedroom with her, helping her dress for her husband's return (222). He constantly returns to one place where they met, to sit at the same table (100). He carries flowers to the grave of a murdered husband, at the behest of the wife who murdered him, and he knows he will keep doing this year after year (311), just as he will visit Sarah twice a week for however long she remains imprisoned.

George's behavior has, at times, a pathologically superstitious quality about it. He reveals that he goes back over the past, and back to places associated with the events of the past, to try to see where the "sequence might have been different, where it might have turned another way" (209). Here he even, enigmatically, adds: "So that this time around, at last, the third time of trying, she won't do it." "But go back, go back to that kitchen before it was the scene of a crime. . . . Rewind the clock. Relive it. . . . It might be different this time" (224). As he sits in his car in Beecham Close on the evening of November 20, 1997, George thinks: "I could stay here all night. As if to prevent it, as if to make it unhappen. A different turn of events this time" (310). If he seriously believes that, perhaps Rita is quite right to think he is mad.

George also omits information and tells lies. He does not tell the reader anything in detail about his marriage with Rachel or about his parents' marriage. It has been noted above how little the reader knows about most of the novel's central characters, because George tells so little about them. He attempts to frame a suspect, and later engages in the sophistry of claiming, at least to himself, that "phoney statements can be true, even if they're not what the witness ever said" (87). "Does anyone tell anyone everything?" he asks. "There are things I can't and won't tell Sarah yet. Perhaps I never will" (237). He lies to her at a crucial point. "'He's on his way home to you,' I lied" (214).

Most strikingly, a very large part of what he tells the reader is invented. It is guesswork; it is surmise. Police work, George informs the reader, is "fifty per cent in your head" (274). He certainly imagines a great deal (just as Unwin does in *Ever After*), for example the voice of the dead Bob from his grave (75), or what Kristina does in Geneva or Dubrovnik (142–44). However, four examples of George's inventing sequences of events stand out among many others. In chapter 10, George recounts the beginning of Bob's acquaintance with Kristina, and in chapter 15 the beginning of their affair and its development. In chapter 27, he tells more about its progress. He is inventing it all. He was not present and never talked to those involved. The use of hypothetical "would" structures sometimes indicates this: "He'd have made himself scarce, he'd have beat a wise retreat" (51).

At other times, he briefly acknowledges he is making things up: "You have to picture the scene" (80); "so I picture it" (145). But he also presents his guesswork as fact. For example, "They shuffle through last year's leaves. . . . She scuffs at something at her feet and stoops and looks" (80–81). But it is all invented. George has not observed the scene. In fact, no one has, for it is purely imaginary.

A second example is George's version of what happened in the Patels' shop when Mr. Patel was stabbed (chap. 28). Again he invents a scene and a narrative, which may or may not be true but for which he has no more than a circumstantial basis. A third example concerns Bob's feelings in the car as he drives back from the airport and, later, in Kristina's apartment (265–66). George presents these feelings in detail. Some he may be able to infer from what Sarah tells him (267), but much is pure conjecture. The fourth and most striking example involves Sarah's actions and feelings as she waits for Bob to come home (219–25, 300–303). What George tells the reader is almost entirely speculation. In part, he acknowledges this: "And she would have thought about it then. . . . And later on she would have placed a bottle. . . . She would have opened the bottle for breathing. . . ." (219). At times, however, he slips into asserting things he cannot know. "She touched up her hair, her face. Lipstick. Scent. . . . She came back downstairs. Now all her agony had condensed into a single minor uncertainty. . . . She knew she might need this last scrap of patience" (221–22).

George must finally be seen as a highly unreliable narrator, a linguistic prankster, manipulative, obsessed to a pathological degree, capable of falsehood, and a figure who invents scenes and occurrences freely and who does not make it entirely clear that he is doing so.[22] The meticulous dating and timing of events, the taxi-driver-like details of roads and junctions can be seen as attempts to conceal this.

Yet that is not all that one can say about George. Wood finds him "very likable."[23] His daughter Helen sticks by him when he is dismissed from the police and her mother leaves him (65–67). Rita clearly thinks he is worth the bother of looking after. He himself does not crumble under the shame of his dismissal. He has a way with words, as his descriptions of people and things show. His devotion to Sarah may be obsessional, but it is genuine and very powerful. He may invent, but his inventions may also be close to the truth. This is a novel of Caravaggio-like shadows (Caravaggio is Helen's favorite artist and one George tries to be interested in [63]), obscurities, and uncertainties.[24] In chapter 65, George mentions that underneath Chislehurst there are mysterious caves. This seemingly irrelevant piece of information is surely far from that, suggesting as it does the mysteries, the questions, and the complexities at the heart of the novel—what is hidden beneath the surface. Perhaps most strikingly, the reader is meant to ask who killed Bob Nash. At the end of his long narrative of the events leading up to the stabbing (events that are, to a large extent, guessed at), George suggests that it was not entirely murder.

> It took two. Something came over him as well.
>
> And, of course, at such a moment, without any practice, without any previous training (another thing Marsh would have to puzzle over), she would have found the spot, the very spot, the only spot that counted. Without even aiming, but without missing, or even striking a rib first. Something takes over. As if her hand was being surely pulled to its mark. (303)

Special pleading? The madness of an obsessed lover? Inspired guesswork? The reader really has to judge for him/herself. Perhaps *The Light of Day* is genuinely a whodunit after all.

It is certainly a highly wrought artistic artifact, deeply self-referential and strongly metafictional. The novel's narrative certainly draws attention to itself by its intricately interwoven composition, while the narrator's voice, as has been noted above, is self-advertisingly distinctive, not only for its informality of vocabulary and pared-down sentences, but for the vividness of its descriptions and its wordplay. The text is also marked by the recurrence of certain motifs, which are an integral part of its meaning, but also shape it as an aesthetic object.[25] Thus, for example, the motif of crossing a line is repeated throughout the novel. "We cross a line," George says at the beginning of the novel (3). "You cross a line" (11). The lines can be physical too. In the florist's shop George watches the sales-assistant come toward him: "The girl steps through the light again as if she's passing through some screen" (14). But usually the lines are metaphorical: the line clients cross when they ask George to spy on their husbands (53); the line George crosses when he falls in love with Sarah (94); George's sudden movement to stand up for Rachel in 1968 (116); the line George's father crosses when he murmurs another woman's name (not his wife's) on his death bed, and the line of knowledge his wife crosses at that point too (163); the line between imprisonment and freedom (195); the line George does not cross when he is following Bob and Kristina ("Keep on your side of the line" [200]). When George imagines Sarah's release from jail, he does so in similar terms: "One day it will be just a case of a simple, small step, across a line that can't even be seen" (323).

Imprisonment, too, is a recurrent motif. When Kristina first arrives at the Nashes' "she just sat there, like a prisoner" (50). George imagines her "as if in some expensive cell" (275). He encounters Sarah in the supermarket and thinks "she looks like she's about to be released" (54). The word "release" is repeated on the next page (55). Sarah, of course, is not released by her husband's return, but is literally imprisoned for much of the novel. However, George also thinks of the dead as being imprisoned in their graves (123). He even imagines Bob in Kristina's apartment after she has left as being imprisoned: "To be reduced to this. A room in Fulham, its four walls closing in on him" (248). George thinks of himself returning Bob to Sarah "as if he was a prisoner set free" (253). Certain words, such as "concession," "falling," "ghost," "refugee," "civilization," and "know," recur, as do the figures of teacher and pupil, father and daughter; but the most striking motif that runs throughout the novel is that of light. It is present in both the title and continually throughout the text. "The sun came in at a low slant through my office window, just like it's doing today," George notes. "Cold outside, warm slabs of sun indoors. It fell like a partition across the desk between us" (10). In the florist's shop, the sales assistant "steps through the light" (14, 178). Both November 20, 1995, and November 20, 1997, are days vibrant with sunlight (23, 26, 28, 34, and many other references). Often these motifs of light overlap with those of imprisonment and line crossing. Like the sales girl in the florist's, Rita, too, "steps through bars of bright light" (5). The sunlight draws George's attention to Sarah's knees, but the jail is present even at this moment: "The bar of sunshine caught her knees and gave them an almost tinselly sheen" (19). He crosses a line of light to shake her hand after their first meeting (28). So all-pervasive is the sunlight that George even allows himself a joke about it and a different kind of light: "Women in the Tanning Centre, doing both sides. The sun in my empty office, touching my desk" (125). As was observed earlier, George sees the sun touching the brickwork at the top of the walls of Sarah's prison (193, 208), and, after visiting her, he comes out into the light of a sunset (251). In the novel's last sentence, he imagines Sarah's release "when she comes back, steps out at last into the clear light of day" (324).

These motifs carry a great deal of meaning. The line one crosses embodies the novel's interest in sudden choices or acts that shape characters' lives, for example, George's falling in love with Sarah, and Sarah's stabbing of Bob. There are varieties of imprisonment in the novel: Kristina's as a refugee; Bob's as a married man who loves someone else; Sarah's literal incarceration; George's empty life before he meets Sarah and his becoming chained to twice-weekly visits to the prison and annual attendance at Bob's grave (an imprisonment that he willingly embraces). The light is the light of knowledge and understanding that, paradoxically on such bright days, proves completely elusive; the light of passion that transfigures the everyday, as George's vivid descriptions light up the mundane and the unglamorous. But these motifs and verbal echoes (of which there are many others in the novel) also render it a closely worked artifact, a thing shaped out of intricate patternings of words and phrases.

George's language even possesses some of the self-referential features of poetry, the lexical and phonological repetitions, the density of metaphor and simile that are often associated with poetic texts. Take the first page of the novel, for example:

Something happens. We cross a line, we open a door we never knew was there. It might never have happened, we might never have known. Most of life, maybe, is only time served. . . .

But she knew even before I did. She's not in this job for nothing, she can pick up a scent. And soon she's going to leave me, any day now, I can tell. I can pick up a scent as well. (3)

One is tempted to set these lines out as verse, and even to attempt a scansion of the first paragraph. However, even without that, the dense metaphorical character (line, door, time served, pick up a scent), the syntactic parallelism ("We cross a line, we open a door"; "might never have happened," "might never have known"; "can pick up a scent"), the recurrence of /s/ and /ʃ/ sounds, suggest poetry. George even rhymes the last two sentences of the above quotation.

George is not only a poet at times, but he is consistently throughout the novel a kind of novelist too. "I can see it. You have to put yourself in the scene," he urges as he imagines Bob's initial response to Kristina (51). As has been discussed previously, he continues to imagine, to infer, to set out his inspired guesswork throughout the novel, as if he were novelist creating character, incident, and scene.[26] The metafictional point is clear. Like George's account of his life and the Nash case, novels have traditionally laid claims to an authority, to an access to the truth. In *The Light of Day*, as in *Waterland* and *Ever After*, Swift demonstrates how that cannot be so in any unproblematic way. Accounts of all kinds (and Swift has been driving home this point since *Shuttlecock*) are partial texts produced from a limited and, indeed, tendentious perspective, verbal artifacts shaped in particular ways, often disingenuously attempting to convince the reader or listener of their veracity. *The Light of Day* rigorously sets out these doubts about narratives, but also, appropriately, plunges the reader into a confusing mire of uncertainty. George is a detective hired to find the truth, a plain man whose narrative is underpinned by dates, times, and documented places, but whose language is at times that of the poet or the verbal prankster, and whose evidence is often pure imagination. He talks of "the clear light of day" (209, 324), but the appropriate metaphor for his story is rather the Chislehurst caves, hidden and of obscure origin and purpose, underlying the quotidian world of high streets and chain stores (315–16). Is he telling the truth? The reader truly cannot tell. Swift's epistemological point is made concrete in the reader's engagement with the text.

It is impossible, however, to end the discussion of either George or "the light of day" at this point. One of the novel's recurrent verbal echoes is that of "falling." When Rachel leaves him, George feels himself "falling. Just falling, in the way you fall when you know there's nothing to land on, endlessly falling, the way people must fall in outer space" (64). He repeats this metaphor later (98). He thinks of Bob, too, as "falling through his life" (79). He also sees the criminal, Dyson "watching me fall" (160), and when he returns to Beecham Close on that night in 1995, George has a sense that "I might have been falling through space" (292). Clearly this metaphor captures the existential and epistemological unease that is so central to the novel. But "falling" also carries religious connotations, as does light.[27] One short phrase focuses this surprising aspect of the novel. When George returns to his office on November 20, 1997, he describes the shabby outer appearance of the building and the cramped staircase, but he also adds that it is "Not the broad way, the narrow way" (318). This is a reference to Matthew 7.13–14, in which the apostle quotes Christ as saying:

Enter ye in at the strait gate for wide is the gate, and broad is the way, that leadeth to destruction, and many there be which go in thereat:

Because strait is the gate, and narrow is the way, which leadeth unto life, and few there be that find it.

Suddenly the connection between *The Light of Day* and Greene's *The End of the Affair* becomes much more substantial and functional. Greene's novel is an examination of the need for transcendence and what might constitute sanctity in a shabby modern world. George's world is a material and fallen one. In such a world, transcendence comes not through the Holy Spirit (for Swift is the most secular of novelists; organized religion might as well not exist for all it appears in his fiction), but with the light of passion and devotion. George enters "the narrow way" of commitment to Sarah, and achieves in this way a kind of salvation. This element adds another dimension to an already complex novel.

The connections of *The Light of Day* to Swift's earlier fiction are clear: it echoes the humdrum world of *The Sweet-Shop Owner* and its devoted protagonist; its fascination with the problems of story and knowledge are shared with *Shuttlecock*, *Waterland*, and *Out of This World*; the dubious, evasive Bill Unwin of *Ever After* is a soul mate of George Webb, bent copper and creative private eye; the "narrow way" that George finds recalls the ritual through which the protagonists of *Last Orders* transcend their humble and mundane world.[28] But, like all Swift's novels, *The Light of Day* stands on its own, a dense, complex, difficult, absorbing text, a major landmark in the career of a major novelist.

Notes

Chapter 1—Understanding Graham Swift

1. The details of Swift's life and a very illuminating account of his career can be found in Nicholas Tredell, "Graham Swift," in *British Novelists since 1960,* ed. Merritt Moseley, *Dictionary of Literary Biography* (Detroit, Washington D.C., and London: Bruccoli Clark Layman/Gale Research, 1998) 194: 262–69. Swift also discusses his biography in an interview with Scott Rosenberg, "Glowing in the Ashes," *Salon* 14 (May 1996): 6–10. http://www.salon.com/weekly/swift960506.html

2. Tredell, "Graham Swift," 265; Hugh Herbert, "Fens for the Memory," *Guardian,* October 1, 1983, 10.

3. Michael Gorra, "Silt and Sluices," *The Nation* 238, no. 12 (31 March 1984): 393; Derwent May, "Booker Books," *Listener,* 20 October 1983, 26; J. L. Carr, "The Complaints of a Violent Family," *Spectator,* 12 March 1998, 28; Lynne Truss, "Out of Focus," *Listener,* 10 March 1988, 21; Hilary Mantel, "Blood Ties," *New York Review of Books,* 11 June 1992, 23–25; Oliver Reynolds, "On the Old Kent Road," *Times Literary Supplement,* 19 January 1996, 25.

4. Harriet Gilbert, "The Lost Boys," *New Statesman,* 11 March 1988, 36; Hermione Lee, "Shutter and Lens," *Observer* (London), 13 March 1988, 43; Truss, "Out of Focus," 21; Lorna Sage, "Unwin Situation," *Times Literary Supplement,* 21 February 1992, 6; Mantel, "Blood Ties," 25.

5. Anne Duchêne, "By the Grace of the Teller," *Times Literary Supplement,* 11–17 March 1988, 275; Stephen Wall, "Self-Slaughters," *London Review of Books,* 12 March 1992, 26; Kirsty Milne, "Static Pools," *New Statesman and Society,* 21 February 1992, 40; Sage, "Unwin Situation," 6; Review of *Waterland* in *Kirkus Reviews,* 1 January 1994, 16; Marion

Glastonbury, "Last Judgements," *New Statesman,* 7 October 1983, 26–27; May, "Booker Books," 26.

6. Michael Gorra, "When Life Closes In," *New York Times Book Review,* 23 June 1985, 12; Hermione Lee, "Norfolk and Nowhere," *Observer,* 2 October 1983, 31; Mantel, "Blood Ties," 25; Michael Wood, "Haunted Places," *New York Review of Books,* 16 August 1984, 48; Del Ivan Janik, "History and the 'Here and Now': The Novels of Graham Swift," *Twentieth-Century Literature* 35, no. 1 (1989): 74; David Leon Higdon, "'Unconfessed Confessions': The Narrators of Graham Swift and Julian Barnes," in *The British and Irish Novel since 1960,* ed. James Acheson (New York: St. Martin's Press), 174.

7. John Banville, "That's Life," *New York Review of Books,* 4 April 1996, 8; Higdon, "Unconfessed Confessions," 186; Mantel, "Blood Ties," 23; MacDonald Harris, "Love among the Ichthyosaurs," *New York Times Book Review,* 29 March 1992, 21; "From *Waterland* to Eternityland," *Economist,* 28 March 1992, 101. See also Tredell, "Graham Swift," 266.

8. Linda Gray Sexton, "The White Silence of Their Lives," *New York Times Book Review,* 11 September 1988, 14; Reynolds, "On the Old Kent Road," 25; Michael Levenson, "Sons and Fathers," *New Republic,* 22 June 1992, 38; Banville, "That's Life," 8.

9. D. J. Taylor, *A Vain Conceit: British Fiction in the 1980s* (London: Bloomsbury, 1989), 114; Valentine Cunningham, "Facing the New," in *New Writing,* ed. Malcolm Bradbury and Judy Cooke (London: Minerva/British Council, 1992), 229–39; Peter Kemp, "British Fiction of the 1980s," in *New Writing,* 216–28; Malcolm Bradbury, *The Modern British Novel* (Harmondsworth: Penguin, 1994), 406.

10. This literary-historical context is discussed in relation to the work of Swift's contemporary, Ian McEwan, in David Malcolm, *Understanding Ian McEwan* (Columbia: University of South Carolina Press, 2002), 6–12.

11. Harris, "Love among the Ichthyosaurs," 21; Banville, "That's Life," 8.

12. Intertextuality is the name given to the very common literary phenomenon whereby texts refer in a variety of ways to other earlier texts, using motifs from them, reworking their story materials, and drawing on or parodying their language and technique. Thus Pope's "The Rape of the Lock" stands in an intertextual relation to Homeric and Virgilian epic, Jean Rhys's *Wide Sargasso Sea* has as its most important intertext Charlotte Brontë's *Jane Eyre,* and Salman Rushdie's *Midnight's Children* draws extensively on narrative strategies and motifs in Laurence Sterne's *Tristram Shandy* and Günter Grass's *The Tin Drum.*

13. William H. Pritchard, "The Body in the River Leem," *New York Times Book Review,* 25 March 1984, 9. See also, for example, Janik, "History and the 'Here and Now,'" 75, 79; Wood, "Haunted Places," 48; Reynolds, "On the Old Kent Road," 25.

14. See the supplement ("Graham Swift's Bookbag") to Rosenberg's interview in *Salon;* Christopher Driver, "Floating," *London Review of Books,* 6 October 1983, 20; Lee, "Shutter and Lens," 43.

15. See Pamela Cooper, "Imperial Topographies: The Spaces of History in *Waterland,*" *Modern Fiction Studies* 42, no. 2 (1996): 374–75; Catherine Bernard, *Graham Swift: La parole chronique. Nouveaux echos de la fiction britannique,* Univers anglo-américain, ed. Claude-Jean Bertrand (n.p.: Presses universitaires de Nancy, 1991): 9–40.

16. George P. Landow, "History, His Story, and Stories in Graham Swift's *Waterland,*" *Studies in the Literary Imagination* 23, no. 2 (fall 1990): 197, 205–7.

17. See Valentine Cunningham, "Fiction '96," *Literature Matters: Newsletter of the British Council Literature Department* 22 (June 1997): 1, 4; Kate Flint, "Looking Backward?: The Relevance of Britishness," in *Unity in Diversity Revisited: British*

Literature and Culture in the 1980s, ed. Barbara Korte and Klaus Peter Müller (Tübingen: Gunter Narr Verlag, 1998), 43–44.

18. Lee, "Norfolk and Nowhere," 31. See also Patrick McGrath, "Shorts: Graham Swift," *Bomb* 26 (winter 1988–89): 20. It is worth noting that Swift has consistently chosen narrators much older than he has been at the time of writing particular novels.

19. For example: Gorra, "When Life Closes In," 11; Patrick Parrinder, "Verbing a Noun," *London Review of Books,* 17 March 1988, 17.

20. Graham Swift, *Last Orders* (New York: Vintage International, 1997), 239.

21. Flint, "Looking Backward?" 40–41.

22. The list of critics and scholars who have noticed this would be very long indeed. One of the best discussions of the matter is in Janik, "History and the 'Here and Now,'" 77, 79, 83–87.

23. Lee, "Shutter and Lens," 43.

24. Banville, "That's Life," 9.

25. There are many such essays. For example, David Leon Higdon, "Double Closures in Postmodern British Fiction: The Example of Graham Swift," *Critical Survey* 3, no. 1 (1991): 88–95; John Schad, "The End of the End of History: Graham Swift's *Waterland,*" *Modern Fiction Studies* 38, no. 4 (winter 1992): 911–25; Del Ivan Janik, "No End of History: Evidence from the Contemporary English Novel," *Twentieth-Century Literature* 41, no. 2 (summer 1995): 160–89. Two of the best book-length treatments of this topic (with extensive discussions of Swift's fiction) are: Frederick M. Holmes, *The Historical Imagination: Postmodernism and the Treatment of the Past in Contemporary British Fiction,* ELS (English Literary Studies) Monograph Series, no. 73 (Victoria: University of Victoria Press, 1997); and Andrzej Gąsiorek, *Post-War British Fiction: Realism and After* (London and New York: Arnold, 1995). Another useful text in this matter is Alison Lee's book *Realism*

and Power: Postmodern British Fiction (London: Routledge, 1990).

Chapter 2—A Narrow World? (I): *The Sweet-Shop Owner* (1980)

1. The reception of *The Sweet-Shop Owner* has always been positive. See Tredell, "Graham Swift," 262; Gorra, "When Life Closes In," 12; Del Ivan Janik, "History and the 'Here and Now,'" 74.

2. Graham Swift, *The Sweet-Shop Owner* (New York: Vintage International, 1993), 9–10. All references in parentheses are to this edition.

3. Hermione Lee, "Boy in the Middle," *Observer* (London), 4 May 1980, 39.

4. Gorra, "When Life Closes In," 12.

5. Ibid.

6. Irene is certainly more complex than Frank Rudman's description of her as "an insistently assertive shrew, a frigid near-hysteric who retreats into illness and invalidism" in his review of *The Sweet-Shop Owner, Spectator,* 26 April 1980, 23.

7. Janik, "History and the 'Here and Now,'" 75.

8. Ibid., 76–77.

9. It is ironic that someone named Chapman should end up as a shopkeeper. The word "chapman" comes from the Old English word "ceapman," which is connected with words associated with buying in various languages. It is an archaic word for someone who buys and sells, a merchant, or a peddler.

Chapter 3—Secrets: *Shuttlecock* (1981)

1. Graham Swift, *Shuttlecock* (New York: Vintage International, 1992). All references in parentheses are to this edition.

2. Like *The Sweet-Shop Owner, Shuttlecock* has generally received favorable attention from critics and scholars. See, for

example, John Mellors, "Beware of the Dog," *London Magazine* 21, no. 8 (November 1981): 89. Additionally, David Leon Higdon argues that Swift finds his distinctive "voice" with *Shuttlecock* in "Unconfessed Confessions," 186.

3. George Steiner, *After Babel: Aspects of Language and Translation* (London, Oxford, and New York: Oxford University Press, 1975), 16–17, 28.

4. Parrinder, "Verbing a Noun," 17.

5. It might be argued that the use of letters of the alphabet for some of the characters' names in *Shuttlecock* (X, Z, etc.) suggests Franz Kafka's *The Trial,* and the quasi-parable type of fiction to which it belongs. But any such echoes are very minor, and are subsumed by the other genres that dominate the novel.

6. A particularly good example is *The Way to the Stars,* dir. Anthony Asquith (Two Cities Films, 1945).

Chapter 4—The Novelist's Workshop: *Learning to Swim and Other Stories* (1982)

1. For British attitudes to short fiction after 1945 see Clare Hanson, "Introduction," in *Re-Reading the Short Story,* ed. Clare Hanson (Basingstoke: Macmillan, 1989), 1–2; Jean Pickering, "The English Short Story in the Sixties," in *The English Short Story: 1945–1980,* ed. Dennis Vannatta (Boston: Twayne, 1985), 75. Swift's stories were first published in respectable journals and collections such as the *London Magazine, Punch, New Stories 3, New Stories 5, Winter's Tales 27,* and *Formations.* "Chemistry" was also broadcast on BBC Radio Three.

2. Jonathan Penner, "In the Laboratory of a Novelist," *Washington Post Book World,* 14 April 1985, 8; Gorra, "When Life Closes In," 11–12; Mantel, "Blood Ties," 23; Jerzy Jarniewicz, "Świat podziurawiony," *Tygodnik Powszechny,* 28 March 1999, 15; Liliane Louvel, "'Cliffedge' de Graham Swift:

l'ambiguïté comme stratégie narrative," *Caliban* 29 (1992): 109–20; Richard Pedot, "'Seraglio' (Graham Swift): Un silence violent," *Journal of the Short Story in English* 33 (autumn 1999): 59–74.

3. Graham Swift, *Learning to Swim and Other Stories* (New York: Washington Square Press, 1986), 29–30, 172–73. All references in parentheses are to this edition.

4. Gorra, "When Life Closes In," 11.

5. Louvel, "'Cliffedge' de Graham Swift," 111, 113.

6. Penner, "In the Laboratory of a Novelist," 8.

7. See, for example, Gorra, "When Life Closes In," 11; Sexton, "The White Silence of Their Lives," 14.

8. Bryn Caless, review of *Learning to Swim, British Book News* (December 1982): 768.

9. An excellent discussion of contemporary British experimental short fiction is provided by the German scholar Birgit Moosmüller in *Die experimentelle englische Kurzgeschichte der Gegenwart* (Munich: Wilhelm Fink Verlag, 1993). See especially section 3, 119–364 ("Experimentelle Tendenzen in der englischen Kurzgeschichte der Gegenwart").

Chapter 5—The Uses of History: *Waterland* (1983)

1. See William Wordsworth, "Ode: Intimations of Immortality from Recollections of Early Childhood" ix, 162–68 ("And see the Children sport upon the shore, / And hear the mighty waters rolling evermore"). In *Waterland,* Tom Crick quotes the "Immortality" ode (v 64) when he talks of children "trailing clouds of glory" (*Waterland* [New York: Vintage International, 1992], 235).

2. Parrinder, "Verbing a Noun," 17.

3. Graham Swift, *Waterland* (New York: Vintage International, 1992, 239–40). All references in parentheses are to this edition.

4. Higdon, "Unconfessed Confessions," 186, 189.

5. George P. Landow, "History, His Story, and Stories in Graham Swift's *Waterland*," 198; Gorra, "When Life Closes In," 11.

6. Gorra, "When Life Closes In," 11.

7. Wood, "Haunted Places," 48.

8. Landow, "History, His Story, and Stories," 204.

9. The U.S. and British editions differ in this phrase. The U.S. edition published by Vintage International omits the word "history." Compare the Picador edition (London, 1984) of *Waterland* (116).

10. Wood, "Haunted Places," 48.

11. Driver, "Floating," 20. See also Lee, "Norfolk and Nowhere," 31; Wood, "Haunted Places," 48.

12. For a rather different reading of these motifs see Janik, "History and the 'Here and Now,'" 84–86.

13. Swift's concern with history as a type of intellectual inquiry has been discussed by many commentators. See, for example, Holmes, *The Historical Imagination;* Ansgar Nünning, "Grenzüberschreitungen: Neue Tendenzen im historischen Roman," in *Radikalität und Mäßigung: Der englische Roman seit 1960,* ed. Annegret Maack and Rüdiger Imhof (Darmstadt: Wissenschaftliche Buchgesellschaft, 1993), 54–73; and Linda Hutcheon, "Historiographic Metafiction," in *Metafiction,* ed. Mark Currie (London and New York: Longman, 1995), 71–91. Very important in this respect is the U.S. scholar Hayden White's book *Metahistory: The Historical Imagination in Nineteenth Century Europe* (1973). Swift's interests in *Waterland* can be directly related to White's scrutiny of the claims of historical narrative to truth.

14. Pritchard, "The Body in the River Leem," 9; Glastonbury, "Last Judgments," 27.

15. Landow, "History, His Story, and Stories," 208.

16. Driver, "Floating," 20.

17. The device of the incomplete utterance (aposiopesis) can be connected with certain silences that mark Crick's narration. These concern, above all, his married life with Mary (passed over very briefly) and his responsibility for his mother's death (122–24, 272–73). The silences that haunt Bill Unwin's account of his life with Ruth in *Ever After* are anticipated here.

18. Glastonbury, "Last Judgments," 27.

19. A good example of a British postwar history textbook that covers the material Crick discusses is Denis Richards and J. W. Hunt, *An Illustrated History of Modern Britain* (London: Longmans, 1950).

20. From 1767, the meridian (0°) at Greenwich, to the East of London, has been used by mariners to calculate their position all over the world. In 1852 a master clock was built at Greenwich Observatory to calculate Greenwich Mean Time. This is still extensively used to indicate a time that is recognizable all over the world (Universal Time).

21. Wood, "Haunted Places," 48.

22. Higdon, "Double Closures in Postmodernist British Fiction," 88–95.

Chapter 6—Witnesses: *Out of This World* (1988)

1. The following are all reviews of *Out of This World*: Gilbert, "The Lost Boys," 35–36; Truss, "Out of Focus," 21; Lee, "Shutter and Lens," 43; Duchêne, "By the Grace of the Teller," 275; Sexton, "The White Silence of Their Lives," 14. The reviews by Gilbert and Truss stress what they see as the schematic, over-intellectualized aspect of the novel.

2. Graham Swift, *Out of This World* (New York: Vintage International, 1993), 90. All references in parentheses are to this edition.

3. Lee, "Shutter and Lens," 43.

4. Gilbert, "The Lost Boys," 36.

5. Parrinder, "Verbing a Noun," 17.

6. Ibid.

7. Sexton, "The White Silence of Their Lives," 14.

8. Lee, "Shutter and Lens," 43.

9. Wood, "Haunted Places," 48.

10. McGrath, "Shorts: Graham Swift," 20.

11. Parrinder, "Verbing a Noun," 17.

12. Lee, "Shutter and Lens," 43.

Chapter 7—Against Transience: *Ever After* (1992)

1. Graham Swift, *Ever After* (New York: Vintage, 1992), 3. All references in parentheses are to this edition.

2. Sir Charles Lyell (1797–1875) was an eminent nineteenth-century geologist whose works such as *The Principles of Geology* (1830–33) and *The Elements of Geology* (1838) argued that the world was very much older than traditional Christian calculations based on the Bible. He is one of the scientists who, like Darwin in *The Origin of Species* (1859) (whose work Lyell endorsed), helped to reshape completely many nineteenth-century intellectuals' view of God, human beings and the universe.

3. James Saynor, "One Hundred Years of Solitude," *Observer* (London), 16 February 1992, 59.

4. Mantel, "Blood Ties," 23–25.

5. Kirsty Milne, "Static Pools," *New Statesman and Society,* 21 February 1992, 40.

6. Wall, "Self-Slaughters," 26.

7. Sage, "Unwin Situation," 6.

8. "From *Waterland* to Eternityland," *Economist,* 28 March 1992, 101.

9. The issue of intertextuality in *Ever After* is discussed in an interesting fashion by Hannah Jacobmeyer at the following internet address: http://webdoc.gwdg.de/edoc/ia/eese/artic98/jacobm/88_98.html

10. It is worth asking whether there are intertextual references in *Ever After* to two earlier British novels that have, on the surface, striking similarities to Swift's novel. These are John Fowles's *The French Lieutenant's Woman* (1969) and A. S. Byatt's *Possession: A Romance* (1990). All three novels have a concern with Darwinian and pre-Darwinian thought and its impact on mid- and late-nineteenth-century attitudes and culture; all three quote and/or imitate a variety of nineteenth-century texts, letters, journals, and poetry; all three move between a twentieth-century present and a nineteenth-century past, stressing continuities and radical differences; all three are strongly metafictional works. There are, however, differences. Fowles's explicit existentialist agenda in *The French Lieutenant's Woman* is lacking in Swift's and Byatt's novels. Neither Swift nor Fowles attempt the same virtuoso pastiches that Byatt achieves. Fowles's and Byatt's texts have pronounced comic elements that are almost nonexistent in Swift's *Ever After*. Fowles's work, generally, stands in an exemplary or paradigmatic relationship to much later British fiction, and, thus, both Byatt's and Swift's novels may well be described as referring to it to some degree. In Swift's case, however, *Ever After* is a negative reflection of *The French Lieutenant's Woman*. Bill Unwin never achieves or even attempts the freedom that Charles Smithson and Sarah Woodruff attain. With regard to Byatt's novel, one can note a similarity of concern and strategy, rather than intertextual reference, when one compares it to *Ever After*. Much British fiction of the 1980s and 1990s delves into the past (and not just the nineteenth-century past) in comparable ways.

11. Isambard Kingdom Brunel (1806–59) was one of the most distinguished of early nineteenth-century British engineers, being the force behind major bridge building, railway construction and shipbuilding projects.

12. Note the incomplete utterances in Unwin's speech when he talks about his wife. In Swift's fiction this device is often a

sign that a narrator cannot (or will not) deal with some emotional issue.

Chapter 8—A Narrow World? (II): *Last Orders* (1996)

1. Graham Swift, *Last Orders* (New York: Vintage, 1997). All references in parentheses refer to this edition. The date the characters set out is clear, although the reader has to search for it somewhat in the text. On page 272 Lenny says "April first yesterday." On page 166 Vince notes that the "'85 Granada Scorpio" he is trying to sell Hussein is "a three-year-old Ford." Jack tells Vic he is going to retire on June 1, 1989, fifty years after his daughter was born (83). Ray has his list of bets up to 1989 when he puts money on Miracle Worker (231). Therefore the journey to Margate must take place in the spring of 1990.

2. The following are reviews of *Last Orders:* Gaby Wood, "Involuntary Memories," *London Review of Books,* 8 February 1996, 20–21; Gary Davenport, "The Novel of Despair," *Sewanee Review* 105, no. 3 (1997): 440–46; Reynolds, "On the Old Kent Road," 25; Adrian Poole, "Hurry up Please, It's Time," *Guardian Weekly,* 28 January 1996, 29; Banville, "That's Life," 8–9.

3. Banville, "That's Life," 8.

4. Ibid.; Rosenberg, "Glowing in the Ashes," 6–10.

5. Banville, "That's Life," 8.

6. Wood, "Involuntary Memories," 20; Banville, "That's Life," 8.

7. Swift's selection of characters might be criticized as too white and too predominantly male. See Kate Flint, "Looking Backward?" 41–43. It is true, however, that—as in his earlier novels—Swift sees his characters in *Last Orders* as an embodiment of an English national history and community.

8. For details see *Oxford Reader's Companion to Dickens,* ed. Paul Schlicke (Oxford: Oxford University Press, 1999). The

entry on Kent is particularly illuminating as regards the Dickensian resonances of the journey to Margate in *Last Orders*.

9. These references are noted by Poole, "Hurry up Please, It's Time," 29, and in Jerzy Jarniewicz, "Podróż urn," *Gazeta Wyborcza*, Books Supplement, 17 February 1998, 2.

10. For a discussion of some of the issues involved in the Faulknerian allusions in *Last Orders*, see Valentine Cunningham, "Fiction '96," 1–4. They are also discussed in Flint, "Looking Backward?" 43–44. Swift talks about the influence of Faulkner on *Last Orders* in the *Salon* interview with Rosenberg (see note 4 above).

11. It seems, however, unfair to call them "debased pilgrims," as Poole does ("Hurry up Please, It's Time," 29).

12. Banville, "That's Life," 8.

13. For the sea as a symbol of infinity, see William Wordsworth, "Ode: Intimations of Immortality from Recollections of Early Childhood" (1807), ix. For the bird as a symbol of the soul, see chapter 5 of James Joyce's *A Portrait of the Artist as a Young Man* (1916): "When the soul of a man is born in this country there are nets flung at it to hold it back from flight."

14. Stephen Gill, *Wordsworth: A Life* (Oxford: Clarendon Press, 1989), 190.

15. See, for example, Poole, "Hurry up Please, It's Time," 29.

Chapter 9—The Narrow Way: *The Light of Day* (2003)

1. The following reviews deal with *The Light of Day*: Michiko Kakutani, untitled review, *International Herald Tribune*, 10–11 May 2003, 20; Anthony Quinn, "Nobody's Perfect," *New York Times Book Review*, 4 May 2003, 6; and D. J. Taylor, "South London Reveries," *Times Literary Supplement*, 28 February 2003, 21–22. It is interesting to compare reviews of Swift's *Ever After* with these reviews.

2. The following are reviews of *The Light of Day*: Anita Desai, "Revenge Tragedy," *New York Review of Books*, 12 June 2003, 38–39; James Wood, "How's the Empress," *London Review of Books*, 17 April 2003, 28–29.

3. Examples of British novels in the Hammett-Chandler manner are those by P. B. Yuill (the pseudonym of Scottish novelist Gordon Williams and celebrated English soccer player and manager Terry Venables): *Hazell Plays Solomon* (1974), *Hazell and the Three-Card Trick* (1975), and *Hazell and the Menacing Jester* (1976).

4. Quinn, "Nobody's Perfect," 6.

5. Swift, *The Light of Day* (New York: Knopf, 2003), 83. All references in parentheses are to this edition.

6. John O'Mahoney, "Graham Swift: Triumph of the Common Man," *Guardian*, 1 March 2003, 20.

7. Quinn,"Nobody's Perfect," 6. Wood finds the suggestion of a connection between the two novels "far-fetched" (28).

8. One kind of intertextual reference in *The Light of Day* is to Swift's own novels. The reader who knows Swift's work well will surely hear resonances of *The Sweet-Shop Owner* and *Last Orders* in the florist who has no choice over his career because he is called Charlie Rose (39). He/she will hear them, too, in George's invocation to civilization (27)—echoing *Waterland* and *Ever After*—in the motifs of incarceration (*Shuttlecock*, *Waterland*, *Last Orders*), golf (*Shuttlecock*), photography (*Out of This World*), and the figure of the teacher (*Waterland*). This is not authorial introversion, but gentle, metafictional reminders of the madeness of any text.

9. This is clearly seen by Quinn, "Nobody's Perfect," 6, and Desai, "Revenge Tragedy," 39.

10. This fixation of characters and narrators with past trauma and their inability to escape it form part of the subject of an

illuminating essay on Swift's fiction by Tamás Bényei, "The Novels of Graham Swift: Family Photos," in *Contemporary British Fiction*, ed. Richard J. Lane, Rod Mengham, and Philip Tew (Oxford: Polity, 2003), 40–55.

11. Kakutani, untitled review, 20.

12. There may be something wrong with George's dates here. The Croatian war of independence from the Yugoslav Federation began in mid-1991 and the initial phase of the war lasted till January 1992. Hostilities continued sporadically between Croats and Serbs (and intensely and brutally in Bosnia Herzegovina) until the Croat advance into Krajina in May 1995. If Kristina came to Britain in late 1992, this would not have been "before the serious trouble began" (44). The reader must decide if this is a deliberate inaccuracy on Swift's part, or an unimportant detail.

13. See Bényei, "The Novels of Graham Swift: Family Photos," 52.

14. Heike Hartung notes an attenuation of the historical in the most recent work of Swift, Salman Rushdie, and Peter Ackroyd (*Die dezentrale Geschichte: Historisches Erzählen und literarische Geschichte(n) bei Peter Ackroyd, Graham Swift, und Salman Rushdie*, Studien zur Anglistischen Literatur- und Sprachwissenschaft 16 [Trier: Wissenschaftlicher Verlag, 2002], 281.)

15. Taylor,"South London Reveries," 21.

16. Ibid.

17. Desai, "Revenge Tragedy," 39.

18. See ibid., 38; Quinn, "Nobody's Perfect," 6; and, above all, Wood, "How's the Empress," 28–29.

19. Wood, "How's the Empress," 28–29.

20. Quinn, "Nobody's Perfect," 6.

21. This is the kind of behavior that Bényei writes about with regard to Swift's earlier fiction. See note 11 above.

22. A recent very thorough treatment of the subject of unreliable narration is *Unreliable Narration: Studien zur Theorie und Praxis unglaubwürdigen Erzählens in der englischsprachigen Erzählliteratur*, ed. Ansgar Nünning (Trier: Wissenschaftlicher Verlag, 1998). Michel Pobloth addresses the issue of unreliable narration in Graham Swift's fiction in a lucid fashion in an essay on pages 131–46.

23. Wood, "How's the Empress," 29.

24. Apart from the shadows, another possible reason for the references to Caravaggio (1573–1610) is that one of the artist's celebrated canvases is that of "Judith Beheading Holofernes" (ca. 1598).

25. Desai notices this ("Revenge Tragedy," 39), and Taylor writes of the "strong figurative undercurrents" in the novel ("South London Reveries," 21).

26. Quinn sees a connection between *The Light of Day* and Greene's *The End of the Affair* in this correlation of the detective and the novelist ("Nobody's Perfect," 6).

27. With regard to light, particularly relevant texts are: Proverbs 4.18; Isaiah 9.2; Matthew 4.16 and 5.14; and Acts 26.18. If there is a reference to Job 3.16, it must be inverted.

28. This issue is addressed by Bényei ("The Novels of Graham Swift: Family Photos," 53–54). See note 11 above.

Bibliography

Works by Graham Swift

The Sweet-Shop Owner. London: Allen Lane, 1980. New York: Washington Square Press, 1985.

Shuttlecock. London: Allen Lane, 1981. New York: Washington Square Press, 1984.

Learning to Swim and Other Stories. London: London Magazine Editions, 1982. New York: Poseidon, 1982.

Waterland. London: Heinemann, 1983. New York: Poseidon, 1983.

Out of This World. London: Viking, 1988. New York: Poseidon, 1988.

Ever After. London: Picador, 1992. New York: Knopf, 1992.

Last Orders. London: Picador, 1996. New York: Knopf, 1996.

The Light of Day. London: Hamish Hamilton, 2003. New York: Knopf, 2003.

Critical Works about Swift

Articles and Book Sections

Banville, John. "That's Life." Review of *Last Orders*. *New York Review of Books,* 4 April 1996, 8–9. A thorough and very positive review by an eminent Irish novelist. Banville admires Swift's technique and his celebration of "small" people's lives.

Bradbury, Malcolm. "Artists of the Floating World: 1979 to the Present" and "An Afterword from the 1990s (1994)." In *The Modern British Novel*, 394–462. Harmondsworth: Penguin, 1994. A very knowledgeable summary of the main features of the fiction of Swift and his contemporaries.

Driver, Christopher. "Floating." Review of *Waterland* and other novels. *London Review of Books,* 6 October 1983, 20–21. A very good discussion of the subjects, organization of motifs, and language of *Waterland*.

Flint, Kate. "Looking Backward?: The Relevance of Britishness." In *Unity in Diversity Revisted?: British Literature and Culture in the 1990s,* ed. Barbara Korte and Klaus Peter Müller. Tübingen: Gunter Narr Verlag, 1998. Interesting comments on the exclusiveness of Swift's social vision in *Last Orders,* and a good exposition of the controversy regarding references to Faulkner.

Găsiorek, Andrzej. *Post-War British Fiction: Realism and After.* London and New York: Arnold, 1995, 147–77. Chapter 7 contains a good discussion of Swift's writing in the context of postmodern debates about historical narrative.

Gilbert, Harriet. "The Lost Boys." Review of *Out of This World. New Statesman,* 11 March 1988, 35–36. This generally positive review expresses unease about "over-schematic" aspects of *Out of This World.*

Glastonbury, Marion. "Last Judgements." Review of *Waterland* and other novels. *New Statesman,* 7 October 1983, 26–27. An amusing, if wrong-headed, rejection of *Waterland.*

Gorra, Michael. "When Life Closes In." Review of *Learning to Swim and Other Stories* and *The Sweet-Shop Owner. New York Times Book Review,* 23 June 1985, 11–12. An early and very intelligent U.S. review of two of Swift's texts. Good analysis of *The Sweet-Shop Owner.*

Higdon, David Leon. "'Unconfessed Confessions': The Narrators of Julian Barnes and Graham Swift." In *The British and Irish Novel since 1960,* ed. James Acheson. New York: St Martin's Press, 1991, 174–91. A good discussion of Swift's retrospective narrators.

———. "Double Closures in Postmodern British Fiction: The Example of Graham Swift." *Critical Survey* 3 (1991): 89–95. An extremely interesting analysis of this aspect of Swift's fiction through *Out of This World.*

Holmes, Frederick M. *The Historical Imagination: Postmodernism and the Treatment of the Past in Contemporary British Fiction.* ELS (English Literary Studies) Monograph Series, no. 73 (Victoria: University of Victoria), 1997. The author discusses Swift's fiction frequently in this stimulating study. He considers Swift and other novelists in relation to theories of history.

Janik, Del Ivan. "History and the 'Here and Now': The Novels of Graham Swift." *Twentieth-Century Literature* 35, no. 1 (1989): 74–88. An important early scholarly study of motifs of history in Swift's fiction through *Waterland*.

Landow, George P. "History, His Story, and Stories in Graham Swift's *Waterland*." *Studies in the Literary Imagination* 23, no. 2 (fall 1990): 197–211. An important scholarly discussion of historiographical and metafictional elements in *Waterland*.

Louvel, Liliane. "'Cliffedge' de Graham Swift: l'ambiguïté comme stratégie narrative." *Caliban*, no. 29 (1992): 109–20. This brilliant analysis shows the potential for interpretation underlying some of Swift's short fiction.

Mantel, Hilary. "Blood Ties." Review of *Ever After. New York Review of Books,* 11 June 1992, 23–25. This long and insightful review is very good on the problems of Swift's choice of narrator.

Nünning, Ansgar. "Grenzüberschreitungen: Neue Tendenzen im historischen Roman." In *Radikalität und Mäßigung: Der englische Roman seit 1960,* ed. Annegret Maack and Rüdiger Imhof. Darmstadt: Wissenschaftliche Buchgesellschaft, 1993. This excellent essay puts Swift in the context of the recent development of the historical novel in Britain.

Parrinder, Patrick. "Verbing a Noun." Review of *Out of This World* and other novels. *London Review of Books,* 17 March 1988, 17–18. A very suggestive discussion of family and history in Swift's fiction through *Out of This World*.

Quinn, Anthony. "Nobody's Perfect." Review of *The Light of Day. New York Times Book Review,* 4 May 2003, 6. The reviewer appreciates the subtlety of Swift's novel but argues it is "somewhat underpowered."

Sage, Lorna, "Unwin Situation." Review of *Ever After. Times Literary Supplement,* 21 February 1992, 6. A useful discussion of loss of faith, Victorian echoes, and language in *Ever After*.

Tredell, Nicolas. "Graham Swift." In *British Novelists since 1960,* 2d ser., ed. Merritt Moseley, 262–69. *Dictionary of Literary Biography,* vol. 194. Detroit, Washington D.C., London: Bruccoli Clark Layman/Gale Research, 1998. An excellent brief discussion of Swift's life and work to date.

Wood, James. "How's the Empress." Review of *The Light of Day. London Review of Books,* 17 April 2003, 28–29. A positive and insightful review, placing Swift's novel in a broad literary context.

Wood, Michael. "Haunted Places." Review of *Waterland* and other novels. *New York Review of Books,* 16 August 1984, 47–48. This review contains some useful observations on Swift's interest in the possibility of freedom from history.

Interviews

Barnard, Catherine, and Giles Menegaldo. Interview with Graham Swift. In Michel Morel, Jean-Jacques Lecercle, Jean-Louis Picot, and Marc Porée, *Graham Swift ou le temps du récit,* 9–18. Paris: Editions Messene, 1996.

Profumo, David. "The Attraction of the Pessimistic View." *Sunday Times,* 6 March 1988, sec. G, 8–9.

Rosenberg, Scott. "Glowing in the Ashes." *Salon* 14 (6–10 May 1996), http://www.salon.com/weekly/swift96056.html

Index

DATE DUE